Scotland's Place-names

David Dorward

is a graduate in Arts and Law of the University of St Andrews. He practised as a solicitor before joining the staff of his old university, where for thirty-two years he enjoyed being an administrator among scholars and occasionally aspired to being a scholar among administrators.

Married, with two sons, he engages in the recreations of golf, gardening and fishing, all of which activities combine happily with his favourite hobby of pondering the meanings of names—personal and of place. *Scottish Surnames* is another of his publications.

SCOTLAND'S PLACE-NAMES

David Dorward

THE MERCAT PRESS
EDINBURGH

First published in 1995 by Mercat Press
James Thin, 53 South Bridge, Edinburgh EH1 1YS

© David Dorward, 1995

ISBN 1873644 507

Typeset in Times New Roman 11 point at Mercat Press

Printed in Great Britain by
The Cromwell Press, Melksham, Wiltshire

For Joy

Contents

Introduction   1
Place-name Elements A to W   15
Postscript   142
Reading List   144
Index   145

Maps

Language groups A.D. 500   4
Some ancient district names   11
The old counties and shires   12
The former Regional Councils   13
The new Councils   14

Introduction

...Ecclefechan, Auchenshuggle, Auchtermuchty and Milngavie
—*Children's Game, c. 1910*

Although the provenance of this tongue-twisting jingle is obscure, and its poetic value none too high, it is perhaps not a bad starting-place for a consideration of Scotland's place-names. This is because it illustrates the fascination that these words—so strange-sounding, yet so familiarly Scottish —exert over many people.

But the place-name enthusiast is concerned with more than sound-patterns, however strange and at times poetic. He seeks above all to discover meaning, significance and function, perhaps with some history and geography added to put a name in context. And although the search may be difficult, the discovery is always theoretically attainable, because all genuine place-names have a lexical meaning, a function and a context.

The four names quoted at the top of the page are genuine and they all have meanings—some more transparent than others; they are discussed later in the book. Their mystery lies in the fact that none of them is in the English language. The tongue that Shakespeare spake has contributed remarkably little to Scotland's place-nomenclature, considering that English (or an approximation of it) is now the language of 99.75% of Scotland's population. It was not always so however, and it is the complicated ethnic and linguistic situation of Scotland up to the early Middle Ages (the time when most place-names were coined) that makes our study at once so difficult and so fascinating.

There are four main languages, or language-groups, to be considered in the study of Scottish place-names, and if what follows is a gross over-simplification it is because this book is intended only as a layperson's introduction to the subject.

P-Celtic
The Celtic language itself can be divided into two main groups, of which

1

P-Celtic is thought to be the older. P-Celtic comprises Welsh, Breton and Cornish, and a version of it was spoken in Scotland during the first eight centuries of the Christian era. Although little is known for certain about the Picts it is generally agreed that a P-Celtic language was current throughout the seven Pictish provinces of Angus, Atholl, Strathearn, Fife, Mar, Moray and Caithness. A similar language or dialect, sometimes known as Cumbric, was spoken in the ancient kingdom of Strathclyde (whose extent was much smaller than the modern region of that name).

The concept of P-Celtic is not an easy one to grasp, and since it might seem a trifle perverse to refer to certain Scottish place-names as having a 'Welsh' or 'Cumbric' origin, the term used in this book to describe the language of the Picts and Strathclyde Britons is 'Brittonic'. Perhaps an easy way to fix it in one's mind is to think of it as the language which would have been spoken in Arthurian times, if not at the court of that legendary monarch.

Q-Celtic

This is the name given by scholars to the second of the Celtic language-groups, comprising Irish Gaelic, Scottish Gaelic and Manx. In this book it is referred to as Gaelic, but remember that we are talking of a language with many dialects, developing over several centuries, and borrowing many terms from Brittonic and other tongues. (For those readers who are curious about the terminology 'P' and 'Q', the explanation is simply that the sound 'p' in the one group is found as a 'k' sound in the other: as an illustration, the word for 'four' in Welsh is *pedwar*, in Gaelic *ceithir*).

Old Norse

The third language group we have to contend with is the Scandinavian—mainly Old Norse, brought to these shores by Viking colonists. As might be expected, the Norse influence is much stronger in the islands and seaboard settlements of the north and west; apparently the east coast did not provide suitable anchorages for the invaders. To complicate matters, however, the English language itself is rich in words of Norse origin, which is not surprising if one considers that at the beginning of the tenth century the Danes were in possession of most of England north-east of a line running from London to Chester.

English

The final language in our survey is of course English, which has been progressively ousting the others since the early Middle Ages. Most (but by no means all) of the place-names in the eastern Border counties and the Lothians are of Anglo-Saxon origin, and of course virtually every modern place-name (such as Helensburgh, Alexandria and Bettyhill) is in the English language. The present English-Scottish Border is of little relevance to place-name scholars, as the majority of names were coined long before the present border was formed; in any case there is usually an enormous time-lag between historical events and linguistic change.

The debate as to whether Scots is a language or a dialect is not one that is to be entered into here; but it is pleasing to be able to record a large number of Lowland place-name elements which can be classified as Scots rather than English: these include *brae, burgh, cleugh, den, fauld, gate, haugh, heugh, kirk, law, loan, moss, neuk, peel, pow, rig* and *toun*. In their way these give as much colour to the place-name vocabulary as do the admittedly more numerous Gaelic terms which will appear in the following pages.

It would be preferable in a book of this limited scope not to deal with history at all, but a word or two is probably necessary. Taking the year A.D. 500 as a snapshot date, we have the broad picture shown on the map overleaf.

A few centuries later this has completely changed. The 'Scots' settlers from Ireland have pushed east and north, the Pictish civilisation has suffered eclipse, and virtually the whole northern kingdom has been united under Kenneth MacAlpin (848). The Scandinavians have settled the islands and the extreme northern mainland, and although their influence diminishes after the Battle of Largs (1263) they remain in Orkney and Shetland until very much later. The northward thrust of the Angles has been halted with their defeat at the Battle of Nectansmere (*Dun Nechtain* or Dunnichen) near Forfar in 685, and they have retreated before the expansionist Scots.

The language-picture which emerges is impossible to reproduce diagramatically, but roughly what has happened is this. Norse has established itself in Orkney, Shetland and the Hebrides, but is already being overlaid on the mainland by Gaelic. Gaelic has spread throughout the north-west and central Highlands, and has reached the eastern coastal plain where it forms a language layer on top of the existing Brittonic. English has established a basis in the Lothians, but has temporarily retreated leaving a sprinkling of Gaelic place-names south of the Forth. Another dialect of Gaelic has found its way into the extreme south-west, covering, but not

SCANDINAVIAN RAIDERS & SETTLERS (*Language – Old Norse*)

(*Language – Brittonic*)

STRATHCLYDE BRITONS
(*Language – Brittonic*)

KINGDOM of NORTHUMBRIA
(*Language – English*)

'SCOTS' INVADERS from IRELAND
(*Language – Gaelic*)

4

obliterating, the existing English and Brittonic place-name pattern.

Even when thus simplified the linguistic situation remains complicated and uncertain. One of the few things that can be said with authority, however, is that Gaelic was never at any time, as is frequently asserted, the language spoken throughout the length and breadth of Scotland.

If we accept the above description and have in our minds the broad language-pattern, we shall avoid the first and worst mistake—that of consulting the wrong dictionary. When trying to ascertain the meaning of a Scottish place-name we must eliminate what is linguistically improbable or even impossible. We should not try, for example, to find a Norse derivation for an Aberdeenshire name, because Viking settlements were almost non-existent thereabouts. Worse, we should not violate language and history by putting an impossible English interpretation on a non-English name—'Danes wark' as an interpretation of Denork in Fife fails on all counts—it is a **dun** name. The time-factor itself is very important: an English etymology for an ancient settlement in the Perthshire Highlands is out of the question, for English was not widely spoken there until the later Middle Ages. Thus, Chesthill in Glenlyon is not what it appears to say in English; it is the Gaelic *seasduil*, meaning plateau.

Another difficulty is that the modern form of a place-name often obscures its origin. When a Brittonic name was taken over by Gaelic speakers, there was perhaps not too much distortion, because of the family likeness between P-Celtic and Q-Celtic. But when a Gaelic word passes into the mouths of English or Scots speakers, the result can be extremely odd. Just as *uisge beatha* becomes 'whisky', so *cinn ghiuthsaich* becomes Kingussie. The reason is that there is little in common between Gaelic and English or even Scots (most of whose vocabulary can be derived from a dialect of northern English). We also have to contend with the process of folk-etymology, whereby an unfamiliar word is adapted so that it becomes familiar. The infant enrolled at the Logie Baird school thought that he was being sent to the Yogi Bear school; and this phenomenon occurs over and over again with place-names, so that *apur crosan* becomes Applecross and *baedd coed*—'boar wood'—becomes Bathgate. One must therefore look behind all the distortions and get to the correct linguistic form of the word; the only way to do this is to consult all the available documentation—old maps, charters, records and the like. Until this has been done, one should never hazard a guess at the form or meaning of a name.

Sometimes however, it is the documentation that is wrong and the correct form of a name is preserved in the pronunciation. The locals speak truer than they know when they pronounce Falkirk as 'Faw-kirk'. *Faw* is an old Scots word meaning dappled or speckled, and the modern spelling of the town name is an attempt at improvement through anglicisation. And if Milngavie is pronounced 'Mill-guy' as it should be—and is, locally—it is not a bad attempt at the Gaelic *muileann gaoithe* or *Dhai*—'windmill' or 'Dave's mill', according to choice.

Once a derivation has been proposed it should be checked against the local topography. Ballantrae looks like the Gaelic *baile nan traigh*—'beach village'—which is exactly what Ballantrae is. It is worth noting that many Gaelic names are simple topographical expressions like this one; indeed any picturesque or 'story-telling' derivation must be regarded with some suspicion. A negative example is Dunbog, which looks as if it should mean 'fort in the swamp', but a glance at the site shows that the settlement was on a hill. 'Bog' is in fact a corruption of *builg*, meaning a bulge or emi-nence. (Who in their right senses would build a fort in a bog anyway?)

One other note of caution. The really ancient names of Scotland belong to a hypothetical pre-Celtic language-group whose nature we can do little more than guess at. River names are usually of much greater antiquity than settlement or hill-names, the reason being that water has been, from the earliest times, such an important element in man's environment. For most of the major Scottish river names no detailed and definitive etymology is possible—only endless research and even speculation. Some classification can be attempted, and there are affinities with other European river systems —Tay with Thames, Ayr and Earn with Rhine, Nairn with Nar and Naro, and so on—and most appear to derive from basic roots meaning water, flowing and the like. Other such names as Spey, Tweed and Stirling (origi-nally a river-name) remain enigmas.

However, Scotland is fortunate in having few factitious or synthetic place-names. There is an entry on p.112 devoted to what one might call fancy names, whose elucidation depends upon anecdote; but by and large every Scottish place-name is meaningful, and Scottish onomatology can be said to have a scientific basis. The same cannot always be claimed of non-abo-riginal Australian and North American place-names, which were sometimes arrived at for sentimental, grandiose or frivolous reasons.

These, then, are the basics of Scottish place-name study, and to illustrate them there follows an alphabetical list of common place-name elements in Brittonic, Gaelic, Norse, Scots and English. Examples of actual names are discussed, with locations and derivations; variant spellings are mainly omitted, but can be found in some of the more scholarly works mentioned in the Reading List. Readers may begin to do their own detective work on uncommon specimens that interest them, and, in company with the author, await the publication of an authoritative and comprehensive dictionary.

It has been a temptation to place the index at the beginning instead of at the end of the book, for it is to the index that the average reader will turn in search of meaning. But this is not intended as a dictionary, and is meant for browsing rather than consultation. Also, lexical meaning is not everything. Hardly less important than *meaning* is *function*. Dallas in Texas is a transplant of Dallas in Moray; the latter has the undisputed lexical meaning of 'meadow station' (see **fas**), which is a singularly inappropriate description of the southern American megalopolis. It is quite unhelpful therefore to be told the dictionary meaning of Dallas: much more meaningful is the information that the Texan Dallas was named after a man whose ancestral roots must have been in Morayshire. The primary meaning is nothing, the function everything. From another viewpoint, it might be said that Dallas 'means' the end of the Kennedy dream. Or is Dallas just a household word whose currency depends on it being the name of a television soap?

The earliest recorded Scottish place-names are tribal in character—such as *Cataibh* (now Sutherland) 'among the cat-men' and *Orcaibh* (Orkney) 'among the Orcs'. Somewhat later come references to the provinces of Lothian, Fife and Atholl; in the early mediaeval period we have territories under the authority of an earl (*comes*) which became counties; and sheriffdoms or shires. Although remaining so for centuries, that type of organisation has largely disappeared with regionalisation; nevertheless to some extent the names of the old unofficial districts—Angus, Badenoch, Rannoch—remain. That these were once important social and political units is reflected in place-names, which very often are grouped round regional divisions. To take the case of Mar, we have a whole string of names identifying parts of the region. Braemar is the upper part (see **brae**); Midmar is probably what it says, although some scholars prefer the earlier form *migmar*, the lower (and wetter) part of the territory. Logie Mar is the 'Howe of Mar' (see **lag**); Craigievar is the 'craigie' (see **craig**) of Mar; Cromar is *crodh Mar*—the bught or cattlefold of Mar. All these terms refer to a name, Mar, which will now mean little to the average Scot. It may be added in passing that the village-name Braemar is a modern coinage; some two centuries ago the eastern part was the Castleton, while the hamlet across the Clunie was Auchendryne ('thornfield') and the parish name was Kindrochit.

At the time of writing, Scotland's administrative divisions are once again in a state of upheaval. The new Councils, replacing the former regional and district councils, incorporate a few administrative improvements; they dismember the mammoth division of Strathclyde, quite useless for pinpointing a place on the map but retain the huge expense of Highland. In this book, therefore, use is made of the historic county names as well as some of the older territorial divisions. A sketch map is included for the benefit of readers whose memories do not go back to the good old days of Perthshire, Roxburgh and Argyll.

When you visit such places as Glen Affric or Rothiemurchus there will be pointed out to you the remnants of a pine forest which allegedly once covered the whole of Scotland. Similarly when you look at a map of a depopulated or wilderness area of the Highlands what you see in the small print is a tiny fragment of the vast treasury of names that must have been current before the passing of the Gaelic language. In the days when the glens were thronged with people, when the hill passes were regularly traversed by drovers with their beasts, when the women and children decamped for the high pastures in summer—in these days every feature of the landscape had its name. Most of these names were never written down, and the survival of those that did was largely fortuitous. Some of them must be regarded as of doubtful place-name status: in the dip between Perthshire's Ben More and Stobinian there appears on the maps the term *Bealach eadar Bheinn*, which is good Gaelic for 'gap between hills'—but one wonders why the capital letters were inserted.

These forgotten names of course were intended to have, and had, only a local currency. That is why the repertoire is restricted and some of the names seem unimaginative and repetitive. Indeed it is this repetitiveness that may have aided their survival, for names that occur frequently like Ben More and Meall Odhar are more likely to remain in the memory. And there was no need for diversification when inhabitants did not stray far from their native glens and loch-sides: the fact that there are two mountains called Sgurr na Lapaich—one in Glen Affric and the other in the neighbouring Glen Cannich—may today be an annoyance to hill-walkers but can scarcely have confused those whose interest in the hills was utilitarian. Similarly the two Dog Hillocks in Glen Clova, much younger names, were probably of interest only to the shepherds who originally bestowed them.

Place-names cannot exist in isolation. Classicists used to use the Greek term απαξ λεγομενον to describe a word that made only a single appearance in the canon. There is probably no such thing in onomastics, and if a name seems singular—like Quirang in Skye (Old Norse *kvi rong*—'crooked enclosure')—its component elements could probably be found in other Old Norse names in Scandinavia if not in Scotland. Names are often repeated in different spellings (sometimes reflecting dialect pronunciations) all over the map; they also arrange themselves naturally according to their component elements, and it seems sensible to study them in groups rather than singly. That is the basis on which this book is arranged.

Selection of names has been a matter for some consideration; the 2 cm to 1 km Ordnance Survey maps of Scotland include about 120,000 names— quite an impossible number for any one person to handle. In the end, all settlement names of over 2,500 inhabitants have been included, plus the names of the principal lochs, rivers and mountains, the main National Trust properties and tourist attractions. Beyond that, the coverage involves a certain amount of serendipity; one name-element in English leads to another in Old Norse, one Scots dialect word suggests its Gaelic counterpart and so on. Also, the importance of a place is no guide to the interest of its name: *Glasgow* is no more rewarding than, say, *Backward* in Aberdeenshire, although the latter is hardly big enough to be called a hamlet.

One is also conscious however that the attention of the general reader will be quickly lost if too many unfamiliar names are included. This has been the problem particularly with Scandinavian names in northern Scotland. For one thing, they have seldom been written down in their original form, and have usually passed into English through the intermediate stage of Gaelic; this gives them a linguistic opacity not often found in names which originate in either of the latter two languages. For another, these names are not in themselves particularly interesting, consisting as they often do of an unidentifiable personal name followed by a generic such as 'farm', or 'stead'. Names of natural features have problems of their own: Old Norse *sker* becomes Gaelic *sgeir*, which in English is 'skerry', a rock surrounded by sea; this would appear to be an example of a straightforward place-name element, yet there is hardly a single familiar 'skerry' name on the map. Worst of all, these Norse names tend to occur in areas of Scotland which are the least densely populated, and so are almost completely unknown to outsiders. Since it is not the purpose in a book of this kind to try to make onomastic points which can be illustrated only by names completely unfamiliar to the average reader, the coverage of Scandinavian names has of necessity been somewhat sketchy.

Apart from a few perhaps idiosyncratic inclusions, the names in effect selected themselves, and settled down at a figure of around 2,500. The coverage of Scotland's place-names contained in this book is therefore far from being comprehensive, but it is difficult even for dictionaries to attain this.

It may be thought that the study of place-names is to be regarded as useless, and unconducive to any practical result. Since names function quite as well when their meaning is unknown or forgotten, why bother to search for it? Yet the fascination of place-name study remains, for the generalist as well as the scholar. And it does help to give a new understanding to the country that we live in. In the Dark Ages, people's horizons were bounded by their tribal provinces; to the Vikings, geography meant mainly safe anchorages; in mediaeval times the feudal system and the clan system held the peasantry in thirlage to the great landowners, and landscape meant the immediate locality. The Victorians tended to see Scotland in terms of railways and waterways—the West Highland Line, the Forth Bridge, the Caledonian Canal. To most of us nowadays, alas, the important thing is the road system, with its M8s and A73s. For the motorist, what lies between Perth and Inverness is the dreaded A9 (does anybody talk about the Great North Road any more?) Place-name enthusiasts on the other hand have a different perspective: we will be aware of crossing the moors and descending into Strathtay, going through the Pass of Killiecrankie, branching up Glengarry, surmounting Drumochter, descending Glen Truim to the Spey Valley with its magnificent views of the Monadhruadh on the right and the Monadhliath on the left, and crossing the high plateau to descend to Strathnairn and the Moray Firth. These are the names that stay in the memory, and that represent the essential features of the terrain, which will still be there when Inveralmond Industrial Estate and Aviemore Leisure Complex are one with Nineveh and Tyre.

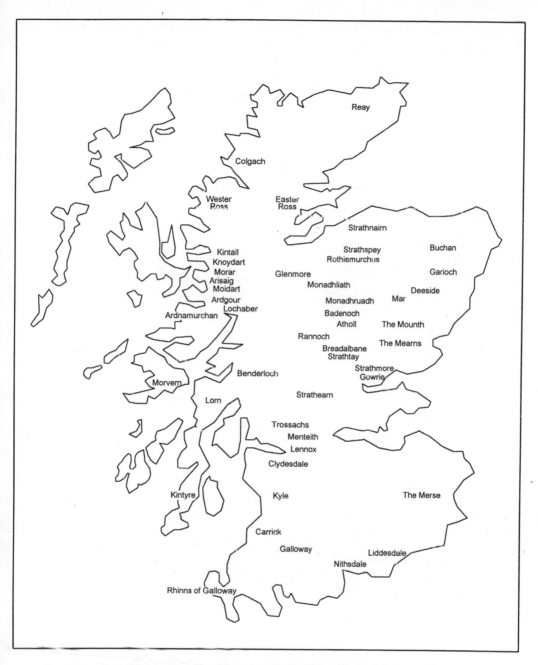

Some Ancient District Names. These traditional names survive in ordinary usage, but in most cases were not adopted by officialdom.

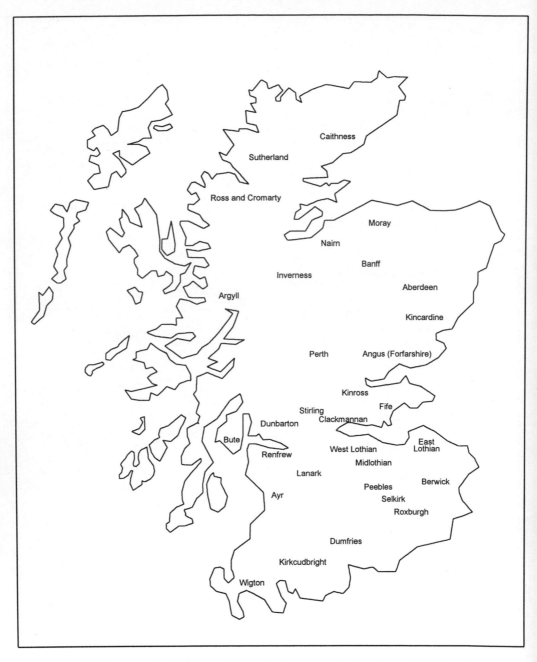

Caithness

Sutherland

Ross and Cromarty

Moray

Nairn

Banff

Inverness

Aberdeen

Argyll

Kincardine

Perth

Angus (Forfarshire)

Kinross

Fife

Stirling

Clackmannan

Dunbarton

Bute

East Lothian

West Lothian

Renfrew

Midlothian

Lanark

Peebles

Berwick

Ayr

Selkirk

Roxburgh

Dumfries

Kirkcudbright

Wigton

The Old Counties and Shires. Although of some antiquity, these administrative divisions as they appeared on the map were essentially the product of modern systems of local government. They existed in various forms until 1975; for the difference between shires and counties, see p.7.

Highland

Grampian

Tayside

Fife

Central

Strathclyde

Lothian

Borders

Dumfries and Galloway

The Former Regional Councils. These divisions existed between 1975 and 1996.

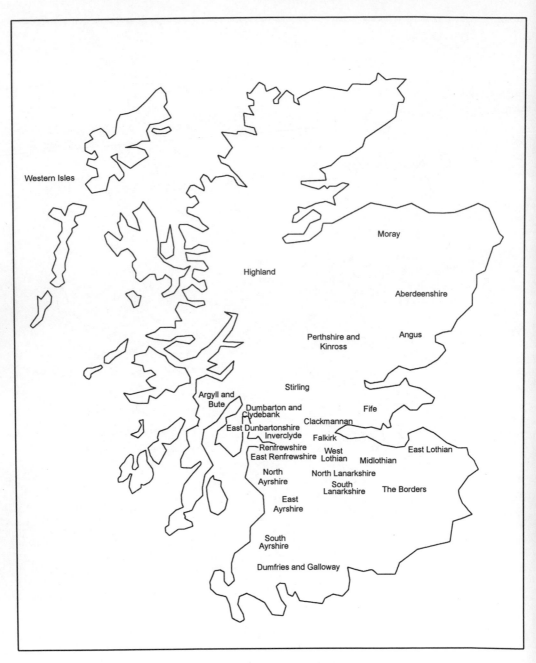

Western Isles

Moray

Highland

Aberdeenshire

Perthshire and
Kinross

Angus

Stirling

Argyll and
Bute

Fife

Dumbarton and
Clydebank

Clackmannan

East Dunbartonshire

Inverclyde

Falkirk

Renfrewshire

West
Lothian

East Renfrewshire

Midlothian

East Lothian

North
Ayrshire

North Lanarkshire

South
Lanarkshire

The Borders

East
Ayrshire

South
Ayrshire

Dumfries and Galloway

The New Councils. These come into existence on 1 April 1996. The cities and the Northern Isles are not included in the map.

A

aber

A Brittonic word with the basic meaning of 'meeting of the waters' when it occurs on the coast, and 'confluence' when it occurs inland. The word never passed into Gaelic speech, but was replaced by **inver**. It follows that *aber* names are older than *inver* ones, and the distribution of the former coincides more or less with historical Pictland (see map on p.4). The *aber* element occurs with great frequency in Wales (the modern home of the Brittonic language) and even in Brittany (Abervrack, Avranches) but never in Ireland (the point of origin of Gaelic).

The first *aber* element that comes to mind is Aberdeen, which is unfortunate because it is a difficult one. Aberdeen was originally two settlements, one of them, 'Abirdoen', being a Pictish ecclesiastical settlement at the mouth of the Don. It is now Old Aberdeen. The other, 'Abirdeon', was a mercantile settlement on the site, more or less, of Modern Aberdeen. The suffix is Gaelic, but unexplained. In 1578 Bishop Leslie referred to Aberdeen as 'an auld toon in twa pairts'; but three centuries before that both the names and the settlements had become confused.

Other *aber* names are Aberfoyle ('pool-mouth'); Aberfeldy (from *peallaidh*, the name of a local water-sprite); Aberdour (*dobhar* is a Brittonic river-word—see **dour**). The Perthshire Abernethy is a largish village at the mouth of a barely discernible stream; the northern Abernethy is a district named after a sizeable tributary of the Spey, Nethy Bridge being the name of the modern settlement; in both cases the name comes from the Nethy (Gaelic *Neitheach*) which apparently means 'the pure one'.

Sometimes the *aber* is contracted, as in Arbroath (originally *Aber brothaig*—'mouth of the little boiling stream'); the stream is still known, locally at least, as the Brothock burn, and there is a Brothock Bridge near the centre of the town, but the term Inverbrothock seems to be a synthetic construct of the last century. Abriachan on Loch Ness was once *Aber Briachan*, from the name (obsolete and unidentified) of a nearby streamlet.

Aber seldom occurs at the end of a name, Lochaber being one of the few examples. It means 'confluence loch', and described the expanse of water where the rivers Lochy and Nevis meet; now it is the name of a district. The water in question was called in Gaelic *an Linne Dhubh* ('the black pool'); the lower part of this large sea-loch was *an Linne Sheilach* ('the brackish pool'—see **sal**). Loch Linnhe as a name is a relatively recent usage, and is a good example of the difference between *meaning* and *function* in a place-name: it would be unhelpful to say simply that Loch Linnhe *means* 'loch pool'—much more useful to explain that the name is not itself meaningful but that it *functions* with reference to a large inlet of the sea.

ach

This is not an expletive but a reduction of the Gaelic *achadh*, meaning field, and it occurs all over the Highlands. If it is less commonly found in the east and south it is probably because in those more populous areas settlement patterns were different: a field in Strathmore is one of thousands, whereas a field in Rannoch is still quite a landmark.

Achnasheen in Wester Ross is 'field of storms', Achnacarry in Lochaber is 'fish-trap field' and Acharn on Loch Tay is 'field of the cairn'. Achlean in Badenoch is *achadh leathainn*—'broad field'. There are dozens of Achmores—'big fields'—some of them farm names.

Rarely is the word *achadh* (or, rather, the sound 'achy') preserved in its entirety in a name, but it is in Breakachy, which is *breac achadh*—'mottled field'. In the south-west, *ach* is frequently rendered into *auch*, which gives us the name of Boswell's family home, Auchinleck—'field of the flag-stones'. Auchenshuggle must be a corruption of something else—possibly of *achadh an t-sabhhail* ('field of the barn'). But do not confuse *auch* with **ath**; they are entirely different Gaelic words, but tended to be confused by the map-makers one with another.

A refinement of *ach* is *tamhnach*—a green or fertile field, which usually appears in names as Tannoch or Tannach (so the fictitious 'Tannochbrae' has some linguistic validity, unlike 'Brigadoon' which is as idiotic as the myth which it perpetuates). Tannach is the name of a village near Wick, and Tannochside in West Lothian is probably the same (despite a claim that it is a corruption of 'St Enoch'). Tannahill in Ayrshire is probably a Gaelic-English hybrid. Tannadice near Forfar appears to be *tamhnach deas* or 'south field'; the name of Dundee United FC's ground comes from the village.

The Old Norse word for field, *vollr*, is to be found in the name Dingwall, which is *thing vollr*, meaning something like 'field of the court of justice' —which it historically was; it may be compared with Tynwald on the Isle of Man.

all

Alloway, Alloa and Alligin embody the early Irish word *all*, meaning rock, a word that is not current in modern Gaelic but is very pervasive in place-names. Alloway and Alloa are probably *all mhagh*—'plain of the rock', the same idea is conveyed in Alva and Alvie, and the Eildons are probably 'rock hills'. The word can occur terminally also: both Kinnell and Kinnoul are thought to be *cinn alla*—'at the head of the crag', and Dowally in Strathtay is Gaelic *duth aille*—'black rock place'.

But this ubiquitous word crops up in other guises. It forms the last three letters of the name Crail in Fife, which was originally *Caraile*—a combination of the Gaelic word *carr* (now current only in its diminutive *carraig*) with *all*, and both meaning rock. Crail therefore says the same thing twice, as do the nearby Carr Rocks—yet another example of the legacy of the Tower of Babel. (See also **carrick**).

The word *all* passed into Gaelic in the form *eileach*, giving Craigellachie—'crag of the rocky place'—and Elcho near Perth. In modern Gaelic *eileach* has the restricted meaning of 'dam'. *All* has its Brittonic equivalent in the word *allt*, meaning cliff or height. It passed straight into Gaelic but with a different meaning (see **allt** below).

At the risk of becoming bogged down in linguistic complexities it is necessary to mention another form of the word *all*, which is the source of several pre-Celtic river-names. Scholars have postulated a form *Alauna*, meaning 'to flow', which gives the names Allan Water, Ale Water, Allander Water and the river Alness, not to speak of several English watercourses called Alne.

allt

This is the Gaelic word for stream, and the map of the Highlands is peppered with the words *Allt na…* this that and the other. Originally the word meant rocky valley but was later applied to the watercourse which invariably was present. Taynuilt is 'house on the stream', and Aultbea is 'birch stream'. Kinaldie in Aberdeenshire and Kinaldy in Fife both mean 'at the end of the burn'. A rivulet or little stream in Gaelic is sometimes *alltan*, which gives the name *Uldeny*, later Udny.

Allt never became part of the English language (as did such terms as glen and loch), but in the eastern and southern Highlands was Scotticised into *auld*. This produces such names as Auldearn—'stream of the Earn' (see **Erin**)—and Auldbar—'stream of the height'. Not unnaturally the word was taken to mean old, and appears in the Aberdeenshire names Old Maud (*allt mad*—see under **con**) and Old Ladders (*allt leitir*—'burn of the hillside').

In most parts of Scotland the prevalent stream name nowadays is *burn*, a word of Anglo-Saxon origin. Sometimes *allt* has been translated into *burn*, preserving the Gaelic word-order and producing such names as Burn of

Sorrow. Burn frequently appears in the Lowlands, but seldom in an interesting way: there are at least a dozen places called Burnfoot, and almost as many called Burnside. Whitburn in West Lothian is 'white burn', and Burnmouth in Berwickshire explains itself. Paradoxically, the word burn passed into Gaelic with the meaning of 'pure water' or drinking water.

annat

In Gaelic, *annaid* is an old word for church (the Latin-derived *eaglais* is more familiar), and properly refers to a church dedicated to a patron saint or containing the relics of its founder. Unadorned the word is to be found in dozens of locations on maps of the Highlands, usually in connection with places of no particular importance and referring to the tiniest of settlements. The name invariably signifies the vicinity of an ancient church or burial-place. Andet (pronounced 'annat') in Aberdeenshire is on the site of a chapel of St Ninian.

Compound-names of this class are more noteworthy. There are several Achnahannets (*achadh na h-annaide*—'field of the annat'); Longannet in Fife is probably *lann annaid*—'church enclosure'—see under **land**; and Craigannet near Stirling will be 'annat rock'.

aonach

This is a term of interest to mountaineers. *Aon* in Gaelic means 'one' (pronounced roughly like the French *une)*, and one of the meanings of *aonach* is a 'coming-together' or 'meeting in a point'; in mountain topography this is a peak or ridge. *Aonach Mor* and *Aonach Beag* are two summits on a 4,000 ft. ridge in the Nevis range; *Aonach Dubh* and *Aonach Eagach* (respectively 'black peak' and 'notched ridge') are in Glencoe, and *Aonach Buidhe* ('yellow ridge') is near Strathcarron. Marcaonach (*a Mharconaich*) near Dalwhinnie is discussed under **marc**. *Aonach Shasuinn* near Loch Affric must mean 'Saxon or Englishman's peak', but no explanation for this name is available.

Aonach had a secondary meaning of 'plain' or 'beach' (presumably also used as a meeting-place). Enochdhu in Strathardle is *an-t aonach dubh*; 'the dark field'; it is pronounced as it was formerly spelt—'Ennochdhu', and, being at the junction of Glen Fearnach and Glen Brerachan may well have been a meeting place of some sort. The old name for Spean Bridge was *Unochan*, also a meeting place, possibly a market. Onich, at the meeting of Loch Leven and Loch Linnhe, might seem to embody a version of this word, but its earlier spelling indicates that it is really *omhanach*—'place of foam'.

18

There was formerly a hamlet in Glen Moriston where Boswell and Dr Johnson spent a night in 1773; it is now Ceannacroc, but Boswell calls it 'Anoch', which may be either *aonach* or **annat**. It is chiefly remembered because Johnson thought that a suitable parting-gift for his host's daughter was a copy of Cocker's *Arithmetic*, which the good doctor had bought in Inverness.

A Gaelic word with a related meaning is *eireachd*—an assembly, probably a place designated for a clan-gathering; such places were prominently situated, often at the confluence of rivers. The Blackwater from Glenshee and the Ardle meet above Blairgowrie in Perthshire, and the river assumes the name Ericht before meeting the Isla a few miles further south; this must have been at one time an assembly place. Glen Errochty near Struan is in Gaelic *gleann Eireachda*—'assembly glen', and Erracht near Fort William has the same sense. Loch Ericht north of Rannoch was yet another assembly place.

ard

To discover the height of anything in Gaelic you could say '*De an aird a tha ann?*' As well as meaning height in the abstract, *aird* can also mean a point of the compass, and is the same as the Scots word *airt* ('direction'). But on the map *aird* (usually spelt 'ard') means a high place, often a promontory. There was a similar word *ardd* in Brittonic, but the occurrence of *ard* in place-names is mainly in the regions that were more recently Gaelic-speaking. Also, promontories and heights are arguably commoner on the deeply indented west coast than elsewhere.

Ardoch—'high place'—occurs at least six times in the Highlands. Ardnamurchan, the most westerly point on the Scottish mainland, is discussed under **muir.** Ardgour may be 'Gabran's promontory' (see **erin**) or possibly *ard ghober*—'goat point'. Ardeer is *aird iar*—'west height'—and Ardersier was originally *aird ros iar*—'height west point'. Ardelve in Lochalsh is 'height of the fallow land'. Ardrossan repeats itself as 'cape of the little cape' (see **ross**), and Ardtornish Point in the Sound of Mull scores a hat-trick by saying the same thing three times—'point of the point of Thori's point' (*nish* being a reduction of **ness**).

Airds is just *aird* with an English plural, and Airdrie (a place which contains more inhabitants than the whole of the Highlands) is possibly *aird ruigh*—'high reach'. But for Airth and Airthrey see **ary.**

arn

The Gaelic word *earran* means a share or division of land, and appears in a

19

modern place-name context as *arn*. Convenient examples are to be found in Perthshire, where Arnclerich, Arnvicar and Arnprior are or were connected with the priory of Inchmahome on the Lake of Menteith. These three names mean 'cleric's portion', 'vicar's portion' and 'prior's portion' respectively. Arngask is also in Perthshire (**gask** means a tongue of land); Arnbrae in Stirlingshire (the gathering-place of the Covenanters in 1676) just means 'high part' (see **brae**). In other parts of the country, *arn* became anglicised to *iron*, as in Irongray and Ironhirst.

A similar Gaelic word with no apparent connection is *fearann*. The heartland of the clan Munro on the Cromarty Firth was called *Fearran Domhnaill*—'Donald's Land'—now Ferindonald. The better-known 'Martin's Land', between the rivers Ythan and Don in Aberdeenshire is the district of Formartin. Ferintosh in Easter Ross is the land of the thane or *toiseach*, a word which gives the Irish *Taoseach* and the surname MacIntosh.

Arthur

Reference is made in the Introduction (p. 2) to the P-Celtic language and to the northern British or Brittonic kingdoms in which it was spoken. These tribal lands (of Dumbarton, Strathclyde and Rheged) suffered the onslaughts of the Angles and Picts in the eighth century, and the language and traditions which characterise them survived mainly in Cornwall, Wales and Brittany.

The so-called 'King' Arthur may have been a Romano-British leader, fighting against the the Anglo-Saxons in the fifth century, about whom legends were circulating by the ninth century. The corpus of Arthurian legend has its basis in a folk memory of this resistance to English expansionism, and the name of Arthur became a sort of fingerprint of the British presence. In 1136 Geoffrey of Monmouth's *Historia Regum Britanniae* popularised Arthur as one of the 'Kings of Britain', giving him a largely fictional biography which included a campaign in Moray against the Picts and Scots, with a victory at Loch Lomond.

When surveying supposedly 'Arthurian' names in Scotland it is by no means necessary to suppose that any of the events related in the legends actually took place in this country (if indeed they took place at all); the most that can be claimed is that Britons tended to describe their terrain in Arthurian terms. This is reflected in the many occurrences of place-names involving the name of Arthur himself. The most notable Arthur's Seat is in Edinburgh, but there were others in the Vale of Leven, on Loch Long, in Angus and in Dumfries. Loch Arthur is in Kirkcudbright, and various rivers and rocks and other natural features in the south-west commemorated the legendary king. Arthur's Fountain in Crawford parish is mentioned (as *fons Arthuri*) in 1239; an old name for Dunbarton Castle was *Castrum Arthuri* ('Arthur's Castle') Arthurlee is in Renfrewshire; a Roman structure on the Carron in Stirlingshire was known in the thirteenth century as 'Arthur's Oven'.

Ben Arthur (often known as 'the Cobbler') in Argyll, and Benarty Hill in Fife are outside traditional British territory, and one is of course left with the possibility that some of these place-names can be attributed to the growing prestige and popularity of Arthur as a forename from the 1150s onwards. It is not coincidence that the clan MacArthur took its name and claimed descent from the 'once and future king'. Arthurstone near Dundee is popularly believed to have taken its name from a megalith locally known as 'Arthur-Stone': it is more likely however the the true source is 'Arthur's toun' (see **ton**).

ary

The Gaelic term *airidh* (pronounced 'ery' and borrowed from Old Norse *erg*) meant originally a hill pasture, and was later applied to the huts or shielings which were built there for the accommodation of the people (mainly women and children) who looked after the cattle in high summer. The changeover from cattle to sheep removed the *raison d'être* of shielings, and most of these sites are now apparent only to antiquarians and archaeologists; a few however became permanent settlements, as at Dalnaspidal on the A9. The word appears occasionally on the map, for example in a little glen north of Callander where there is a lonely cottage marked as Arivurichardich—'Murcharty's shieling'. It has been claimed that Airth and Airthrie are of this origin, but neither answers to the description of a green place among hills.

The word *airidh* occurs in place-names mainly in the ending *-ary*. Glassary must mean 'grey or green shieling', and there are many such names in the Western Isles, Sutherland and Caithness, where *airidh* often had the more ordinary meaning of settlement. Ardarie is *aird airidh* ('high shieling') and Fiunary is *fionn airidh* ('white shieling'). Scourie in Sutherland went through a Norse stage (*sjoga-erg*) and re-emerged in the Gaelic form *Sgogairigh*—'shaw place'. Glen Dessary in Lochaber looks very like *deas airidh* (literally 'South Shields', but an incomparably more beautiful name).

Another Gaelic term for a grazing was *ruighe* (pronounced 'roo-ye' and meaning literally a 'reach' or 'forearm'). This word was widely used in the Cairngorm and Deeside area to indicate a shieling, and although these have largely vanished, the maps preserve their names in Ryvoan (*Ruighe a' Bhothain* or 'bothy-shieling') and Ryenettin and Renatton ('juniper shieling').

auchter

In everyday Gaelic *air uachdair* means 'on top of'; *uachdair* can be the upper part of anything, e.g. cream (the top of the milk). In a place-name context it is the high ground. So we have Auchtermuchty, a name which seems to exercise a perennial fascination, and means 'high ground of the pig-rearing'. Drumochter on the A9 is 'spine of the high ground'—and still appears a ridge of some height when you cross it on a bicycle. Auchterderran ih Fife is 'high ground with thickets' and Ochtertyre near Crieff is just 'high land'. The topographical use of the word *uachdair* does not seem to have been common in the north-west, and 'auchter' names are pretty well confined to the Highland fringes and the Lowlands.

The opposite of *uachdair* in Gaelic is *iochdair* (pronounced 'eech-kir'), the bottom part of anything, claimed as the origin of Glasgow's Yoker. A more productive term however is the little word *fo*, meaning under. '*Na biodh bhur cridhe fo thrioblaid*'—'Let not your heart be troubled' (John 14:1), that is, 'under trouble'. This term occurs in Fowlis, which is really *fo-ghlais*—'sub-stream' or tributary ; Fowlis Easter is near Dundee, and Fowlis Wester near Crieff. Foulis Castle in Easter Ross is the ancestral home of the Munro chiefs; and the surname has the same origin. Fortrose, which is pronounced locally 'fortress', is possibly *fo terros*—'subsidiary cape', and Forres is *fo-rais* or 'sub copse').

avon

This familiar river-name is perhaps associated more with Shakespearean England; nevertheless there are several Avons in Scotland, and the ramifications of the term as a place-name element are extensive. Scholarship has now established that the Indo-European root is *ab*, which simply means water or river. Its Welsh or Brittonic cognate (see Introduction) is *afon*, and the Gaelic is *abhainn* (pronounced 'ah-von'). There were equivalents also, in Gaulish and Breton, which provide several *avon*-type river-names on the continent, including five rivers Avon in France. The rivers Avon in West Lothian and Lanark, and the Evan Water in Dumfriesshire probably come from the Brittonic source; Strathaven, elided in pronunciation to 'strayven', means of course 'valley of the Aven'. The Aven in Aberdeen/ Kincardine may be Gaelic in origin.

The Banffshire Avon (with its offshoots of Loch Avon and Ben Avon) is thought to be different: these should all be pronounced 'A'an' (which they frequently are) and spelt in the same way (which they seldom are).

There is a respectable tradition that the river was named after *Athfionn* ('very bright one') the legendary wife of *Fionn mac Cumhaill* (Finn Maccool); as is always the case, the hill and loch names followed suit.

The name Kelvin is said to derive from *caol abhuinn*—'narrow river'; there is also a Kelvin in East Kilbride. Kelvingrove (the parliamentary division of Glasgow) and Kelvinside (the municipal ward) are recent derivatives, as is the barony bestowed on the enunciator of the second law of dynamics.

Going back to the root-word *ab*, we have the rivers Almond in West Lothian and Perthshire; the same stem gives Loch Awe and its derivatives Bonawe (see **bon**) and Inverawe (see **inver**). Avoch in Easter Ross (pronounced 'auch') comes from a related Gaelic word *abhach* meaning 'stream place', and Loch Oich in Inverness-shire has a similar sense.

Ayr

The Gaelic for Ayr is *Inbhir air*, meaning 'Ayr mouth'; but the actual meaning of the river-name is more problematical. The root word is thought to be *ara*, meaning something like 'watercourse', and is the basis of many European river-names from the Aare in Switzerland to the Oare in Somerset. The nearby River Irvine, from which the town takes its name, may have a broadly similar etymology; and it is possible that the Scottish river-names Earn, Findhorn and Deveron are originally from this root-word rather than the ones suggested under **Erin**.

B

bal

A baillie is a municipal officer, and in Gaelic the word *baile* means town or village, sometimes a feudal holding, both words no doubt coming originally from the Latin *ballium*, meaning an enclosure. The Gaelic word is pronounced 'balla' (and often so rendered into English).

Names beginning with *bal* are legion, and indeed this element was the standard one used by Gaelic-speakers in describing any settlement. It completely superseded the earlier Brittonic term **pit**, which to the Gael had a somewhat specialised and anatomical meaning. (To this day Gaelic-speakers prefer to say Bailechlochrie rather than Pitlochry.)

Bal names are scattered over Scotland, Highland and Lowland, and are found everywhere except the far north-east and the eastern Border areas (where Gaelic was never the majority language). They are particularly concentrated in Galloway and the upper Forth valley, Fife, Angus, East Perthshire, the Mearns, Easter Ross and Inverness. Historians have been able to find parallels between the spread of *bal* names from the Dalriadic settlements in the south-west and the growing ascendancy of Gaeldom over Pictland in the ninth century (see Introduction).

There are four Balgowans and two Balnagowans on the map, all deriving from *baile a'ghobhainn*—'village of the smiths'. There are four Balfours—'pasture village'—(see **four**), and other examples are Balquhidder—'fodder village'—and Ballinluig ('township in the hollow'— see **lag**). Ballachulish is discussed under **kyle** and Ballantrae under **traigh**.

In a genuine *bal* name the stress is never on the *bal* but always on the following syllable. This means that Balloch at the foot of Loch Lomond cannot mean 'lake village': in fact it comes from **bealach**. Similarly the stress on the first syllable of Ballater (discussed under **letter**) means that it is unlikely to be a genuine *bal* name. On the other hand, Bellshill in Lanarkshire has been claimed as a *bal* name, with an English suffix: the bell bit certainly does not refer either to the surname or to the object, but no satisfactory etymology has been found.

balg

This is the Gaelic term for bag or belly, no doubt a loan-word from Latin *balga*—a pouch, which gives the additional word 'bulge'. In a place-name context it often refers to a bag-shaped river-pool, as at Bridge of Balgie in Glen Lyon. More familiar, if less obvious, is the River Bogie in Buchan, with its bag-like pools, which gives its name to Strathbogie (of which a better spelling is preserved in the peerage title of 'Strabolgi'). There are two hills in Angus, The Builg in the Mearns, and Bulg near Edzell, which are correctly described as 'bulges'; more notable than either is the Cairnwell, a mountain that found itself celebrated with the boom in wintersports at Glenshee; in Gaelic it is *Carn Bhuilg*—'hill of bulges'. Lynwilg in Strathspey is *linne bhuilg*—'pool of the bag'; Bawkie Bay, the west bay of Dunoon, is a variant of the same usage.

A curious use of *balg* meaning 'bag' or 'bay' is found in the name Ardvorlich, which occurs on both Loch Lomond and Loch Earn. The earlier form is *ard mhur (bh)laig*—'promontory of the sea bag', the term having been transferred from a salt-water bay to an inlet on a freshwater loch. Even more curious, these two tiny inlets have given their name to the two Ben Vorlichs, among the most notable peaks in the southern Highlands. The early spelling of these names leaves the etymology in no doubt.

One of the summits of Beinn a Ghlo in Atholl (popularly, 'mountain of mist') is called on the map *Braigh Coire Chruinn-bhalgain*. This appears to mean 'top of the corrie of the round bulges', and is interesting for two reasons: first, it illustrates the doggedly unromantic nature of most Scottish mountain-nomenclature, and secondly it is usable only by Gaelic speakers. Without the permanance conferred by the map-makers' print, it would surely, like thousands of other such names, have disappeared without trace.

Later the term *balg* tended to be assimilated to another Gaelic word *bog* meaning wet (see under **mig**); Dunbog in Fife is probably *dun builg* ('fort of the bulge') as its toponomy would indicate, rather than 'bog fort'. But beware of confusion with the Gaelic prefix **bal**.

barr

In Gaelic this means literally 'a crop'. But the English word crop is really the top of anything—the head of the corn, the sprouting of the hair, that which requires to be cut. The Gaelic word *barr* has all these meanings and more, including the tip of a fishing-rod, the point of a needle or even (in Lewis) the cream on the milk; in place-names it usually signifies 'crest' or 'height'. The village of Barr in Ayrshire means just that, and Barrhead says much the same thing twice over. Bargeddie near Coatbridge is 'top ridge', and Dunbar is probably 'fort on the height'. Barcaldine is *barr calltuin*— 'hazel height'—and Barlinnie once had pleasanter associations—with a **linn**, or pool—than it now does. Barrie in Angus is probably a *barr* name, although this element is not commonly found in these parts, and the ending remains obscure.

Notice that all these names are taken from the Lowlands and the southern Highlands: *barr* as a place-name element is not found north of Fort William. And do not be misled by Barra, which is probably St Barr's Island.

bealach

This Gaelic word, pronounced 'b-yal-ugh', means a pass, and is used in much the same way as **lairig**. The two words co-exist in the Cairngorms and upper Deeside area. The Lairig Ghru and the Lairig an Laoigh show the word *lairig* in its usual sense of mountain-route, while *bealach* can be simply a gap in the hills (or even in a wall or fence); it can occasionally mean a 'stream-crossing', as is probably the case with Ballochbuie ('yellow pass'), which does not seem to describe a hill-crossing but is now the name of a deer forest.

There are two passes called Bealach nam Bo ('pass of the cattle'), discussed under **tarff**. Bealach a' Mhargaidh ('pass of the market') is at the head of Glen Kinglas, leading over to Loch Lomond, and apparently got its name from being the location of a summer cattle-market in bygone days. Loch a Vealloch in Sutherland is a somewhat feeble English approximation to *Loch a Bhealaich*—'Loch of the Gap'.

In the Lowlands the term usually becomes Balloch, and there are six places so-called. Confusion with **bal** names is a contingency, but the stress is a good indication. Balloch near Loch Lomond is discussed under **bal**. Kenmore at the foot of Loch Tay was also called Balloch until quite recently. The elegaic poet Gray, when staying there in 1777, referred to the old name and opined that it was 'changed for decency'—no doubt he pronounced it in such a way that it sounded like the vulgar word for testicle. Elsewhere the term *bealach* has been transferred from the pass to the range: there are several Ballo Hills on the Highland fringe.

A narrower pass is covered by the Gaelic word *agaidh,* which is the basis of Aviemore ('great gap'), a reference to the conspicuous cleft of the Spey valley at this point; a small defile in the Cairngorms not far away used to be known as *Agaidh Beag* or 'little gap'. Advie on the lower Spey is of the same origin. The Lowland village of Glamis is also thought to mean 'cleft', but through an obsolete Gaelic word *glamphus* which comes ultimately from the Old English verb *cleofan*—'to cleave'.

Beauly

It would be pleasant, in celebration of the five hundredth anniversary of the Auld Alliance between our two countries, to include a paragraph or two concerning names of French origin. Alas, this is not easy, because most place-nomenclature was well established long before the inception of the Alliance.

Beauly is probably the most obviously French of our place-names; it is of course *beau lieu* ('fine place') an early but contrived name for a monastery originally known as *Manachainn 'ic Shimidh* (Mac Shimidh being the patronymic of the Frasers of Lovat); Beaufort was another surname in the Fraser pedigree, which made it ('fine fort') a very appropriate name for the nearby clan headquarters. Fontainebleau, the hunting-palace of the French kings, became a fashionable name for Scottish residences in the eighteenth century; there are three Fountainbleaus in Aberdeenshire and one near Dundee—the grandeur being somewhat diminished in the vernacular rendering of 'The Funtins'.

The odd Aberdeenshire name of The Barmekin (which occurs twice) comes from the Norman-French term *barbican*; originally a watch-tower, it was used locally (in Echt and Keig) to mean a hill-fort.

A number of our frenchified place-names originated as Norman sur-names, such as Melville which occurs several times in the Lothians and Fife, not to speak of the several castles, houses and streets so called. The surname no doubt originated in a Norman place-name, whose apparent ety-mology (? 'bad town') is less complimentary than that of Beauly. Belses near Hawick is said to derive from 'de Bel Assize', the name of a Norman knight.

Champfleurie near Linlithgow and Floors in the Borders refer to flow-ers; Burdiehouse in Edinburgh is supposed to be a corruption of 'Bordeaux house'. Much later than the Alliance is the name Hopeman on the Moray coast; it is apparently *haut mont*, and is an early nineteenth-century coin-age.

Sciennes (pronounced 'sheens') is Italian and not French, but is worth including in this not very impressive rag-bag. It was the site of the monas-tery of St Catherine of Siena. The one or two Belmonts on the Scottish map are there to stress the cosmopolitan taste of the proprietors and to reinforce the Italian reputation for beauty.

ben

It is hardly necessary to explain that *ben* means mountain, of which the Highands boast many. But not every Scottish mountain has the prefix *ben*, and of the 280 Munros (mountains over 3,000 feet in height) fewer than half are *bens*. The others have such designations as *creag* (crag), *carn* (see **cairn**), *bidean* (pinnacle), *braighe* (see **brae**), *gob* (point), **meall** (lump), **mullach** (top), **sgurr** (rocky peak), *stac* and *stob* (see under **stuc**).

Hill names are always the subject of curiosity to visitors, but the truth is that hills themselves were never very important in human terms (compared with valleys and plains); so it is not too surprising that some of the most spectacular mountains are named after insignificant streams which rise in them. Scotland's biggest ben is named after the River Nevis; and the temp-tation must be resisted to relate Ben Nevis to the Latin *nebula*, however appropriate that might seem. (*Nevis* is probably linked to the Gaelic *neimh*, pronounced 'nev', and meaning 'poison' or 'venom'. Glen Nevis in the late mediaeval period had a reputation for evil; the name is shared with Loch Nevis in the north-west).

Ben is the Gaelic word *beinn*, which has the secondary meaning of 'horn'. The early settlers, tenders of cattle and hunters of deer—who never went nearer to the mountains than they had to—must have seen the resemblance between mountain-peaks and the horns of animals; and it is surely no coincidence that 'horn' (Matterhorn, Wetterhorn, Fischerhorn) occurs so frequently in Swiss mountain terminology.

Horns do not have to be vertical, and there was another Gaelic adjective *beannach* which described horn-like bends on river or loch. Loch Vennacher in the Trossachs is *Bheannchair*—'horn loch', and its diminutive is to be found in the two Lochs Beanncharain in the Straths of Conon and Farrar. There are many other Glen Banchors and Tullybanchors with horn-like attributes; and Banchory on the Dee signifies a river-bend. Bangor in Wales has a similar derivation: but note that the stress on the second syllable of Bangour in Midlothian suggests *beinn ghobher*—'goat hill'.

Two other variants of the word 'ben' deserve mention. The genitive is *bian*, so that Bidean nam Bian in Glencoe means nothing more romantic than 'peaks of the ben'. (The pronunciation incidentally is 'beech-an'). An older adjectival form of the word is *bannog*, which survives in the name Bannockburn. *Bannoch* (which happens also to be the Gaelic word for 'bannock') is thought to refer to the hilly area above the Carron valley which is drained by the burn which gave its name to the site of Bruce's great victory. The strangest *ben* name must be Benbecula, which is in Gaelic *beinn a bhaodhla* and means literally 'hill of the fordable water'; the last bit is clear enough, as Benbecula lies between the two Uists, and the channels are referred to as the North and South Fords—but it is more obviously an island than a hill.

black

Although a huge number of Lowland place-names have a Gaelic stem, in many cases there is an English-language prefix which long ago became an integral part of the name. By far the commonest prefix of this kind is the adjective black, and an example is the River Blackadder. *Adder* is a pre-Celtic word probably just signifying 'watercourse', and is related to the German Oder.

Other examples of an English specific being added to a Celtic generic are Blackcraig ('black rock'), of which there are three, and Blackness ('black point') of which there are two. More recent names combine 'black' with an English stem: there are six Blacklaws, three Blackfords, two Blackwoods and no fewer than nine Blackwaters. Most of the dozen Black Lochs and the six Black Burns and the nine Black Hills will be modern or will be translations from the Gaelic. The Black Mount south of Glencoe is a modern coinage, as is the one in East Lanark. The Black Isle was formerly *Ardmeanach* ('middle point')—it is not an island but a peninsula between the Moray and Cromarty Firths.

'Black' in place names is much commoner than other adjectives of colour;

this is because it is very often just a differential rather than a description: the pairings of Blackadder/Whitadder and Devon/Black Devon illustrate this point, but see under **den** for the meaning of Devon. Note however that Blacklunans in Glen Isla is not a 'black' name of any kind: it is a corruption of *baile cluanean*—'steading of the meadows' (see **cluny**).

blair

The word *blar* in modern Gaelic usually means 'a battle', as in *blar Culodair*, the Battle of Culloden. Less celebrated, but hardly less bloody, is *blar na leine*, the Battle of the Shirts, which took place between the Frasers and the Clanranald Macdonalds in 1544 and was so called because the warriors stripped in the heat of the conflict. Topographically, *blar* means a piece of cleared land, but no doubt in the turbulent days of clan warfare any spare bit of ground served as a venue for a fight.

There are several places in Scotland called Blair, signifying a plot of land, or sometimes a plain. The two best known are Blair Atholl and Blairgowrie (both discussed under **erin**). There are a Blairmore and a Blairbeg on Loch Long, meaning 'big' and 'little plot'. Blair Logie near Stirling is *blar luig*—'land of the hollow' (see **lag**). Blairingone, also near Stirling, is *blar nan gobhainn*—'field of the smiths'. Blawrainy near Kirkcudbright gives a better idea of the Gaelic pronunciation: the name is *blar raineach*—'ferny place'—and the second element appears more familiarly in Rannoch. In Ross-shire there are three places called Balblair— 'village on the plain'; and Balblairs was the camp site of the Hanoverian army on the eve of Culloden. Blairadam took its name from that of the proprietor.

bon/bun

These two Gaelic words, although of different origin, have much the same meaning 'bottom'—and both make a considerable impact on Highland place-nomenclature. Bonawe is at the foot of the Awe, and Bunrannoch is at the end of Loch Rannoch; Bunessan in Mull is 'foot of the waterfalls', and Bunchrew near Inverness is probably 'tree-stump' (see **crieff**). Bonar Bridge was earlier *am Bonnath*—'the bottom ford' (across the Kyle of Sutherland at low tide); Bonaly in the Pentlands looks like 'foot of the rocky place'; and Bonskeid near Pitlochry is thought to be 'foot of the corner'. The Border name of Bonjedward is unusual: topographically it is at the mouth of the Jed, but literally it means 'Jedburgh-foot', and the supposition is that a Gaelic prefix has been added to an existing English name whose meaning was misunderstood (see also under **worth**).

After a preposition, the initial letter of both *bun* and *bon* becomes 'm':

thus, Moness near Aberfeldy is 'at the foot of the waterfall', and Munlochy in the Black Isle means 'near the loch'.

Lowland names beginning with *bon-* give the misleading impression that they incorporate the Scots word *bonny* meaning 'handsome'; this may possibly be the case with the occasional croft or farm but is not the origin of the several Bonnytons and Bonningtons in the Lothians. These names are of Scandinavian origin, and the prefix could be either Old Norse *bonde* or the personal name Bondi: their meaning would be either 'peasant farm' or 'Bondi's farm'. Bonnyrigg near Lasswade is really 'bannock ridge' or 'bannock-shaped (i.e. round) field'—see **rig**; the field name became that of a village in the eighteenth century. Bonnybridge near Falkirk takes its name from the River Bonny, of obscure origin.

brae

This is a very pervasive place-name element in Scotland. It appears in English dictionaries as a Scots dialect-word, and of course means 'hill-slope'. Its origin is Old Norse *bra*, and it is in this pure and unadorned form that it appears in Shetland, in the village of Brae. The various settlements known as Braehead were probably Scots coinages rather than Scandinavian, as is also the case when the word is used in the plural to indicate a district; the Braes in Skye is the bit between Portree and Sligachan, where the crofters' 'battle' took place in 1882. Similarly, the terminology 'Braes of Abernethy', 'Braes of Balquhidder' and 'Braes of Doune' is modern, although the names involved are ancient.

There are two similar-sounding Gaelic words *braighe* and *braghad*, which mean 'neck' or 'upper part'. The latter gives the name Breadalbane, in Gaelic *Braghad Alban* or 'high land of Scotia'; Braemar and Braemoray incorporate the same word, and mean the uplands of Mar and Moray respectively. Braeriach, second highest of the Cairngorms, means literally 'rough neck' or 'rugged height'.

The Braid Hills in Edinburgh have the same sense of height, although the Scots word *braid*—'broad'—has crept into the spelling.

It should be mentioned that there is yet another Gaelic word *bruach*, meaning bank or edge, which has sometimes caused confusion. Tighnabruaich is 'house on the bank' (not on the brae), and Bruachladdich looks like 'shore bank'. Breich in West Lothian shows the word in its uncompounded state; and Ballinbreich in Fife is 'bank-stead'.

The corresponding English terminology is more straightforward. There are six Bankheads, three Bankends, a Bankfoot and a Banknock, all with meanings too obvious to need clarification. Clydebank is a useful nineteenth century coinage for a shipbuilding village on the river. But in the far north there is confusion with the Norse word *bakki*. Bakki is said to be the name of thirty farms in Iceland: be that as it may, there are or were many settlements in the Northern and Western Isles with such names as Back, Bachd, Bakki and Bacca—all meaning 'bank'.

breck

Breac in Gaelic has several meanings, one of which is smallpox. Alan Breck in *Kidnapped* was so-called because of his pockmarked appearance. More pleasantly, the Gaelic word for trout is *breac*, or 'speckled one'. In its plural form of *breacan* the word means tartan.

In place-names *breac* usually has the sense of speckled. Ben Vrackie is 'speckled mountain' and so are Ben Bhraggie and Ben Bhreac. Breakachy near Beauly is 'dappled field', and the three places in Aberdeenshire called Bracco also have this sense; so does Braco near Crieff. Ardvreck on Loch Assynt is probably 'speckled point', but Altnabreac in Caithness must surely be 'troutbeck' and Braclinn near Callander looks very like 'trout pool'.

Brechin in Angus is thought to be indirectly a *breac* name, through Brychan, an Irish prince who lived in the fifth century and who gave his name also to Brecon in Wales; Brychan (which may have meant 'spotted' or conceivably 'tartan-clad') is probably the same name if not the same person that figures in Corrievreckan (see **corrie**). Affric in Gaelic is *ath bhreac*, literally 'very dappled'—but this rather puzzling name has been assumed to be that of a river-goddess.

Our word salmon comes from the Latin *salmo*, the root word being *salire* 'to leap'; the Gaelic equivalent is *bradan*. Neither it nor the English word figure in any Scottish place-names. But *lax*, the Old Norse word for salmon (and current in one form or another in most of the Germanic languages), gives Laxford in Sutherland, Lax Firth in Shetland, Laxay in Lewis, Laxadale in Harris, and Laxdale in Lewis; the respective meanings are 'salmon-loch, -river, and -valley'. There are no salmon names in Orkney; and there are no salmon found in Shetland, although the name Laxo ('salmon voe') would seem to indicate that this was not always so.

bridge

Bridges have always been important in terms of human geography, as providing nuclei of settlements and hubs for road systems and trading routes. There are upwards of fifty Lowland settlements in Scotland whose names contain the word bridge or its Scots variant brig: there are at least fifteen Bridgends, and numerous Brigtons and Bridgefoots. The beginning of

Bishopbriggs refers unambiguously to the episcopate, but the suffix is more doubtful—it might be **rig**. One of the more interesting bridge-names is Stockbridge in Edinburgh, which comes from Old English *stoc* meaning a stave, also found in 'stockade'.

Bridge is hardly less frequent in the Highlands, where it has largely replaced the Gaelic word *drochaid*; although we still have Drumnadrochit and Kindrochit (meaning respectively 'bridge' and 'bridge-head') they are nothing to the large number of modern formations of the 'Bridge of Orchy' type. As their Gaelic word-order indicates, these names are probably translations, and are earlier than formations such as Bonar Bridge or Coatbridge (the bridge was built in 1800 and took its name from the much older settlement of Coats, i.e. 'cottar-houses'); even more modern is the use of the definite article—*The* Erskine Bridge, *The* Moncreiffe Bridge.

burgh

As a common noun, burgh is more familiar in Scotland than in England, where the allied form of 'borough' is preferred. Both come from Old English *burg* or *burh*, meaning a cluster of houses round about and dependent upon a fort or monastery; there are cognates in Old Norse (*borg*) and modern German (*Burg*), but not in the Celtic languages. As one might expect, therefore, Scottish place-names incorporating the term burgh are found mainly in areas where English replaced a Celtic language at an early date, or where the name is modern—or where the name comes direct from Old Norse. An example of the latter is Borve, which occurs five times in the Hebrides and which just means 'fort'. The metathesised form Brough occurs more often in England, but there is an isolated example in Shetland. The Hebridean Boreraig was originally *borg-wic* ('fort-bay') and Boreray is 'fort-isle'; Burghead in Moray and Broughton in the Borders probably have a similar origin, but with an English suffix. Another variant is Borgue near Kirkcudbright, and there is a Burra in the Northern Isles.

The three original Scottish burghs were Edinburgh, Roxburgh and Winchburgh, dating from the time when the word meant strictly a fortified place. The name Edinburgh, earlier *Dineidin*, is discussed under **dun**. Roxburgh, described in the twelfth century as the fourth largest burgh in Scotland, was destroyed after the tragic death of James II at the siege of its castle in 1460; the name was 'Hroc's burgh'. Winchburgh suffered arrested development: it is now no more than a village in the central belt. Musselburgh dates from the eleventh century, the reference being to a nearby musselbed in the Forth estuary. Jedburgh is not a proper 'burgh' name: it was originally *Jedworth*, the Old English term **worth** (meaning 'enclosed village') having dropped out of use around the seventeenth century.

At one time the award of burgh status was a royal prerogative, and conferred certain trading rights on the recipient, but rarely involved a change of name; Perth and Crail are two examples. Royal burghs in the mid-thirteenth century tended to be English-speaking enclaves in a still large Gaelic-speaking population, and were a rallying point for Flemish, Norman and Anglian settlers. Royal control of the west coast from the Clyde northwards was not sufficiently secure to establish burghs in that area for several hundred years: burgh names in the West Highlands are without exception modern. In the Lowlands the more recent burgh-names include Fraserburgh, founded by one of the Frasers of Phillorth at the end of the seventeenth century; its earlier name was *Faithlie*, and its modern nickname is *The Broch*. Helensburgh was feued in 1776 by Sir James Colquhoun of Luss and later named for his wife; Osnaburgh was an attempt (1823) to rename the village of Dairsie in Fife after osnaburgs, a coarse cloth which was processed there, but the new name survives only on the map.

by

The Old Norse word *byr* meant farm or hamlet, and appears as the termination of several place-names in the far north. Duncansby Head (you can't get much further north) has as its first component Dungad's *byr* (he is probably the tenth-century chief referred to in the *Orkneyinga Saga*); the nearby Canisbay is probably 'canon's farm'. Golspie is 'Gulli's farm', or just possibly 'gold farm', an etymology made more plausible by the presence of that metal in the vicinity.

However, names of this type are even more numerous in the extreme south of Scotland; over thirty of them are recorded in Dumfriesshire alone. They are quite common in England also—Whitby, Kirkby and Derby are examples that come to mind—and they are found in regions of former Danish and Norwegian settlement of the English midlands and north. This only serves to remind us that Scottish place-names cannot be studied in isolation from those of England, for, despite dialectal differences, southern Scotland shares a common linguistic heritage with its neighbour.

Bie is a variant of *by*. Canonbie is 'canon's farm'—the same in fact as Canisbay; Lockerbie is 'Lockhart's farm'. Sorbie is Old Norse *saur byr*—'muddy farm'—and reappears in Yorkshire as Sowerby. Humbie is probably 'hound's farm': its *bie* ending is rare in eastern Scotland, and names of this type are notably absent from the Central Lowlands.

33

C

caer

It would be a very incurious person who did not make the mental link between the Welsh Caernarvon and the Dumfries Caerlaverock: the connection is the P-Celtic word *caer* which means a stone fort, often Roman rather than native in origin. In Scotland, the element *caer* usually indicates something more modest—a fortified homestead, sometimes just a hill or a farm (incidentally, Caerlaverock from its early spellings appears to be not 'larkhill' but 'elm hill'); the term is confined to the area south of the Forth-Clyde line, where a Cumbric form of P-Celtic was current between the ninth and eleventh centuries. *Caer* does not occur between Cumbria and Wales, possibly due to the fact that by the mid-seventh century the Northumbrians had driven a wedge between north-west England and the Mersey.

Caer is a fugitive term which tends to be put to flight by stronger words such as **kirk** and **cairn**. Cairnryan in Galloway is thought to be *Caer Rion* —'fort of the king'; Kirkcaldy was originally *caer caled din*—'fort on the hard hill', and Kirkintilloch is *caer cinn tulaich*—'hill-head fort'. Cathcart had the earlier spelling of *Kirkart,* and means 'fort on the River Cart'. *Caer* frequently becomes *car*: Carmyle near Glasgow and Carmyllie in Angus mean 'warrior's fort', and Carfrae on the A68 is 'hill farm'. Carmunnock was earlier *Carmannoc*—'monks' close', and Carluke has an obscure stem which is discussed under **lag**. Occasionally *caer* is contracted out of recognition: Cramond on the Forth is *caer Almond*—'fort on the Almond'.

The Gaelic form of *caer* is *cathair* (which in ordinary usage means a chair) and both may well be related to the Latin *castrum*, 'a camp' (as is the English name Chester, by no means unknown on the map of Scotland although often no more than a farm name). *Cathair* is a very common place-name element in Ireland, but for some reason is only found in the east of Scotland, and that rarely. Stracathro in Angus was *srath cathrach*— 'strath of the fort'—and the term may well be repeated in the neighbouring hill forts of Caterthun. Carnegie in the same county is *cathair an eige*— 'fort in the gap'—and Catterline (the ending being pronounced 'linn') is *cathair linne*—'pool fort'.

A related element is Keir, which is a mangled version of either *caer* or *cathair*. Keir was once so frequent in the central belt of Scotland as to be a common noun rather than a proper name; the best-known survivor is near Stirling.

cairn

In Gaelic *carn* means a heap of stones, and by extension a rocky hill. It is one of the commonest words in mountain terminology, and the map of the Grampians is peppered with carns and cairns. The most notable are Cairngorm and Cairn Toul (respectively 'blue hill' and 'barn hill'); Cairn o Mount is discussed under **monadh**.

The word cairn is used by Scots people as a common noun, usually with reference to the heaps of stones which indicate a mountain path or a summit. It is in its primary sense of a stone-heap that it appears outside mountain areas.

The village of Cairn near New Cumnock will have this derivation; Carntyne near Glasgow is *carn tinneadh* ('fire cairn' or beacon); and Carnwath in Lanarkshire shows the Brittonic form (see Introduction) of *carn gwydd* or 'cairn of the wood'. But beware that Cardney and Cairney can have their source in **carden**; Cairnryan is discussed under **caer**.

Carnoustie has posed problems, not only for golfers. *Carn fheusta* ('cairn of the feast') and *carn giuthais* ('cairn of the pines') have been proposed; the first seems unlikely and the second misses the mark phonetically; bearing in mind that *carn* could also mean a grave, one might point as a possible alternative to the near-homonym Carn Aosda, the name of a hill near Braemar (meaning 'ancient cairn').

calder

This appears as a name at least two dozen times on the map of Scotland, mostly as a river-name; in Lothian, however, it has become that of a district, with East, West and Mid Calder. The element has its origin in the Brittonic words *caled dobhar* ('hard water') and is also familiar in the form Cawdor in Nairn. Kelty in Fife is a version of the same formation; there are three other villages called Keltie on the southern Highland fringe.

Achallader on the Black Mount means 'field of Calder', the original name of the water of Talla. Callater near Braemar is similar, as is Callander near Crieff. (But Callander on the Teith was taken from Callander Park near Falkirk and has a slightly different etymology: it probably means 'hard shore'). Invercauld and Inverkeillor refer to the confluences of streams which earlier bore the Calder name or some variant of it; all mean 'hard water'.

35

cambus

Camas is a bay or creek, sometimes just a bend. Camusericht is the bay in Loch Rannoch into which the River Ericht (prior to hydro-electrification) discharged its waters. (Ericht and the nearby Glen Errochty are discussed under **aonach**). In the Lowlands a mediant letter 'b' creeps in: and it is on the winding rivers of Clyde and Forth that the term *cambus* is most commonly found: Cambuslang is *camas long*—'ships' bay'—the highest tidal bay in the Clyde, and Cambusnethan is 'Neithon's bend' (also on the Clyde). Cambus and Cambuskenneth near Alloa are two examples on the the Forth, with obvious meanings. Cambusbarron near Stirling must be 'bend of the heights'. Cambus o' May in Aberdeenshire is discussed under **may**.

cardine

The Brittonic word *cardden* meant copse or thicket. Its most obvious occurrence is in the name Kincardine which appears in at least seven different places on the Scottish map; it means 'at the head of the wood'. The best-known is Kincardine on Forth, not for its earldom but for its bridge. The Mearns village of Kincardine, however, which gave its name to the county, suffered from arrested development and has virtually disappeared off the map. Kincardine o' Neill mentions the old thanage of Neil to distinguish it from its Deeside counterpart.

The oldest occurrence of the name, mentioned by Adamnan, the biographer of Columba, is *Airchardan*, meaning 'at the woods'. Its modern form is Urquhart, the name of a parish in Inverness-shire, but even more familiar as a surname. Orchy is probably from the same source. Cardenden in Fife is 'thicket-glen' (the word *den* is nearly always used in the Lowlands where you would find 'glen' in the Highlands). Pluscarden probably contains the Brittonic word *plas*—'wooded estate'. Fettercairn is originally *fothair cardden*—'wooded slope', Drumchardine near Beauly is 'copse ridge' and Cardno in Buchan is 'copse place'.

carrick

The Gaelic term *carraig* is one of the oldest place-name elements in Scotland; it is also familiar in names such as the Irish Carrickfergus. The word means basically 'rock', and occurs mainly on the southwest coast where it gave the name to the ancient district of Carrick. More specifically it meant a rock serving as a quay or fishing-station, and its occurrence in several unimportant coastal place-names is taken as evidence of early Gaelic settlement (see Introduction). Carradale in Kintyre is probably the best-known of these.

Sometimes the suffix disappears, and we are left with names like Carrbridge (a bridge over a rocky gorge) and the Carr Rocks—see also under **all**.

When the suffix is replaced by the genitive *ann* we get the river name Carron. There are rivers Carron in the shires of Nairn, Banff, Kincardine, Stirling and Dumfries, some at least of which have distinctive rocky beds. Loch Carron in Wester Ross probably takes its name from the river which runs into it. But beware that in print *carr* can masquerade as two other elements, **caer** and **carn**.

A similar Gaelic word is *creag*. Creag Dubh is one of the commonest hill-names in Scotland, and just means 'black crag'. Creag a Bhinnean in Atholl is 'rock of the pinnacle', and Craig Phadrick near Inverness is 'Patrick's Rock', thought by some to mark the site of King Brude's fortress. A number of craig names have quasi-historical associations: Creag Righ Harailt in Badenoch marks in popular history the grave of King Harold, said to have been defeated in the vicinity by a Pictish force at an unspecified date. Craigellachie (battle cry of the Clan Grant) is 'crag of the rocky place'; Craiglockhart is probably 'rock of the encampment' (cf. Luichart) rather than 'of Lockhart'. The word also occurs terminally, as in Kincraig ('head of the crag'), and the adjectival form, *creagach* ('rocky'), gives the numerous Craigies. Craik is the form found in the Borders.

castle

The earliest historical settlements in Scotland were not towns and villages or even farms, but 'touns' or 'clachans'—clusters of houses formed for mutual assistance and protection. Often these touns were associated with a church, when they became known as 'kirktons', dozens of examples of which are to be found both in Highlands and Lowlands (see under **ton**). Only slightly less common were the clachans surrounding the laird's fortified house, and these were known as 'castletons'. Some of these became proper names, as in Castleton on Loch Fyne and Castletown near Thurso. More often however only the differential was preserved: thus, Castleton of Braemar became simply Braemar (see also p. 7). In Liddesdale, Old Castleton has been overtaken in size and importance by Newcastleton (built in the 1790s). When the defensive castles came to be replaced by grand mansions, as at Taymouth and Inveraray, some of the old castletons were cleared in the late eighteenth century to make way for the model villages which so delight the modern visitor.

There are of course many other 'castle' names like Castlehill (eight of them) and Castle Law (six) which do not refer to settlements; and places like Castlecary and Castle Douglas embody proper names. Castlebay on Barra is modern.

clunie

In Gaelic, *cluain* is a plain, meadow or pasture, and its diminutive *cluaineag* (pronounced 'cloon-eeg') is a lawn or patch of green. A handy term for a place-name, one might think; and the Highlands are full of Clunies in various spellings. Working from north to south we find Cluanie on Loch Duich, Clunie in Banffshire and Cluny in Badenoch (better known perhaps as the territorial designation of the MacPherson chiefs). Clunes in Lochaber is *cluain fhas* or 'meadow stance'; and there are at least half a dozen other places involving *cluain*, usually in the dative form of the word; the most notable perhaps are Clunie dam near Pitlochry and Loch Clunie near Blairgowrie, both called after a nearby settlement. Compound forms such as Aldclune near Killiecrankie are quite common—*allt chluain* is 'burn of the meadow'.

The Gaelic word *uaine* (pronounced 'oon-ye') means green, but is invariably used as an adjective and not as a noun. In the Cairngorms there are at least five tarns which are called Lochan Uaine; and the same word occurs in Arduaine ('green point') in Argyll, not to speak of the Ardoyne in Ulster.

The adjective green is a very familiar component of Lowland place-names: there are at least five Greenhills, a Greenlaw and a Greenloaning (see **loan**). Just as often the word appears as a noun, as in Rullion Green, Kenly Green, Pitcairngreen and many others. But Greenock is misleading, being a rendering of the Gaelic *grianaig* 'at the sunny knoll'.

coille

Coille in Gaelic is a wood; it is pronounced 'cull-ye'. *Coille mor* ('great wood') by Loch Alsh, formerly the home of sixty-seven families, is now deserted and does not even appear on the map. Coille Bhrochan near Bonskeid in Strathtummel means 'porridge wood', and traditionally is the spot where Robert the Bruce rested his men after the disastrous battle of Methven in 1306: they recruited their strength on porridge supplied by the locals. Ardchyle near Killin is probably *ard choille* ('wood-height'), and Coilantogle in the Trossachs has the same prefix; the suffix is possibly an **ochil**-type word. Coilacriech near Ballater is *coille a' crithich*—'aspen

38

wood', and the Coyles of Muick embody the same word (although originally the reference was to the one wooded hill).

The word can occur terminally as in Kinkell (*ceann na coille* or 'wood-end'), the name of places in Aberdeenshire, Perthshire, Ross, Kincardine and Fife.

The derivative form *coillteach* (pronounced 'cull-tuch') means a woodland or forest and is even more productive of place-names, usually in the spelling Cults. There is a Cults in the Dee valley, another in north-east Fife and yet another in Wigton. The suffixes of Cultybraggan near Comrie and Cultoquhey near Crieff are personal names—the latter thought to be *Ce*, one of the seven legendary princes of Pictland.

Unfortunately however there are other similar Gaelic terms such as *caol* (**kyle**), **cul** (back) and *cuil* (**neuk**) which sometimes get confused with woodland-names; and there are Old English and Norse personal names such as Cola and Colbane which make matters worse: Colinton in Edinburgh was 'Colbane's toun', and Collieston in Buchan and Colliston in Angus both refer to persons unknown. So probably do Collafirth in Shetland and Collin near Dumfries.

Another woodland term is Keith. When it appears on the map of Scotland it is usually a rendering of a Brittonic word *coet* (Welsh *coed*), meaning forest or wood. So Dalkeith means 'wood dale' and Inchkeith 'wood island'. Keithock near Brechin is 'wooded place' and the various settlements called Keith in Banffshire, East Lothian and Ayrshire have much the same sense. (But note that the Keithing burn which gives its name to Inverkeithing seems to have a different and unknown origin, while Keith in Caithness represents the lost personal name *Caidh*). In some names a semblance of the original Brittonic word is preserved, as in Pencaitland—see under **pen**; Bathgate was once spelled *Bathchet*, and was originally *baedd coed*—'boar wood'.

The handy Gaelic word *bad*, which means a clump or bunch, has several uses; *bad chaorach* for example, is a flock of sheep; *bad coille* is a clump of trees or thicket, and it is in this latter sense that we usually find it in place-names. Badcall in Sutherland is 'hazel thicket', and is repeated near Kirkintilloch in the bizarre spelling of Bedcow; Baddidarach is 'oakwood', and Badbea in Wester Ross is 'birchwood'. Badanden in Angus is 'hill-thicket'; Badachro in Gairloch is explained under **tarff**. There are dozens of *bad*-names in Aberdeenshire.

Another Gaelic word in this category is *doire*, meaning a copse or grove (earlier, an oakwood). The example that comes most readily to mind is Glen Derry in the Cairngorms, but of course Ireland has an even more celebrated

39

one. Loch Derry in Wigtonshire is of similar origin. Dargavel near Erskine is *doire gabhail* ('copse of the fork'). But Loch Derry in Sutherland is from *dithreabh* ('wilderness').

Woodland names are even commoner in the Lowlands. There are dozens of Woodlands, Woodsides and Blackwoods, all with meanings which are too obvious to need explanation.

colm

Columba, Celtic princeling and Christian missionary, crossed the Irish sea in the mid-sixth century to become 'an exile for Christ'. As an ecclesiastical statesman in the then Irish colony of Dalriada (equivalent in extent to the modern Argyll) he founded the monastery of Iona and many others in the western Highlands. His personal fame and prestige and his ability to move easily in royal circles contributed both to the christianisation of neighbouring Pictland and the ultimate ascendancy of Dalriadic Scotland. Known in Gaelic as *Colum Cille* ('Columba of the cell'—a reference to his monastic way of life) he became the foremost of Scotland's saints and a considerable cult figure in later mediaeval times.

It was the contemporary practice to name monasteries, abbacies and lesser foundations after the founder, and Columba's name is commemorated in several places in Scotland (as well, of course, in such surnames as Malcolm and MacCallum). The chief of these is *Icolmkill* ('Columba's isle') which was the old and correct form of the name Iona (itself probably a scribal error—see under **ey**). Other examples are Kilmacolm ('cell of my Columba') and Inchcolm (see **inch**).

Most of what we know of Columba—fact as well as legend—is derived from his biographer Adamnan, ninth abbot of Iona, who flourished some hundred years after the saint. He also was canonised (in the vernacular, *Saunct Eunan*), and his personal name survives in the north-eastern surnames Younie and Tewnion. Several religious foundations were named after him, and these include Ardeonaig on Loch Tay (formerly *Ard Eodhnain*—'Adamnan's cape') and Rowardennan on Loch Lomond (see under **rubha**). Killeonan in Kintyre is 'St Adamnan's sanctuary', and there were many others which never achieved the dignity of print at the hands of the Ordinance Survey.

con

One of the first words that one learns in Gaelic is *cu*, a dog; in the genitive and the plural it becomes *coin*, reflecting its origin in the Greek κυων; on the map it is usually shown as *con*. The word was very popular as a stream-name, not in commemoration of any particular dog but rather of the mythic qualities of the animal. Conon in Ross is 'dog stream', and the same meaning is found in Glen Conglass (one in Banffshire, the other in Argyll); even Glen Kinglass (one in Perthshire, the other in Argyll) was originally *Chonglais*. There are numerous Loch Chons, and Balgonie in Perthshire and East Lothian are both 'dogs' stead'. Cononish near Tyndrum looks very like *con innis*, which could be 'dog enclosure' (see **inch**). There is a spectacular cliff in the Cairngorms called in Gaelic *Creag an Leth-choin* (crag of the cross-breed, literally 'half dog'), which is familiarly known as 'The Lurcher's Crag'; this may however be a mistranslation, because some maps call it *Creag na Leacainn*, which has the much more general meaning of 'hill-slope'.

Another Gaelic word for dog is *madadh* (pronounced 'matt-a'); *madadh ruadh* is 'red dog' or fox and a wolf is either *madadh geal* ('white dog') or *madadh allaidh* 'fierce dog'. It is impossible without the qualifying adjective and in the absence of other evidence to know which animal is referred to in any particular case, although Lochmaddy in North Uist is said to be named after three rocks in the bay called *Na Maidhean*—'the hounds'. There are a few Highland hills called Creag Mhadaidh, sometimes spelt and always pronounced 'Craig Maddy'; in Aberdeenshire the suffix was dropped, giving frequent *mad* names of which the most notable is Old Maud (*allt mad*—'dog/fox/wolf burn'); and let us not forget such names as Dog Hillock that survive in areas where Gaelic had died out.

The word wolf was a very common component of Germanic personal names, which favoured ferocious and macho associations; examples such as Wolfgang, Wulfram and Wulfstan come to mind, and Wolf figures in many English place-names like Wolstanton and Wolverhampton. In the Scottish Lowlands we have several names such as Wolfhill in Perthshire (there is another in Angus) and Wolflee near Hawick, where the reference is likely to be not to the personal name but to the animal itself (the last wolf in Scotland was killed in the eighteenth century). Further north one sees the Norse influence, in places like Ulbster near Wick ('Wolf's abode') and Ulva in the Hebrides ('Wolf isle') which may well involve personal names.

Perhaps more remarkable is the use of 'cat' in place-names. The Pictish tribes were in the habit of calling themselves after animals, and one such were the *Cataibh*, who inhabited an area in east Sutherland. They gave their name to Caithness, which means 'cat headland'. The word cat is the same in Gaelic, so we don't always know the linguistic origin of a cat-name: for example, the Catlaw in Angus may be either English or a form of an earlier Celtic name, while Lochan a Chait in the Ben Lawers corrie is surely of Gaelic origin. It may be assumed that the reference is to the wildcat rather than the domestic tabby.

corrie

Phoilead, cur an choire air would be Gaelic for 'Polly, put the kettle on'. But of course a kettle did not always have a spout, lid and handle: a paint kettle or a fish kettle is simply a metal cup or cauldron, and it is in this sense that the word *coire*, or 'corrie', is used when it appears on the hill maps. A hollow in a Highland hill is nearly always called a corrie, and skiers in the Cairngorms are familiar with Coire Cas—'steep corrie'—and Coire na Ciste—'corrie of the chest or coffin'. A nondescript brown corrie would be *coire odhar*, and there are numerous Corrours in the Highlands. Corgarff in Strathdon is now the name of a district, but was originally *coire garbh*—'rough corrie'. More spectacular is Coruisk in Skye—'water corrie'.

Cauldron is implicit in the name of the Corrieshalloch gorge in Wester Ross, where the reference is to willows (*saileach*); and a different type of cauldron appears in the name Corrievreckan: it is 'whirlpool of Brecon', who perished there with all his company of fifty ships, as related in the *Book of Ballymote*.

The word 'corrie' is not to be found outside the Highlands. Currie in Midlothian and Cora Linn on the Clyde both come from another word, *currach*, meaning 'marshy plain'.

Although 'kettle' is a perfectly good translation of the Gaelic *coire*, when occurring in place-names it does not normally have a topographical reference: it is, rather, from Thurkettil, a Scandinavian forename, which is the basis of such surnames as Thirkell and MacCorquodale. Kettla Ness in Shetland and Kettletoft in Orkney are pure Norse; they mean respectively 'Kettil's point' and 'Kettil's croft'. Names such as Kettleshiel in Berwickshire, Kirkettle and Kettleston in the Lothians, are not in themselves of Old Norse origin but are interesting as showing evidence of the presence of Scandinavian settlers in these areas. On the other hand, Kingskettle in Fife was on the edge of the royal hunting preserve of Falkland and is thought to embody the Brittonic word *cuddial* meaning 'preserve'.

crath

This Gaelic verb (the 'th' is silent) means shake, agitate, wave, and is the basis for such diverse place-names as Crathie near Balmoral (there is another in Badenoch and another in Angus); Crathes on Deeside; Craichie near Forfar; Cray in Glenshee and Loch Achray in the Trossachs.

It is not easy to see what these names can have in common. The Ballater Crathie possibly has its origin in the *Moine Craichidh* ('shaking bogs') up the hill from the Crathie burn; Loch Achray is probably *ath crathaidh*— 'ford of the shaking'. The others must contain some reference to a local feature or event, long forgotten and never now to be explained.

crieff

The word for tree is *craobh*, which is the basis of the name Crieff (and not a bad approximation of how it is pronounced in Gaelic). Pittencrieff in Fife is a Brittonic term for 'place of trees' and Ballencrieff in East Lothian is the Gaelic version (see Introduction). Pitcrievie is *peit craobhaigh* or 'wooded part', and Bunchrew is either 'tree stump' or 'tree foot'; it is by no means unlikely that a single tree would produce a settlement-name. Auchencruive in Aberdeenshire is 'tree field'—see **ach.**

On his famous visit in 1773 Dr Johnson complained of a treeless Scottish landscape, but it was not always thus. Place-names testify to an abundance of tree-cover, even though the varieties are not great. The commonest tree-word is *giuthas* or *giubhas* (pronounced 'g-yoo-as'), the Gaelic word for fir or pine. The most celebrated is Kingussie, which is discussed under **kin,** but in roughly the same area are to be found Glen Giubhasach near Lochnagar ('glen abounding in fir') and Glen Geusachan off Glen Dee ('glen of the little fir wood'). There is a Guisachan estate in Strathglass, and in Strathtay we find Dalguise, which was originally *dal giuthas* ('fir heugh').

The next commonest tree-name is probably birch, in Gaelic *beith* (pronounced 'bay'). and connected with Latin *betula*. The village of Beath in Cunningham and the parish of that name in Fife both record birchwoods, as does Aultbea ('birch burn') in Wester Ross; Badbea, Baddybae and Bodiebac all refer to clumps of birches. The allied word *beitheach* ('birchwood') gives Dalbeathie, Tayside, and probably Dalbeattie, and possibly Beattock and the last syllable of Cowdenbeath (the first two are discussed below). The Scots word for birch is *birk* and tends to be found in names of more recent coinage, such as Birkhill and Birks of Abergeldie.

Fearn (pronounced 'fee-arn') is the Gaelic for alder, a very common tree in the Highlands. Fearn in Ross and Cromarty has this meaning, as does Fern near Brechin; Fearnan on Loch Tay was earlier *Stronfearna* ('alder point'); Fernie in Fife and Elderslie in the Borders mean 'alder-place'; Glen Fernate in Perthshire is 'glen of the alder water'. Ferniehirst, near Jedburgh, however seems to have an English derivation, involving the Old English *hyrst*, meaning a forest—thus, 'ferny wood'.

Cowden is often a Lowland version of the Gaelic word *calltuin*, meaning hazel. Cowdenknowes are hazel knolls: but note the stress on the first syllable, and contrast Cowden in Kent, which means 'cow-den', and is so pronounced. The original Gaelic word is preserved in Barcaldine, Argyll, meaning 'hazel-height'. The Cowden of Cowdenbeath is certainly not *calltuin*; it may be nearer to the Kentish name in origin.

Willow trees have always been common in Scotland, and we find place-names which can derive either from Gaelic or Scots: Achnashellach in Wester Ross and Salachan in Morvern are from the Gaelic *sailech*, while Sauchie, Sauchieburn and Sauchiehall may just as easily be from the Lowland dialect word *sauch*. Saughton in Midlothian is a twelfth century name with a Celtic beginning and an Anglo-Saxon ending.

Oak woods were less common, and the Gaelic word (*darach*) for that noblest of trees tends to be found sparsely; Craigendarroch at Ballater is a reminder of the oakwoods of Deeside, while Drumindarroch ('oak ridge') and Rhidorroch (*rubha darach*—'oak point') are places in the far north-west where oaks will not now be found.

Beeches appeared in Scotland largely as a result of eighteenth century land-improvement, and while there are plenty of Lowland place-names of the Beechwood/Beechgrove variety, the Gaelic term for beech (*faibhle*, pronounced 'fyvla') is scarcely to be found on the map. Similarly the Gaelic word for ash (*uinnse*) did not take up the cartographers' time, but this kind of tree figures quite commonly in Lowland names like Ashkirk and Ashestiel (Old English *ash stael*—'ash place'). Elms were equally uncommon, and although *leamhan* (pronounced 'levan') seems familiar enough it is probably a false etymology (see **Leven**).

The word for yew is *iubhar* (pronounced 'yoo-ur'), and this is to be found in Craignure on Mull (*creag an iubhair*—'yew-tree rock') and Glenure in Argyll. Loch Iubhair in Glen Dochart is similar, as is Dunure in Ayrshire.

crioch

This Gaelic word means boundary or end: *tha an latha a' tighinn gu crioch*— 'the day is ending'. The parish of Creich in Sutherland and the village of Creich in north-east Fife must have been named for some frontier quality, and Crichie in Buchan probably expresses the same idea. The word when combined with Scots 'toun', gives Crichton in Midlothian (and the surname Crighton is of this origin). Similarly, Crimond in Aberdeenshire was earlier *Criechmont*—boundary moor.

A similar idea is expressed by the Gaelic word *airbhe* (pronounced 'ervy'), meaning 'frontier wall'; Altnaharra in Sutherland is *allt na -h airbhe*, literally 'burn of the dividing wall', or 'boundary stream'. Clachnaharry near Inverness looks like 'march stone' but see the comments under **stone**; Balharvie in Fife and Balhary in Glen Isla both embody the word *airbhe*, probably just with reference to common-or-garden walls; and Auchenharvie in Ayrshire is probably 'walled fields'. The Brittonic language had its own term for boundary: Tantallon is *din talgwn*—'high frontier fort'.

In the days before the precise line of the Scottish/English Border (known as 'the March') was established, what lay on either side of it was the 'Debatable Land'. Although this historic name is now largely forgotten, there are other portions of land whose title is not clear, and these were known as 'threap' land, from a Scots verb meaning to argue, dispute or debate. There is a Threepland in Biggar, another in Banff, a Threepneuk and several Threepwoods; the Threepland Burn is in Renfrewshire, and Threipmuir is in the Pentlands. Clearly none of these places was the subject of a Border dispute, nevertheless they were all once debatable lands and their names are there to remind us.

crom

Crom in Gaelic means 'bend' or 'bent', depending on whether it is noun, verb or adjective. A *cromag* is a hook, hence a shepherd's crook or staff. Cromdale in Moray is 'bent haugh' caused by the configuration of the Spey; Cromalt in Sutherland looks like 'bent stream'. Cromlet near Nigg is *crom leathad*—'crooked slope'; Cromlix appears to have the word *leac* as its suffix—'crooked stone'. Cromarty is the same concept but the precise etymology remains doubtful.

Crombie is a stream name in Banffshire, and Abercrombie in Fife is the old parish name of St Monans; both refer to a bendy watercourse.

Crom has its equivalent in German *krumm* and indeed in the Scots word *crommie*, used for a cow with a crumpled horn. Ancrum shows the word as a noun: originally *Alnecrum*, it refers to a bend on the River Ale in the Borders. The Roxburgh name Cromrig ('bent field or ridge') has probably a Scots rather than a Gaelic origin.

Another Gaelic word for bend or twist is *car*, in the genitive *cuir*. Strachur in Argyll is *srath chuir*—'strath of the bend', and this also offers a reasonable etymology for Strathyre—there never was a Highland glen without a bend. Twechar in Dunbartonshire has been explained as *tuath a'chuir*—'north of the bend'.

Loop in Gaelic is *luib*, probably a loan-word from English. Luib in Glen Dochart is just a bend in the river, as is Luib in Corgarff. Luban ('little loop'), a croft in upper Glen Lyon, must have been flooded by the enlargement of the loch, for it no longer appears on the map. Loch Lubnaig is thought to be 'the crooked or winding loch'.

cross

The cross is the most potent symbol in Christendom, and this is reflected in the numerous place-names which include the word. But a cross is also very important in human geography, in terms of crossroads, crossing-places and market crosses. Furthermore, the word cross occurs in recognisable form in Old English, Old Norse, Brittonic and Gaelic as well as in English, and historical as well as linguistic considerations have to be taken into account when arriving at etymologies.

Lowland names like Mearns Cross in Renfrewshire and Fishcross near Alloa are of the 'market-cross' variety and present no problems; likewise Crossgates in Fife refers to crossroads, and the various Crossfords, Crossburns and Crosslees are obvious enough. Crossmichael will have a religious origin, as will Crosshill in Dunbartonshire; Crossmyloof (ignore the palmistry involved in the folk-etymology) is *crois Maoldhuibh*—'Malduff's cross'. The numerous places called Crosbie (Old Norse *krossa byr*—'cross farm') in the north of England have their counterpart in Scotland in the metathesised form Corsby which occurs in the shires of Ayr, Wigton and Berwick. Metathesis persists in the other Lowland names Corsehill, Corsemill, Corsewall and Corseford, whose meaning will be obvious enough. Crossraguel (pronounced 'cross-ray-gle' with the stress on the 'ray') in Ayrshire is interesting in showing Norse words in a Gaelic word-order; the meaning is 'Riegal's Cross', the name probably relating to Latin *regula*, a rule. Corstorphine in Edinburgh ('Thorfinn's cross') is a similar formation.

The Gaelic equivalent is *crois*, but it appears in place-names mainly in its related form *crasg*, genitive *croisg*, and with the specific meaning of 'crossing'. Thus Loch a' Chroisg in Sutherland means 'loch of the crossing', as does Loch Rosque in Wester Ross, where the map-makers helpfully supplied a phonetic spelling. Glencorse signifies the glen which crosses the Pentlands. Applecross has an oddly English appearance for a settlement in the far north-west; its original form was *apur crossan*, and while the etymology is problematical, the generally accepted meaning is 'confluence'.

The Old Norse version, *kross*, remains as Kross in Iceland but is usually anglicised on the maps—as in Cross, Crose and Corse in Orkney. Crossipoll on Coll is 'cross farm' and so is Crossbost in Lewis (see under **ster**); Crossnish in Skye is 'cross point'.

46

Cross in the sense of 'athwart' is the meaning of The Trossachs, in Gaelic *na Trosaichean*, a small range of hillocks between Loch Katrine and Loch Achray which lie against the contours of the area.

cul

This is a handy little Gaelic word which means the back of anything; *air do chul* is 'behind you'. It derives from the Latin *culus* (buttocks, 'backside') and relates to the French *cul*, with the same meaning; its use in Gaelic is not however impolite. In the place-name context it nearly always combines with another noun: *cul tir* ('back land') gives Coulter in Aberdeenshire; *cul tref* ('back place') gives Coultrie in Inverness-shire and Coultra in Fife; and *cul beinne* ('back of the mountains') is Culbin. Culloden has the harmless meaning of 'at the back of the little pool'. Culreach (*culriabhach*) on Deeside means 'brindled back'.

Very often *cul* has been translated into English, so that streams formerly known as *Cul allt* are now 'Back Burn'. There are also numerous Backmuirs and Backburns, while expressions like 'Back Road' hover on the brink of becoming place-names proper.

The problem is that there is another Old Gaelic word with the same pronunciation, spelt *cuil* and meaning 'nook, corner' (it is discussed under **neuk**). Another culprit is **coille**. It is not always possible to distinguish between these in place-names; *cul, cuil* and *coille* are little words that struggle for survival, and their particular combination of letters is sometimes taken over by a stronger one; for example Culross in Fife is from *cuileann* ('holly').

D

dale

Dale is an English word with cognates in Old Norse (*dalr*), Brittonic (*dol*) and Gaelic (*dail*), and it is found in those guises all over Scotland. It does not, however, appear in Ireland, which may suggest that the Scottish Gaelic version is a Brittonic loan-word.

Of the English form, typical examples are Clydesdale, Liddesdale, Tweeddale and Nithsdale—all in the south. (Nobody would ever refer to 'Taydale' or 'Dondale'). Annandale is a valley-name which became a district name, and by back-formation produced the town of Annan; as a river-name Annan is very ancient, possibly pre-Celtic, and likely to mean no more than 'water'.

As one would expect, the Norse form occurs exclusively in the extreme north and west, and it takes on an English spelling on the maps. Borrodale is 'fort dale', Helmsdale is 'Hjalmund's dale', Berriedale is 'Beri's dale', and Armadale (transported from Sutherland to West Lothian and thence to Australia) is 'arms valley'. Knapdale is *knappr* ('knob dale'). Spinningdale is 'spangle-dale'; Swordale is 'sward-dale'. Rodel in Harris is 'red dale'. Strathalladale is a pleonastic form, the Gaelic term *srath* having been prefixed to the Norse 'holy dale'.

Notice that in English and Norse the generic term (in this case *dale*) occurs at the end of the word. In Celtic languages the order is different: it is the specific, or qualifying part that comes at the end—and with it the stress. Thus Dalmore and Dalbreck have the accent on the second syllable; in Gaelic they are *dal mor* and *dail breac*, meaning 'big dale' and 'dappled haugh' respectively. It has to be added that *dail* in Gaelic normally has the meaning of field, as it does in Dollar. There are at least five Dalreochs, three in Perthshire, one in Angus and one in Dunbartonshire: the meaning is 'rough field'. Dalnaspidal and Dalwhinnie, villages off the A9, mean 'hospice field' (see **spital**) and 'champion's field'. Dalbeattie is 'birch haugh', and Dalmarnock is associated with St Mernoc. Dalmally makes reference to an obscure Saint Maillidh (also commemorated in Kilmally).

The genitive form *dalach* is seen in Ballindalloch on the Spey and Ballendollo in Angus; both mean 'haugh village'. (Names in Fife and Angus which end in 'o' very often show an earlier -*ach* ending, which dropped off when it ceased to be understood). Kindallachan on the A9 seems to be 'at the head of the fields'.

The Brittonic form of the word appears to be preserved in Dull in Strathtay, as also in Glen Doll in Angus and the Doll in Strathbrora. A curious formation crops up in some Aberdeenshire names, such as Burntdales. This is thought to represent the old Scots term *dale*, meaning share or allotment or piece of land (cf. English 'deal'). It is just conceivable that this may provide the etymology of Edzell—i.e. 'Esk-land'; it certainly cannot be 'Eskdale', and no satisfactory alternative has been offered.

deer

The Old Norse word *dýr* means a wild beast, and can include deer, foxes and wolves. It is the origin of the names Durness in Sutherland, Deerness in Orkney and Duirnish in Skye, all of which mean 'deer cape'. Jura is thought to mean 'deer isle' (see **ey**).

Gaelic is usually more specific with its animal-names, although members of the canine family are sometimes lumped together (see **wolf**). The generic term for deer in Gaelic is *fiadh*, plural *feidh* (pronounced 'fay'). *Cabar feidh* means 'antlers' and is the badge of the MacKenzies; but it is difficult to think of a place-name which embodies these terms. A stag is properly *damh cabrach feidh*—literally a 'horned ox', but when this is abbreviated to *damh* as in Inchnadamh it is impossible to tell which animal is meant. *Boc* is a buck, and tends to be assimilated to the English word: Buccleuch ('buck glen') incorporates the Scots word *cleugh* (see under **den**).

Roe deer in Gaelic is *earb*, but again does not seem to figure in Highland place-names. Raeburn however is a familiar enough Lowland surname, deriving from a stream-name and producing the settlement of Raeburnfoot. Raecleuch ('roe glen'), now obsolete, was a companion name for Buccleuch.

The commonest deer-name is probably hart, found all over the Lowlands, and the normal Scots term for a stag in the fourteenth century. Hartlaws and Hartfells are common in the Border country; Harthill is now best known as a service-station on the M8. Hind names are not unknown, as witness Hindside in Berwickshire; but Glasgow's Hyndland is 'back-land'.

den

A den has been defined as a narrow valley, especially one with trees, and it is the characteristic term for that topographical feature wherever it occurs in the Lowlands. The word 'den' comes from the Old English *denu*, and passed into modern English (but not Scots) as 'dene'. The connotation of an animal's lair is secondary, although the concept of a place of safety remains. The word still operates as a common noun in rural Scotland, and any wooded defile is liable to be referred to as 'the den'. The Den of Alyth and Dura Den (see **dour**) are examples from the east of Scotland.

There are four villages in the Lowlands with the name of Denhead—two in Angus, one in Fife and one in Aberdeenshire: the meaning is 'top of the valley'. Kirkden is almost as common—'church valley'. Dryden near Roslin means what it says, and Foulden is 'bird valley'. Denny near Falkirk appears to preserve the word *denu*, and Dennyloanhead will be 'end of the Denny lane'. Forgandenny however is different—it means St Eithne's Forgan (see **forgan**).

Bearsden is a modern and probably fanciful reference to a lair; Denby in Dumfries, like its homonyms in England, means 'Danes' village'.

Den-names in the Highlands are very rare and always modern; it would be tempting to say the same of glen-names in the Lowlands, but that would be unfair to the sizeable number of genuine southern names such as Glencorse, Glentress, Glenmuir, Glenapp, Glentrool, Glenlee, the Glenkens,

Glendhu, Glentanner, and Glenkitten. The egregious name Glenrothes is discussed under **glen**.

Smaller than a den is a *cleugh*, an old Scots word meaning a ravine; it appears in such names as Ben Cleugh in the Ochils and Caldcleugh in Roxburgh and in the Pentlands; Buccleuch is discussed under **deer**.

In common speech *cleuch* later began to acquire a somewhat different, almost opposite meaning, that of cliff; this may have been caused by the attraction of another Scots word *heugh*, which means a hill: compare the English place-name element *hoe*, as in Plymouth Hoe. This gives us Minto, which is the Brittonic *minit* (see **monadh**) followed by *heugh*, with the meaning of 'moor hill'. Kelso,whose earliest recorded spelling is 'Calkou'—from the Old English *cealk* (chalk, cf. Latin *calx*)—has the same suffix, giving some such meaning as 'lime hill'. Gretna is more difficult and obscure: the name has been interpreted as *greten ho*, 'at the great hill'. Redheugh near Berwick gives the surname Riddoch.

doch

A contraction of the Gaelic word *dabhach*, which means literally a tub or vat, and is found in the history-books as davach, the characteristic measurement or unit of arable land in the Highlands. The supposition is that the area in question corresponded in some way with the seed-content of the vat; the extent of the land would vary according to its quality, but was usually in excess of four hundred acres. 'The Daugh' is a common farm name in Aberdeenshire; it represents the Gaelic pronunciation which survived after the meaning of the name had been lost.

Doch is found in place-names such as Dochfour (*dabhach phuir*—'pasture davach'), Findochty ('white davach') and Dochgarroch ('davoch of the rough land'—now a lock on the Caledonian Canal); Mugdock in Strathblane is *magh a dhabaich*—'davach plain'.

More commonly however a fraction of a davach is involved: Lettoch in the Black Isle is *leth dabhach*, or half-davoch, and the same idea is expressed in Scots in the Aberdeenshire Haddo. (But note that Glen and Loch Dochart in Perthshire have a different origin—possibly shared with the Irish surname Docherty, which means something like 'unlucky'.)

Sometimes land-measurement place-names record only the fraction involved. Trinafour in Perthshire is *trian a phuir* ('pasture third'); Kirriemuir in Angus is *ceathramh gearr*—'short quarter'; and Coigach in Wester Ross is 'place of fifths'.

Arrochar takes its name from the vernacular version of Latin *aratrum*, a plough. The ploughgate was a measurement of land that could be cultivated by a team of eight oxen in a year—apparently something over a hundred acres.

What the davoch was to the north, the 'carrucate' was to the south of Scotland. This technical word does not appear in place-names, but a related term,'oxgang', does. There are several Oxgangs—near Grangemouth, Kirkintilloch and Dumfries, not to speak of the Edinburgh suburb. An oxgang was as much land as an ox could 'gang over' (plough) in a day.

dour

It is reasonably certain that an early form of the Celtic language was spoken at one time or another in most of the British Isles, and it is not difficult to trace a linguistic connection between Dover in the extreme south of England and Aberdour on the east coast of Scotland. The common element is the early Celtic word *dubron*, Welsh *dwr*, Gaelic *dobhar*, all meaning water (and having no connection with the Scots word *dour*, which is from Latin *durus*, hard).

Dover is probably 'at the water' and Aberdour in Fife was the name of a parish on the Dour 'water'. The 'bh' sound in Gaelic is silent, and so *dobhar* usually appears in place-names as *der*. Aberarder is *aber ard dobhar*—'confluence of high water'—and Auchterarder is 'upland of high water'. Glen Fender in Atholl is *fionn dobhar* (see **fionn**)—and Morar is *mor dobhar* or 'big water'. Ben Alder is from *all dhobhar*—'rock water' (describing a stream which falls down the mountainside). Dura and Durie in Fife are also *dobhar* names.

Another familiar combination with *dubron* is the Brittonic word *caled*, the whole meaning 'hard water', usually found in the form **calder**. The diminutive, *dobhran*, occurs in in Ben Doran—'hill of the streamlet'—and Inveroran—'mouth of the streamlet'—both names occurring on the Black Mount. Another Gaelic word, *dobhran*, with a similar root, means 'otter', and gives Craigendoran or 'otter crag'.

drum

The Gaels tended to see landscape in anatomical terms, and one of the most common topographical words is *druim*, meaning back, spine or ridge. The great ridge of Scotland, separating the Picts in the east from the 'Scots' in the west, was known in the Dark Ages as Drumalbyn.

The correct pronunciation of the word is preserved in Drem in East Lothian, but 'drum' names are commonest in the Highlands. There are numerous Drumbegs and Drummores—little and big ridges respectively—and other examples are Drumchapel (*druim chapull*—'mare's back')—and

51

Drumnadrochit ('bridge-ridge'). Dunrobin in Sutherland is properly *drum rabhain*—'ridge of the long grass'. There are several examples of *druim buidhe* ('yellow ridge')—Drumbuie in Wester Ross and Newton Stewart, Drumbowie in Lanarkshire and Drumboy in Ayrshire. (Drambuie however is a made-up word, meaning 'golden dram', cf. English drachm, a measure of liquor). Notice also that Drumsheugh in Edinburgh is a contraction of 'Meldrum's haugh' and is of Lowland Scots origin.

Drymen and Drummond are from the related word *drumein*—'at the ridge'.

., Shoulder in Gaelic is *guala* or *gualainn*, and Ben Gulabin at the head of Glenshee looks very like a duplication—'hill shoulder hill'. An even worse example is Drumgoldrum in Aberdeenshire—'ridge of the shoulder ridge'. But Kingoldrum in Angus makes more sense with 'head of the shoulder ridge'. From *guallain* comes Gullane (the Gaelic pronunciation is 'goo-allin', and gives no basis for the Edinburgh pronunciation of 'Gillan').

Slugan in Gaelic means throat or gullet—in place-names, something like a pit. It is the basis for the Sluggan pass in Rothiemurchus, and of Slugain and the Sluggan in Braemar, the latter being the name of a ravine near Invercauld. Slug is a Lowland rendering of the term. There is a related Gaelic word *sloc* or *slochd* with the same meaning, to be found in the Slochd summit, the highest part of the railway and the A9 just south of Inverness; the resemblance to the German word *Schlucht*—'gorge'—is probably fortuitous.

Another handy term is 'fist', which in Gaelic is *dorn,* and in a place-name context has the extended meaning of 'rounded fist-sized pebble'; with the *-ach* suffix one gets 'pebbly place', which is the meaning of Dornoch in Sutherland and Dornock in Dumfries. The ending has been mutilated in Durno in Aberdeenshire; and the compound forms Mundurno, Drumdurno and Edindurno (all in that county) mean respectively 'mount', 'ridge' and 'face' of the pebbles. Dornie in Kintail shows the dative form—'at the pebbly place'. Dorniegills on Meggat Water has an added reference to the whiteness of the pebbles (*geal* is Gaelic for bright or white).

Other Gaelic anatomical terms which figure in place-names are *ceann* ('head'—see **kin**), and *sron* ('nose'—see **ness**). The word for neck is *braghad* (see **brae**) and Ben Cruachan is 'haunch mountain'. *Mam* means a rounded hill, the name obviously deriving from its mamillary shape: examples are Mambeg, Mamore and Mam Ratagan (Ratagan is the loch-side settlement, thought to be a person's name). More explicitly, Bennachie (stress on the last syllable) is 'breast hill', and Beinn na Ciochan ('hill of paps') was an old name for Lochnagar; the metaphor is preserved in the more modern names Little Pap and Meikle Pap, referring to the summits of that mountain. Most 'pap' names are English translations of *cioch*—like the Pap of Glencoe and the Paps of Jura—although the Maiden Paps near Hawick would be locally inspired. Dunsinane is thought to be *dun sineachan*—'hill of nipples'. It would be possible to multiply examples, but since Gaelic is not a squeamish language perhaps the matter might be left to private research.

dun

In Gaelic this word means a fortress, castle, hill or mound. It had its place in Brittonic place-nomenclature also, and is found throughout Scotland, as well as in Wales and Ireland. For that matter it is found on the Continent in names like Dunkerque and Thun. In Anglo-Saxon it usually just meant hill, as in the Downs and in the endings of names such as Wimbledon.

Although *dun* can appear on its own, in names such as Doune in Perthshire and Duns in Berwickshire (note the English plural), it is commonest as a prefix. The more straightforward *dun*-names are Dunalastair in Rannoch—'Fort Alexander'—a name given to the residence of the Robertson chiefs in the eighteenth century, and now applying also to the new reservoir. Dunoon is *dun obhainn*—'river fort'; and Duntroon in Argyll and Duntrune near Dundee both commemorate a person called Tren. Dundas, now much more familiar as a surname and hence a street-name, is thought to be *dun deas*—'south fort'. Dunblane is said to have been the site of the chief monastery of Blaan, bishop of Kingarth in Bute; Dunnichen is *dun Nechtain*—'Nechtan's fort' where Brude, king of the Picts, defeated the Angles in 685. The site was known historically as 'Nectansmere'. Dunfermline is a very problematical name; but from one of its early spellings (*Dumferlin*) it has been taken by some to be 'fort of Parlan' (he from whom the MacFarlanes claim descent).

Dundee is *dun Deagh*, probably from the personal name Daig, deriving from an old Celtic word for fire. (The city's soubriquet *Dei donum*—'gift of God'—is a clever if doubtfully appropriate Latin pun, with no etymological relevance.) Dunkeld is 'fort of the Caledonians' (the name given by the Romans to the Picts). Dumbarton was earlier *dun breatainn*—'fort of the Britons', and the capital of the ancient British kingdom of Strathclyde. (Dunbarton was nonsensically created by officialdom to distinguish county from town.)

Dun Eideann is the Gaelic version of Edinburgh (see under **edin**). The diminutive of *dun* is *dunan* (stress on the first syllable); it means 'little hill', indeed sometimes a dunghill, but the former interpretation is preferred in such names as Dunan (a hamlet on the road to Rannoch) and Dunning in Perthshire.

Dun usually became *dum* when followed by a palatal, as in Dumbarton. Similarly, Dumyat, a summit in the Ochils, is *dun Myat*, 'fort of the Maetae', a Pictish tribe mentioned in the period of Roman occupation. The temptation to derive Dumfries from 'fort of the Friesians' is strong, but as regards the second element there is no historical evidence of a connection with Friesians, and the -fries bit is probably Gaelic *preas*—a thicket. It is true that in some of the earlier spellings of Dumfries there is a persistent 'r' after the initial 'd', which casts doubt on its classification as a *dun* name; but the likelihood is that these variants refer to neighbouring places involving such elements as **drum** and *dronn*. (It is necessary to say a word about the latter: *dronn* meaning 'a hump' occurs fairly frequently, notably in Fife and Angus, where there is a farm and a parish of Dron; the genitive form *druinne* is possibly the origin of Loch Drunkie in Perthshire.)

So the consensus is that the Queen of the South probably gets her name from *dun phreas*—'copse fort'; and one might add that *preas* crops up in Pearsie in Glen Prosen and Persey in Glen Shee, which both mean 'copse place'.

Dun is a satisfying prefix and attracted a number of analogical formations, such as Dunrobin (see **drum**). But be careful with Don and Doon: these are river-names which celebrate the goddess Devona (see also Devon).

E

eas

Eas, pronounced 'ess' is the Gaelic for waterfall, of which there are not a few in the Highlands. Dalness in Glen Etive is *dail an easa*—'valley of the cataracts'. Bunessan in Mull seems to be 'foot of the falls', and Glen Moriston is from *mor easan*—'big falls'. Fetteresso involves the locative form *easach*—'slope at the waterfalls', and this also gives Essich in Inverness-shire, the two Essies in Aberdeenshire and Eassie in Angus (although in the latter three cases the flat terrain must render the etymology a trifle suspect).

The equivalent Old Norse term is *fors*, which gives Forse in Sutherland, the River Forsa in Mull and the first syllable of Forsinard (which is followed by the Gaelic *aird*, the whole meaning 'cataract on the height'). The north of England term 'force' meaning a waterfall (as in High Force in Upper Teesdale) is from Old Norse *forss* and is not from the English word 'force'.

There is a cascade on the River Nevis which is called on the map Steall;

this is the Gaelic word *steall* (pronounced 'st-yall') meaning a spout, but as it does not seem to figure elsewhere on the map its permanence as a place-name must be in doubt.

eccles

The Low Latin word for church was *ecclesia*, familiar in many English place-names, notably Eccles near Manchester. The word passed into Brittonic as *egles*, and into Gaelic as *eaglais*; and the occurrence of an 'eccles' name in Scotland is taken to indicate the presence of an early church. There are places called Eccles in Tweeddale, Dumfries and Berwickshire, and an Ecclesmachan in West Lothian. Ecclefechan in Dumfries is *egles Fichan*, and *ecclesia Cyrici* was the old name for St Cyrus near Montrose; the name is preserved in a nearby property called Ecclesgreig. Gleneagles (discussed under **glen**) is really an 'eccles' name, as is Eaglesham, a 'planned village' in Ayrshire, which has the additional curiosity of an English **-ham** ending. Terregles in Kirkcudbright is *tref yr eglwys*—or 'church stead'. Eccles-names are not found in the Highlands, the characteristic ecclesiastical term being **kil.**

The word for 'abbacy' or 'abbey land' is *appin*; it comes from the Middle Irish *abdaine*. Appin is the name of a district on the east side of Loch Linnhe in Argyll, famous for a Jacobite assassination in 1752; Appin of Dull in Perthshire is another 'abbey land'. There is also an estate of the name near Dunfermline, and a burn so called in Dumfriesshire.

Paisley is probably of Brittonic origin; it comes originally from the Latin *basilica* meaning church. *Provan* is the Scots form of prebend, the share of the revenues of a cathedral accruing to the clergy. Provan near Glasgow was held by the prebendary of Barlanark, who was one of the canons of Glasgow cathedral.

edin

This familiar prefix is usually a version of the Brittonic word *eiddyn* (Gaelic *aodann*, pronounced someway between Eden and 'oo-dun') and meaning 'face', or in a place-name context 'hill-face'. We are on fairly firm ground with Edinbane ('white face'), Edinkillie ('copse face') and Edinglassie ('streamy face'). Edinchip near Lochearnhead and Edinkip are both 'hill face of the block' (*ceap*) while Edinample on Loch Earn is *aodann ambuill*— 'face of the vat', through Latin *ampulla*, an amphora.

Its most famous exemplar, Edinburgh, is however a complicated name; the present day Gaelic version is *Dun Eideann*, and it was exported to New Zealand in the simplified form of Dunedin; these seem to recall the earlier *eiddyn* form, and 'hill slope fort' would certainly fit with the topography. But as an etymology for Edinburgh this does not completely satisfy scholars, who suspect that the Gaels may have adopted the prefix without having understood it. Furthermore, Edinburgh was a Northumbrian capital before it was a Scottish one, and an Anglian root might be more likely. What is certain is that the origin of the name is not 'Edwin's burgh', for the name of the city was current long before Edwin of Northumbria ever saw the light of day.

Erin

If it is true that 'no Gael ever set foot on British soil save from a vessel that had put out from Ireland', then we should expect to find much evidence in Scottish place-names of our Irish origins. And we shall not be disappointed.

Traditionally, the leaders of the first invasion from Ireland were Fergus, Loarn and Angus, the three sons of Erc. The kindred of Angus occupied Islay and Jura; Loarn's took Lorn; Fergus had two sons whose names were Comgall and Gabran, and they are commemorated in Cowal and Gowrie.

Drum Albyn—literally 'the spine of Scotland'—was the original frontier of Irish settlement, but was later breached by the expansionist Gaels. Just as later emigrants named part of North America 'Nova Scotia', so these early settlers liked to think that they were in New Ireland. They used several words to convey this idea, one of which was the word *eilgin*, diminutive of *elg*, which are preserved in the names Elgin and Glenelg. Another ancient name for Ireland was Fodla, and it has been maintained that Atholl is *ath Fhodla*—'the next Ireland'.

There is also evidence that a form of the word *erin*, Gaelic *Eireann*—meaning 'of Ireland'—was applied to Strathearn in Perthshire. This cannot be proved, and some scholars hold that *earn* is instead a pre-Celtic water word, cognate with Rhine and Rhone (see also **Ayr**). They also point to the connection between the river name Earn and the Findhorn, whose former name was *fionn eren*—'white water'—as contrasted with the Deveron, or *dubh eren*—'black water'.

eun

Eun (pronounced 'en') is Gaelic for 'bird', the plural being *eoin* (pronounced 'yoin'). There are at least half a dozen little lochs in the Highlands styled 'nan Eun' or 'nan Eoin'. Dirnanean in Strathardle is *doire nan eun*—'bird thicket'.

Of individual bird-names, eagle is the most notable: not Gleneagles, for which see **eaglais**, but in the Gaelic form *iolair* (pronounced 'yoolur'):

there are a number of hills with names such as Carn or Craig Iolaire, of interest mainly to hillwalkers. The Old Norse word for eagle (*örn*, cf. Scots *erne*) crops up many times in the far north and west: Arnaval in Skye ('erne fell'), Arnamul in Mingulay ('eagle-headland'); Arnish and Arnisort ('eagle ness fjord'). Unst in Shetland is *örn vist*—'eagle dwelling'.

Raven occurs in four Lowland places all named Ravenscraig, which seems to have been a fashionable name for a castle; the Gaelic equivalent is Creag an Fhitheach (pronounced 'ee-uch'), found in a few Highland locations, notably on Ben Lawers. Hawk is found in Dundee's Hawkhill and in various Highland names such as Craig an t-Seabhag (pronounced 'shevig'), not uncommonly found in the Cairngorm area.

The Scandinavian word for swan (*svannr*) is to be found in Swanney ('swan isle') in Orkney and many other Northern places; but beware confusion with the personal name Sven, which has the different etymology of 'swain', meaning 'servant', and is the basis of Swanston near Edinburgh. We are on surer ground with the Gaelic *eala*: *loch nan eala* is Loch Nell or 'swan-loch' near Oban.

Gaelic took over the Old Norse word for cormorant—*scarfr*—and rendered it into *sgarbh*. Skarskerry near Dunnet Head is 'cormorant rock'; Scarba and Scarpa both mean 'cormorant isle'. Marsco in Skye is supposed to be Old Norse *mar skogr*—'sea-mew wood'.

The general Scandinavian word for bird is *fugla*, represented by the numerous Foglas, Foulas and Fulas in the Hebrides and the Northern Isles.

ey

Ey is the Old Norse term for island, and so widespread is the word that one has to think hard to produce examples of Scottish islands whose names *don't* end in a 'y' sound. There are over 500 islands off the Scottish coast between Kintyre and Sutherland, and apart from Arran, Mull, Rum, Eigg, Uist, Harris and Lewis, they nearly all embody forms of the word *ey*.

Not all the names are translatable, but Jura appears to be 'Diorad's isle', a personal name meaning 'deer'. Raasay is difficult but may mean 'roe-deer isle'; and Skye is from the Gaelic *sgiath*, 'a wing'—hence 'winged' or 'divided isle', which probably refers to its shape. Scalpa and Scalpay are 'boat-shaped' from Old Norse *skalpr*, whence comes also Scapa Flow. Soay is *sautha*—'sheep'. Pabay is originally Norse *pap ey*—'priest isle'—and Papa Stour is 'great priest-isle'. (The Old Norse *stor* is usually a prefix, but gives Stoer in Sutherland), Ulva is from Old Norse *ulfr* 'a wolf'—and the Cumbraes are the 'Cumbric isles' (*Cumbri* being another name for the Brittonic-speaking inhabitants of Strathclyde, cf. Welsh *Cymri*). Eriskay, once thought to be 'Erik's isle' is probably Gaelic *uruisg* 'a water-sprite'; but Rothesay is Roderick's isle. Berneray, of which there are six, is Bjorn's isle; Boreray is 'fortress isle' (see **burgh**). Shellay (one in Harris, the other in North Uist) is 'seal isle' and the name is reduplicated in translation along the west coast; Sellafield and Sellafirth will be from the same source.

The most beautiful name (and island) of all, Iona, is a scribal error for 'Ioua', and its meaning is uncertain. Perhaps the error was deliberate, for Iona is a transliteration of Jona, a Hebrew name meaning 'dove', and the Latin for dove is *columba*. Even as late as Dr Johnson's visit in 1779, the island was known as Icolmkill—*ey Colum cille*—'isle of Columba of the church'.

The meanings of most of the island names not involving the word *ey* are unexplained; but Mull probably has the sense of 'lofty, high', Eigg is 'notched isle', and Harris on the face of it is *na-h-earaidh*, meaning 'higher' (than its neighbour Lewis). Shetland is also unexplained, but *yell* is Old Norse for 'barren' (in Scots a cow that won't yield milk is a 'yell coo'). Whalsay is 'whale's isle', and Gigha is thought to be 'God isle' or 'good isle'. Arran may derive from its kidney shape (Gaelic *airne*).

Orkney (the *Orcades* of Nennius) is discussed under **muc**; Hoy is *ha ey* or tall isle. Rousay and South Ronaldsay refer to Rolf and Ronald (but North Ronaldsay is said to be a corruption of Ringan or Ninian). The Isle of May in the Firth of Forth has been explained as *ma ey*—'sea-mew isle'— but it is difficult to believe that a Norse name penetrated so far south; it may be from the equivalent Scots term 'sea maw'.

The Gaelic language has its own words for island, namely *eilean* and *innis* (see **inch**). *Eilean* is familiar in Eilean Donan castle on Loch Duich, and Loch an Eilean in Strathspey. Eilean Mhunna near Ballachulish (St Munn's Island) is named for an associate of St Columba. Innellan in the Firth of Clyde seems to be *en eilean*—'bird isle'. A few others occur, but you will rarely find *eilean* applied to sea-girt isles, for the Norsemen made them their own.

F

fada

This is the everyday Gaelic adjective 'long', and the maps are peppered with it, sometimes in a disguised form. There are at least six lochs Fada ('long lochs', but note that Loch Long itself means 'ship-loch'), and a Druim Fada ('long ridge') above Loch Eil. Beinn Fhada is in Glencoe, and there is another on Mull; Ben Attow in Kintail is an anglicised spelling of the same name, which looks odd but gives a reasonable indication of the Gaelic pronunciation; Attadale is the same.

The opposite of *fada* is *gearr* (pronounced 'g-yarr') which means 'short' as an adjective and 'to cut' as a verb. Loch Gair, an inlet of Loch Fyne, is well described, as is Gairloch further north; (but Gairlochy is under suspicion as a **caer** word). Garmouth on the Spey is correctly *gearr magh*—'short plain'; but although the town of Girvan takes its name from the Water of Girvan, an attempted derivation from *gearr abhainn*—'short river'—will not do. Obscurity reigns.

fas

A Brittonic term which did not pass into Gaelic; it means a stance, a pitch, a spot where a drover might have rested his beasts for the night. Fasnakyle in Glen Affric is *fas na coille*—'station of the wood'; Fasnacloich in Appin is 'station of the stone'; Dallas is 'meadow station' and Duffus is 'black station'. Rothes involves the word *rath* meaning 'grace, good fortune'—Rothes must have been considered a lucky pitch.

An allied word is *fasadh*, which has much the same function in the place-name vocabulary; *am Fasadh Fearna* on Loch Eil became Fassiefern —'alder station'. The Braes of Foss in Strathtummel are in Gaelic *Braigh Fasaidh*. Barassie near Troon is *barr fhasaidh*—'summit of the station'.

fauld

The Scots term for a cattle or sheep-pen, the same as the English 'fold' with the related meaning of 'to envelop'. There are a few not very well known Lowland place-names of this type such as Broomfaulds and Gilliesfaulds. Fallside in Lanarkshire is another example.

A Gaelic word *fal*, with the meaning of fold or pen, is probably the origin of Glen Falloch near Loch Lomond, and of Fala in Lanarkshire. Falkirk is however different (see under **kirk**) and may be compared with Falside/ Fallside which occurs four times in the south of Scotland. Falkland is thought to be a reminder of its origin as a place for hunting with falcons. Falmouth near Cullen is traditionally a reduction of 'whale mouth'.

fell

This is an Old Norse term, much less familiar in Scotland than in the North of England, whither it was brought by the Danes; there are reckoned to be well over fifty *fell*-names in Cumbria alone. *Fell* does occur frequently in southern Scotland, but most often, as it were, without a capital letter: Borgue fell ('fort hill') for example is a construction akin to 'Birnam hill', where the second element is not an integral part of the name; the Campsie Fells are similar, and are known locally simply as 'the Campsies' (see **shee**).

Fell (Old Norse *fjall*) is much more productive of place-names in areas of Scandinavian colonisation, i.e. the far north and the Hebrides. It means of course 'hill', and the best-known example is Goatfell in Arran—which seems certain to be *geita fjall* or 'goat hill' rather than the more enticing *gaoth fjall* or 'wind hill'. Ben Loyal in Sutherland is *laga fjall*—'law hill', and Suilven in Wester Ross is thought to be *sul-fjall*—'pillar hill'. But Conavel in Sutherland not a *fell* name; it is the Gaelic *conmheall* or 'high lump' (see **meall**)—the highest part of Ben More Assynt.

There are very many Hebridean hills whose original '-al' ending shows a lost *fjall* ; examples are Blaven in the Cuillin which was formerly *bla fjal* ('blue hill'); the form *Blabheinn* is a Gaelic/Norse hybrid. In the Northern Isles the *fjall* suffix often takes the form '-field' or '-fiold', giving Fugla Field ('bird hill') in Shetland and Sand Fiold ('sand hill') in Orkney.

fetter

The name Foyers on Loch Ness has posed etymological problems of an unusual sort. The site is a terraced slope, and there are other forgotten place-names around the loch which apply to similar terrain: an obsolete Gaelic word *fathair* or *fothair* has been reactivated, and has been linked to forms such as Fetter which still appear on the map. (Those interested in further etymological excavation may wish to refer to the current Gaelic words *fo* and *tir*, which mean 'below' and 'land' and perhaps relate to the concept of 'terrace').

Foyers means 'terraced slopes' (the plural 's' is an English addition). Fettercairn, Fetteresso and Fetterangus, the first two in the Mearns and the third in Buchan, mean respectively 'wooded', 'waterfall' and 'Angus's' slope. Forteviot is another 'fetter' name, but the -teviot ending is obscure and unlikely to relate to the equally difficult Border river-name. The term occurs terminally in Dunottar ('fort slope'); Fodderty in Ross and Fedderat in Aberdeenshire both mean 'place of terraces'. The oddest perversion of the term is to be seen on a wayside notice-board on the A9 in Badenoch which reads Phones; this has nothing to do with telecommunications but is an attempt to anglicise *Fotharais*, which means 'slope of the wood'. The name Forfar has always posed great difficulties; the suggested etymology of *fothair faire* ('watch-slope') is mere speculation, and Forfar must remain in the class of 'etymology unknown' names.

The modern Gaelic word for hill-slope is *leathad*, usually contracted to 'led' in place-names but pronounced something like 'l-ya-ud'. This produces the relatively simple names of Ledbeg and Ledmore (little and big slopes), Ledcrieff ('tree-slope') and Ledard ('slope of the height'). Lednock in Strathearn is 'knoll slope', and Ledaig at Connel contains the Old Norse element *eitja* meaning 'to hinder' (possibly a reference to the nearby Falls of Lora). Lethnot in Angus is probably 'naked slope', as is Lightnot in Aberdeenshire; and Ben Ledi is popularly derived from *Leathad Dia* 'slope of God'.

Two more types of slope may be mentioned here. The first is *sliabhach*, meaning 'place of slopes', which accounts for Sleach in Glengairn, Slioch at Drumblade and Slioch, the mountain in Wester Ross overlooking Loch Maree. ('Sloping place' is rather an understatement in this particular case). The word is of course an extension of *sliabh*, a high moor or mountain; it is very common as a place-name element in Ireland (e.g Slieve Donard), but in Scotland is virtually confined to the south-west corner which was formerly known as Dalriada. The second and final 'slope' name comes from the Old English *sceot*, and gives us the Lanarkshire name Shotts (unconnected, be it said, with Aldershot and Bagshot).

fionn

Fionn pronounced ('f-yunn') is Gaelic for white, and is the component of several Highland personal names such as Fingal, Finlay and Fiona. In the place-name vocabulary it is very often paired with its opposite *dubh*, meaning black. Thus *fionnghlais* means 'white stream' and gives Glen Finlas in the Trossachs as well as the River Finlas which joins Loch Lomond, and Glen Finglas in Ayrshire. Its counterpart is *dubhghlais*, which was a stream name before it became the place- and personal name Douglas (see **glas**). Findhorn and Deveron—two neighbouring rivers—are discussed under **Erin**. Finnart on Loch Fyne and in Rannoch are both *fionn aird* ('white point'), and Finlarig on Loch Tay is 'white pass'. *Fionn tref* means 'white stead' and gives Fintry in Stirlingshire and Dundee, and also the two Fintrays in Aberdeenshire. Fincastle in Atholl, Fionnphort in Mull (see under **port**) and the various Fionn Lochs all have obvious meanings. (But beware that Foinaven (*Foinne Bheinn*) in Sutherland, after which the oilfield was named, means 'wart mountain'). Findon, the name of a village in Kincardineshire, probably contains the element *fionn*; the local pronunciation—'finnan'— gave rise to the term 'finnan haddie'—a haddock cured in the smoke of green wood. Glenfinnan is however a much more august name, discussed under **saint**.

firth

This term appears in our standard dictionaries, and as an English word it occurs in names of places ranging from Solway to Pentland. (It is worth noting that that the Old Norse word for Pict was *Petr,* and that the Norsemen called the channel between Orkney and Caithness the 'Pettland' firth. The name of Edinburgh's Pentland hills is discussed under **land**).

The original form of firth, however, is Old Norse *fjordr,* modern Norwegian fjord. Gaelic speakers found great difficulty in saying this word, and it appears in place-names in the aspirated and truncated forms of *ort* and *art.* There are many of these, notable examples being Moidart ('Mundi's bay'), Knoydart ('Cnut's fjord'), Sunart ('Sven's fjord') and Snizort ('Sni's fjord'). The Scandinavians, like the Anglo-Saxons, were given to naming places after people; the Gaels did this sparingly, unless to commemorate one of their innumerable saints.

Not infrequently the *fjordr* element becomes anglicised to *ford,* which accounts for Laxford in Sutherland, meaning 'salmon loch'; Melfort is *melr fjord*—'sandbank loch' (cf. the first part of Milford Haven). In Melvich and Melvaig, the suffix means 'bay'. Broadford in Skye, however, is modern and has no Norse ancestry (see next entry below).

ford

Crossing-points on rivers, whether in the form of fords or bridges, are very significant in terms of human geography, and, as we should expect, these words occur in many place-names. The best-known was probably the Fords of Frew, now of no consequence at all but at one time the first place above Stirling where the Forth was fordable (the Jacobite army crossed it on its southward march in 1745). Frew incidentally means 'current' (as in Renfrew—see under **ness**), and the reference is to the thin water at that point in the river's course; in Gaelic the fords were referred to as *na Friuthachan* and in Scots as 'the Frews'.

On the face of it, names like Blackford, Whiteford, and Redford will be relatively modern, for they are simple descriptive English terms, with obvious meanings. The Fortunes in East Lothian also display the 'ford' element. Sometimes however these are translations of much earlier names, often involving the Gaelic word for ford, which is *ath.* Broadford in Skye is just a translation of the Gaelic *an Ath Leathan.* Galla Ford in Midlothian is really *geal ath* ford, or 'Whiteford-ford'.

The trouble is that *ath* is a fugitive word, the 'th' being silent and very often swallowed by the following consonant. Amulree in Perthshire is *ath Maol Ruibhe*—'St Maolrubha's ford' and Aboyne is *ath bo fhionn*—'white cattle ford'. Ethie in Angus is an *ath* name, meaning something like 'ford-place'. Sometimes *ath* masquerades as **ach**, so that *ath Thorcuil* becomes Acharacle ('Torquil's ford'). When *ath* occurs at the end of a name it becomes a short 'a' sound: Dava in Moray is *damh ath*, literally 'Oxford', and Dunira in Strathearn was originally *dun iar ath*—'fort on the west ford'. Most confusing is Alford which is probably a 'ford' name but not in the obvious way: the local pronunciation is 'Aff-ord' and the Gaelic form would be *ath-ord,* 'ford of the height'.

Now for the inevitable pitfalls. Atholl incorporates a completely different Gaelic word *ath* meaning 'next' or 'new'; the name is discussed under **Erin.** The English word ford itself is often a rendering of the Gaelic *fothair*; Fordell in Fife and Fordoun in the Mearns are probably **fetter** rather than ford-names. And Glassford in Lanarkshire is really the Brittonic *glas ffrid*—'green forest'.

An Old English word for ford was *waed*, giving the Lothian name Lasswade—*laes waed,* or 'ford in the meadowland'.

fort

It is time to pause in our etymologising and consider a few fragments of history. .

In 1597, in an attempt to curb the lawlessness of the Gaels, the Scottish Parliament enacted that burghs should be created to maintain the cause of 'civility and policy' in the West Highlands. In those days decisions appear to have taken even longer to carry out than they do now, for it was not until 1655 that a fort was built in Lochaber by General Monk. It was rebuilt under William of Orange nearly fifty years later, and called Fort William after him. The nearby village was named *Maryburgh,* after his consort. When the Gordon family acquired the estates in the eighteenth century they re-named the village *Gordonburgh*; later still Sir Duncan Cameron of Fassifern bought the property, and the village for a time rejoiced in the name of *Duncansburgh.* The native Gaels persisted in calling the place *an Gearasdan*; this name was heard until comparatively recently—it means 'The Garrison'. Eventually town and fort became one; Mary and Gordon and Duncan were all forgotten, and Fort William has become the metropolis of the north-west. (Just to complete the record, the original site of the fort was called *achadh an todhair*—'dung field').

All this is a useful reminder that in bygone days place-names were not the fixities that they are now, and tended to change from generation to generation. It was only with the mass-production of maps in the late-Victorian era that the natural development of place-nomenclature was arrested; and indeed modern maps of the Highlands abound in stream and hill names in nineteenth century Gaelic which are no longer used by anyone.

Fort Augustus is of somewhat later origin, having been built after the Rising of 1715. It was named in honour of William Augustus, Duke of Cumberland, which is appropriate because it was around this spot that his soldiers perpetrated some of their more barbaric outrages. The earlier name of the place was *Cilcumein* (*cill Cummein*—'the cell of Cummein', abbot of Iona).

The third fort in the trio, Fort George on the Moray Firth, was named after George II. Built too late to be involved in any action, it is a perfectly preserved eighteenth century military installation.

Fortingall is a much older name than the three above, the fort element in this case being a reduction of the Brittonic *gwerthyr*. The *gall* part is a corruption of the Gaelic *ceall* (see **kil**). Fortingall is thus 'fortress church'. (The beguiling etymology of 'fort in Gaul' must be strenuously rejected for reasons linguistic, geographical and historical.) Forter in Glenisla probably has the same derivation, while Kirkforthar in Fife is possibly *caer gwerthyr* 'fort-fort'.

Forteviot and Fortrose are not fort names. The former is discussed under **fetter** and the latter under **fo**.

fraoch

The Gaelic word for heather is *fraoch*, pronounced approximately as 'free-ugh'. In its simplest form it is found in such names as Fraoch (a hill in Kintyre) and Fraoch Eilean ('heather island') on Loch Awe; with the locative ending it becomes Fraochaidh, a hill near Ballachulish ('at the heather'), which in anglicised spelling is rendered as Freuchie, the name of a loch in Perthshire, a village in Fife, and the old name for Grantown-on-Spey. Auchnafree in Glen Almond is 'heathfield'. East and West Freugh in Wigtonshire are of similar origin. The oddest development of this term is to be found in Angus, where in 1824 the name of Friock Feus ('heather-lands') was formally changed by its germanophile proprietor to Friockheim.

The Old Norse word for heather is *lyng*, whence our 'ling', and there are no fewer than four islands in Shetland and the Hebrides called Linga. There are similarly named places in Norway and it has been suggested that the bestowal of the name may as often have been nostalgic as descriptive.

Place-names involving the word 'heath' are common in England, but 'heather' names in Scotland are thin on the ground. Heatherwick in Aberdeenshire and Hedderwick in East Lothian and Angus are the only ancient ones that come to mind, the others probably being fairly recent.

G

gair

This Gaelic word means 'cry' or 'roar', and in a place-name context even 'outcry' or 'uproar', possibly with reference to the noise of the wind. This certainly seems to be the sense of Lochan na Gaire, a tarn which unaccountably gave its name to one of Scotland's finest mountains. (It must be said that Lochnagar as applied to the mountain is a relatively modern name, its currency no doubt reinforced by Byron's poem entitled, in the corrupt eighteenth century spelling, *Lachin y Gair*). An earlier and alternative name is *Beinn nan Chiochan* ('hill of paps'), two of the summits still being known as 'Little Pap' and 'Meikle Pap'; the whole massif was known as 'the White Mounth' (see **monadh**). The word *gair* also gives *gairneag* ('crying one'), which is the meaning of Glen Girnock on Deeside and Glen Girnaig in Atholl. Garnock in Ayrshire and Dalgarnock in Dumfriesshire are similar. Bridge of Gaur in Rannoch is from the *Abhain Gaoir*, or River Gaur, which derives from the Gaelic *geamradh*—'winter'.

A comparable word to *gair* is *labhair*, pronounced 'lavir', meaning 'speak'. *Labhairt* is the usual term for a sermon, and *labhar* is (with less dignity) 'a chattering one'. This is precisely the sense behind Lawers; Ben Lawers, Perthshire's highest mountain, is named after the village of Lawers, which in turn was called after a chattering little stream on which the old settlement stood and which drove the mill that gave the place its *raison d'être*. (The present village of Lawers is insignificant compared with the old loch-side settlement which boasted a kirk, a cemetery, a mill, a laird's house and a pier, all now in picturesque ruin). The Lawers estate in Strathearn imported its name from Loch Tay-side. The opposite of *labhar* would be *balbhag* ('little dumb one'), which gives us the name of the River Balvaig in Strathyre.

Alphabetically the last of the chattering streams to be mentioned is the Aberdeenshire Ythan, which has as its root the Brittonic word *iaith* meaning 'language'. But one might for good measure include a very odd Gaelic dialect word *eibh* (pronounced 'ev'), which is defined in an old-fashioned dictionary as 'a long-continued cry, as when women hear of some disastrous catastrophe'. If that seems melodramatic, at least it is reasonably certain that Moniaive in Dumfries means 'moor of the cry'.

gall

Gall is a pervasive and significant adjective in Highland history: it has the opposite sense to Gael, and means 'strange, foreign'. The word for the Lowlands was *Galldachd,* and the sense of oppression at the hands of their more powerful neighbours was summed up by the Gaels in the phrase *mi-run mor nan Gall*—'the great hatred of the Lowlanders'. The surname Gall would be given originally to a non-Gaelic speaker; more specifically, Galbraith was 'stranger Briton', an inhabitant of the old British kingdom of Strathclyde.

The tribal province of Galloway, which earlier covered a much larger area comprising Renfrew, Ayr and Dumfries, was perceived as the place of freebooting Norse-Hebridean settlers or *Gall Ghaidhil* ('stranger Gaels'), and was called *Gall Gaidhealabhaidh* (pronounced approximately as 'Galloway', believe it or not). Galston, a later settlement in Ayrshire with an English suffix, expresses the same idea, as apparently does Loch Goil in Argyll.

Similarly, the Hebrides—the *Ebudae* of Ptolemy, meaning unknown— although originally Celtic, were under Norse domination for a sufficiently long period to be known as *Innse Gall*—'islands of the stranger'. To complete the picture, it may be added that the district of Argyll (which formerly stretched as far north as Ullapool) is *Oirer Ghaidheal*—'coastland of the Gael'. (But note that the numerous settlements known as Gallatown, Gallowflat, Gallowgate and Gallow Hill all have this in common, that they refer to the instrument of execution.)

Historically, the Scots were a Gaelic-speaking people from Ireland who co-existed with English-speaking Lowlanders and Norse-speaking Northerners, and at one time these racial groupings were fairly well defined; this is reflected in the prevalence within Scotland of the surname Scott, and one or two place-names bear similar witness. Scotscalder was traditionally that part of the Calder valley in Caithness that was inhabited by Scots as contrasted with the nearby Norse-speaking Norncalder. There are numerous Scotstons and Scotstowns in Aberdeenshire as well as Scotstoun in Glasgow; these would perhaps refer to a Gaelic-speaking settlement in the Lowlands; but Scotlandwell near Kinross makes an early appearance in the records in the Latinate form *Fons Scotiae,* a clear reference to the national name.

gaoth

This Gaelic word, pronounced between 'goo' and 'guy', means wind (also, as in English, 'flatulence', but that does not concern us here). It might be thought that the adjective 'windy' (*gaothaich*) would apply to most parts of Scotland, but place-names indicate that some are more stormy than others. Ardgay on the Dornoch Firth is 'windy height'. Goatfell in Arran has usually been taken literally, but 'windy fell' may be another possibility; Guthrie in Angus is *gaotharachd*—'windiness'.

Now for the inevitable *caveat*: there was another Gaelic word *gaoth* (pronounced 'goo'), now obsolete, which turns up in some place-names and which means a marsh (as though there weren't already enough Gaelic words for that—see **mig**). Sometimes it is impossible to distinguish wind from wet, but notable examples of the latter are the two places called Gight (pronounced 'gecht') in Aberdeenshire; Bog of Gight in effect says the same thing twice. Guay on the Tay seems also to be a candidate for the wet option, as does Irongath near Linlithgow (*earran-gaoithe*—'marsh part'). Balgay in Dundee has been interpreted as 'windy village' but, like Milngavie near Glasgow (discussed in the Introduction), remains undecided.

gart

This is a difficult element, because the word appears in the four of the languages with which we have to deal—Old Norse (*gardr*), Brittonic (*garth*), Gaelic (*garradh*) and Old English *(geard*—'yard/garden'). The Gaelic is thought to be a borrowing from Old Norse; the name Garth near Aberfeldy could be either Gaelic or Brittonic.

The biggest cluster of *gart* names in Scotland occurs in the area now covered by greater Glasgow: Garscadden—'herring yard'; Gartcosh—'foot of the yard'; Gartloch—'lake enclosure'; Gartness—'waterfall place'; Gartcraig—'crag place' and Gartnavel—'apple yard'. Others nearby include Gargunnock—probably 'hillock-place', Garscube—'sheaf field', and Gartocharn—'garden of the cairn'. Kingarth in Bute is 'end of the enclosure' and Gartsherrie at Coatbridge is *gart searraigh*—'colt field'. Boat of Garten is a modern name referring to a ferry over the Spey, but incorporates the term *garradh*. So probably do Grandtully in Strathtay and Gartly in Aberdeenshire—'hillock-enclosure' (see **tulloch**). All these are pure Gaelic.

The Norse *gardr* is usually seen in its Gaelicised form of *gearraidh*, and spelt 'garry'. This gives us the names Calgary ('Kali's enclosure'), Flodigarry ('fleet enclosure') and Mingary ('big enclosure'). But these are not to be confused with the 'garry' of Glengarry, Loch Garry and Invergarry, which derive from *garbh* (see **garve**).

The English word 'yard' is not of common occurrence in place-names, the only one that comes to mind being Guardbridge in Fife, which is really 'yard (enclosure) bridge'.

Another Gaelic term for a garden or enclosure (especially of a monastery) is *lios*. Lesmahagow in Lanarkshire (modern pronunciation 'lez-ma-hay-go', with the stress on the 'hay') was once *Lios mo Fhegu*—'enclosure of my Fechin' (see under **saint**). Lismore in the Firth of Lorn is 'great garden', or possibly 'enclosure', referring to the monastery of St Moluag. Pitlessie in Fife is 'garden place'. Auchterless in Aberdeenshire is 'upper enclosure'. The Lowland name Leys may be *lios* in disguise, but is probably the plural of lea meaning meadow.

The Brittonic version of *lios* is *llys*, which, combined with *celyn* ('holly') gives the unfamiliar name *Lescelin*: but simplify it to Leslie, and we get the name of a twelfth century barony in Aberdeenshire. It became a well-known surname, that of the earls of Rothes; through them it was adopted as the name of a paper-making town in Fife. Its use as a Christian name (Lesley for girls) is fairly modern.

garve

A well-used Gaelic adjective which means rough, coarse, harsh, brawny; in the old language it is *garbh*, pronounced 'garav'. *Garbh Chriochan* are 'the rough bounds' (of Knoydart and other areas). As a noun the word means 'rough place', as exemplified in Garve near Ullapool. Garvellach is 'rough, rocky place', and the same meaning is found in Garioch, which was *Garbheach* in Gaelic (the early spellings do not support the local pronunciation 'Geary'). In mountain terminology the word features countless times in names such as *Meall Gharbh* ('rough lump') and *Garbh choire* ('rough corrie', sometimes anglicised to Garrachory); and *Garbh allt* (Garvalt) is a very common name for a brawling stream.

Most familiar of all is the water-name Garry, whose origin is the continental Celtic *garu*; as well as being the name of two separate Highland rivers, and the even better-known Glen and Loch Garry, it is the basis of the lowland river Yarrow, the English Yar and Yare and the French Garonne. All have the basic meaning of 'rough, turbulent'.

It says a lot about the terrain of the Highlands that *garbh* is very much more commonly found in place-names than is its opposite *min*, meaning smooth. The north side of Loch Rannoch was known as *Slios Min*—'smooth slope', in contrast to the southern shore, but there are very few areas to which that adjective could be applied.

The Old Norse word for smooth was *slettr*, which provides the etymology of Sleat in Skye—certainly the least mountainous part of the island. Slattadale is 'smooth valley'.

gate

In Scots, *gate* or *gait* means a thoroughfare rather than a portal; it comes from Old English *geat*, which has the primary meaning of 'way' as is evidenced by the street-names Trongate ('weighbridge street'), Cowgate, Nethergate ('low road') and Skinnergate (the lane of the skinners or hide-strippers), occurring in Glasgow, Edinburgh, Dundee and Perth. But there are numerous settlement-names in Scotland which incorporate the word 'gate'. In Fife we have Crossgates ('crossroads') and Windygates (which must mean 'twisty roads'). There are at least ten wayside hamlets called Gateside. These names are all relatively modern, and date from a time when the English language had become established in Lowland Scotland. But 'gate' names of this type are characteristically Scottish; in England, oddly enough, names such as Gateshead in Durham and Gatwick in Surrey have a different origin, namely 'goat'.

glas

The Gaels seem to have had no great liking for primary colours, or at least their adjectives of colour appear to be slightly ambiguous. *Gorm* is 'bluish green', as in Cairngorm; *ruadh* is 'reddish-brown', as in Monadhruadh (the old name for the Cairngorm range); and *buidhe* is 'golden yellow', as in Achiltibuie (which is probably *achadh uillte buidhe*—'field of the yellow brook', although local tradition maintains that it is *achadh a ghille buidhe*— 'field of the golden-haired lad').

Glas can be either 'grey' or 'green'. The *bodach glas* is the spectre that appears in Scott's *Waverley*, where the meaning is explicitly 'grey'. But Glasgow is the Brittonic *glas cau*—'green hollow'—and the correct pronunciation, 'Glesca' is heard daily on the lips of native Glaswegians.

The term *glas* occurs in many types of place-name. We have numerous examples of Ben Glas (*beinn glas*—'grey mountain'), and in its inverted form Glasven, which reminds us that in older Gaelic the adjective did not invariably follow the noun. Glas Maol ('grey lump') at the head of Glen Isla, is discussed under **maol**; Glas Tulachan to the west is 'grey hillocks'; and Glassary in Argyll is probably *glas airidh*—'grey or green shieling'.

But now for the inevitable pitfalls. There is an older Brittonic word *glas*, meaning water, which occurs with great frequency in place-names. Take Douglas, which embodies the Brittonic words *du* (black) and *glas* (stream); this is found all over Lowland Scotland as a stream name and

69

gave rise to a surname which in turn became a baptismal name. There are places called Douglas in Ireland and the Isle of Man; in Wales the spelling is Dulais and in England it is Dawlish; combined with the prefix **inver**, the name Inveruglas emerges. The opposite of *du glas* is *fionn ghlais* or Finglas. More accessible are Strath Glass—'stream vale', and Kinglassie in Fife and Strathkinlas in Argyll. The last two give the idea of 'at the head of the stream'. Erchless is *air glais*—'on the River Glass'. But Glen Kinglass is different—see **con.**

The upshot of all this is that if you see the element *glas* in a place-name you cannot by linguistic evidence alone tell whether the reference is to the colour grey or the colour green or to a stream; but you can be pretty sure that glazing is not involved.

glen

The Gaelic word *gleann* has become so thoroughly internationalised that there are now 'glens' in Canada and Australia—indeed wherever the Scots have settled. Properly speaking, however, there are no genuine glens outside the Scottish Highlands and a few parts of the Southern Uplands, and Gaelic usage prescribes that *glen* always precedes the other components of the name. Where that does not occur, as in Alva Glen and Pittencrieff Glen, the name was not bestowed by Gaelic-speakers. 'The Sma' Glen', to take another example, is a product of the tourist trade—it merely describes a narrow and picturesque part of Glen Almond. In the Lowlands the topography does not produce so many glens, and the term for a dell or defile is **den**. In the Borders the characteristic term is **dale** as in Tweeddale and Teviotdale.

The great majority of Highland glens are named after the streams that drain them: Glen Almond is 'stream glen' and Glen Lyon is 'flood glen', from the names of these Perthshire rivers. (There is another River Almond near Edinburgh, with the same meaning; the word is cognate with **avon**). Glen Roy (*ruaidhe*) is not 'red glen' but rather 'glen of the red river', and Glen Devon is from the river name *Devona*.

Not all *glen* names derive from streams, however; there are at least ten Glenmores ('great glens') in the Highlands, apart from the one which now seems to have lost its name to 'the Caledonian Canal'. Glencoe is still popularly supposed to mean 'the glen of weeping'; but the weeping did not begin until 1692, and the name is much older than that—anyway, singularly few Scottish place-names commemorate events in history. In Gaelic the name is *gleann comhann* meaning 'narrow glen', but this may be a rationalisation from the topography: more likely the second part comes from the River Coe, whose etymology is obscure.

70

Gleneagles has nothing to do with the king of birds (or even with golf); it is discussed under **eccles**. Glenfinnan is 'Fingon's glen': he was a four-teenth century abbot of Iona, and is also remembered in the surname Mackinnon. Glen Fiddich, famous for its malt whisky, may be from an ancient personal name meaning 'woodsman' (but see under **staff**); Glen Grant, an equally famous name, does not exist except on bottle-labels.

The oddest *glen* name is perhaps Glenrothes, which was coined around fifty years ago for a new town in Fife. The *rothes* part (see **rath**) is unex-ceptionable, for the earls of Rothes had an estate of that name nearby, but why did the authorities create a glen where none exists in nature? 'Newtonrothes' might not have have been so helpful in attracting Ameri-can industry, but it would have been more in touch with both topography and common sense.

Gordon

This is an example, by no means unusual, of a place-name which achieved much greater fame as a surname and in turn produced more place-names. Gordon, a parish and village in Berwickshire, is thought to come from the Brittonic words *gor dun*, meaning 'great fort'. (So probably does Gourdon in Kincardineshire). Adam of Gordon was rewarded by Robert the Bruce with the lordship of Strathbogie; he adopted the Border village-name as his own, and it became highly influential in the north-east. Various landed Gordon families gave their names to Gordon Castle, Fochabers, to Port Gordon, Gordonstown near Elgin (purchased in 1638 by Sir Robert Gordon, vice-chamberlain of Scotland), and to the estate of Gordonstoun (formerly known as 'Bog of Plewlands') which became a famous school. Invergordon was called after Sir Alexander Gordon, its proprietor in the eighteenth cen-tury. Two centuries later the name Gordon was (rather maladroitly) conferred on an administrative district in Aberdeenshire

The Gordon take-over of the north-east did not end there. Another celebrated name in the area is Huntly, whose etymology is purely Eng-lish—'hunt-lea', or 'hunting meadow'. It would be impossible to have an ancient name of this kind in the solidly Gaelic milieu of Strathbogie; and the explanation is that it was transplanted from the Borders when a Gordon heir was created lord of Strathbogie in the early fifteenth century. The place-name Huntly now seems to have disappeared from the Borders; all that remains are the 'Huntlie Bank' on which lay Thomas the Rhymer in the famous ballad, and a farm called Huntlywood.

'Hunt' names are not uncommon in Scotland, although not so plentiful as south of the Border. England has Huntingdon ('hunt hill'), three

Huntingtons, a Huntingfield and a Huntley (with the same meaning as ours). Scotland has Hunthill in Roxburgh and Huntingtower near Perth, seat of the Lords of Ruthven and locus of the Gowrie conspiracy. The Gaelic word for hunt is *sealg* (pronounced 'shalg'); but it yields only Dunshalt ('hunting fort'), situated near Falkland, itself the hunting-palace of the early Scottish kings, and whose very name may derive from Old English *fealca*— a falcon.

If hunting in the Highlands is perceived as a cruel sport nowadays it was very much worse in the past. An age-old method of deer-hunting was to drive the animals into a trap, for which the Gaelic term is *eilerg*, where they would be slaughtered in vast numbers by arrows and mauled by hounds. These traps were usually V-shaped defiles in the hills, and appear on the maps as Elrick. Meikle and Little Elrick were two such in upper Deeside, and there are at least three Carn Elricks in the Cairngorms; but the term is found throughout the Highlands, sometimes as Ellick.

gowan

The Gaelic word for blacksmith is *gobh* (the surname Gow shows the pronunciation); in its variant form of *gobhainn* it is responsible for the many place-names such as Balgowan and Balnagowan—all meaning something like 'smith's stead'. But Balgownie is a **poll** name; and beware that *gowan* in Scots means 'daisy', and gives names like Gowanbank near Arbroath and Gowanhill in Aberdeenshire; it achieves its true place in Victorian house-names like Gowanlea, 'daisy meadow'.

There are only one or two 'smith' names in Scotland; Smithfield is just across the Border, and Smithton near Inverness must be modern (and possibly from the surname). The best examples are the numerous Lowland hamlets called Smiddy Green.

Shoemaker in Scots is *souter*, which gives, as well as a familiar surname, the Soutars of Cromarty, eminences on the north and south of the Firth which were supposed to be the workstools of two giant cobblers. Souterford, Souterhill and Souterton are Aberdeenshire hamlets. The Gaelic equivalent is *greusaich* (more familiar in the surname Grassick, which shows the approximate pronunciation); Pitgersie in Foveran is *peit an ghreasaighe*—'cobbler's place'; Cairngressie, Dalgrassick and Gressiehill are other Aberdeenshire places named after the trade.

Not many other Gaelic trades are commemorated on the map, but one that comes to mind is Stronaclachar on Loch Katrine: *clachair* is a mason, and *sron* is discussed under **ness**. Beinn a Chlachair in Badenoch recalls another anonymous practitioner of the trade.

72

Grampians

The name given to the massif extending from Dumbarton in the south west to Stonehaven in the east, and comprising the Cairngorm and Perthshire mountains. The origin of the term is a pregnant phrase in the *Life of Agricola* by his son-in-law, the Roman historian Tacitus: *ad montem Graupium pervenit.* Unfortunately for posterity, Tacitus was interested only in the result and not the site of the battle of Mons Graupius, and the latter (although now thought to be somewhere in the Mearns) is still uncertain. Tacitus's rendering of the name may be a Latinised version of some Brittonic word such as *crwb* ('hump'); the 'm' originates in a misreading taken from an edition of Tacitus printed in Italy in the fifteenth century. An etymology of the word Grampian is therefore as elusive as is a definitive location of the battlefield.

The term Grampian, whatever its origin, was never in common currency. The eastern range was formerly known as The Mounth; but in 1975 the name Grampian was borrowed for an administrative region, with an artificially restricted reference to the area between The Mounth and the Moray Firth. Somewhat later it was adopted as the name of a television company which enjoys the broadcasting franchise for that particular area. Thus does a mountain-range become a channel, and a typographical error a household word.

H

hall

When these four letters occur in a Scottish place-name they very seldom represent the English word for a large house. Larkhall in Lanarkshire, although unambiguously documented (originally in the Scots form Laverock Hall) would really make better sense as laverock **haugh**, larks being not much given to frequenting halls. The word hall is usually represented in place-names in its Scots form 'ha-'; there are at least seven Hattons on the map, some of them originally farm-names, and the meaning is 'farmstead associated with a large house', or manor-farm in English terminology.

Halkirk in Orkney is 'high church' (the 'l' does not appear until the seventeenth century, and may be, as in Falkirk, an attempt at 'improvement'). Halbeath in Fife is really *coille beath*—'birchwood'. Hallival (there is one on Rum and another on Skye) is Old Norse *hjalli fjal*—'ledge or terrace hill'.

Sometimes the word 'holy' is indicated, as in Halladale in Sutherland (Norse for 'holy dale'). The English term is found in Holy Island in Lamlash Bay on Arran; called *Melansay* in the sagas ('St Melan's Isle'), it is now a Buddhist retreat. (Lamlash itself is a contraction of *Eilean mo Laise*, the village being named after the island.) Holyrood is of course 'holy cross'; according to popular legend King David I founded the abbey on the spot where a fragment of the True Cross miraculously came into his hands after an encounter with a giant stag; the palace followed some time later. Holy Loch is associated with St Munna, cf. nearby Kilmun, and is a translation of Gaelic *Loch Seanta*; (the Shiants are *na h-eileanan Seanta*—'the hallowed isles'). Holytown is near Coatbridge, and Hollywood in Dumfriesshire was formerly called *Darycongall* ('St Congal's wood').

ham

This Old English word, meaning dwelling, house, village, estate (take your pick) is a very common place-name element in England (see further under **tref**). It usually indicates the homestead of a tribal leader, whose name forms the first component of the term: thus Birmingham is 'home of the sons of Beorn'. The word *ham* apparently became obsolete early in the Anglo-Saxon period, and is found most often in areas of earlier conquest.

In Scotland, as might be expected, there are only a few *hams*, and these are all in the south-east: Birgham is 'bridge homestead' and Coldingham is 'village of the settlers of Colud'; Oxnam is an abbreviation of Oxenham ('oxen village'), Ednam of Edenham ('village on the Eden'), and Midlem of 'middle ham'.

Yetholm appears from its earlier spelling to be a 'ham' name in disguise—thus 'yett ham' or 'gatehouse'. Smailholm and Smallholm are really 'small homestead'.

In the cases of the East Lothian villages of Tyninghame ('Tyne-dwellers' village') and Whittingehame ('homestead of Hwita's people'), the final 'e' adds a touch of Scottish colour.

Bottle is another English place-name element which strayed across the Border at several points and cannot be ignored in a survey of Scottish names. The Old English word *botl* meant a house or dwelling, and gives the name Bootle which is to be found in Cumbria as well as in Liverpool; the exact Scottish counterpart is Buittle in Kirkcudbright. Morebattle in Roxburgh is *mere-botl* ('lake house'); Newbattle in Midlothian is named in contrast to Eldbotle ('old house') in the neighbouring county to the east.

74

Another *botl*-derivative gives Bolton ('dwelling-enclosure'), common in England but with only a solitary occurrence in East Lothian. Tarbolton in Ayrshire is another example—it is *tor botl toun*—meaning something like 'hill of the dwelling house'.

har

The old English word *har*, meaning 'grey with age or cold', passed into Modern English as hoary. It retains its original form in some Scottish place-names, with the principal meaning of 'old'.

The familiar name Hare Stane (found several times in Aberdeenshire) refers not to the animal but to an ancient stone, very often marking a boundary; there is one in Edinburgh, and a Harestanes near Dundee. Hartree near Biggar is named after some venerable tree, and Harburn near Carnwath is 'boundary stream'. Hare Cairn and Harewood are also found, and Hairmyres near Glasgow comes into the same category. Most notable is Harlaw in Aberdeenshire, site of a bloody battle in 1411 between the Lord of the Isles and a royal army led by the earl of Mar: the meaning is taken to be 'boundary hill', and assumes the existence of an ancient march-stone.

haven

A common English noun which occurs in many southern place-names such as Milford Haven. In Scotland it is heavily localised, on the east coast, between Aberdeen and Dunbar, where there were thought to be Frisian settlements in the Dark Ages. (Certainly the word *haven* occurs also in Dutch, with the meaning of 'inlet' or 'harbour'; and it was probably brought to the east coast from the Low Countries). Reading from north to south along the coast we have Long Haven, North Haven, Twa Havens, Stonehaven, Castle Haven (at Dunottar), Johnshaven and East Haven. In Fife there are the outliers of Woodhaven and Buckhaven, and further south we find Newhaven and Belhaven; these all mean what they say, Newhaven having been created by James IV in 1536. (Doubt has been cast on the first syllable of Stonehaven, which is discussed under **stone**; its vernacular form, 'Steenhive', seems to embody in its ending the Old English word *hythe*, meaning 'landing stage'. If this is correct it would be a unique example in Scotland of this term, common in Thames-side—names such as Rotherhithe and Maidenhead).

Nowhere else does the word haven appear on the map of Scotland, although the Old Norse equivalent, *hafnar*, gives Hamna Voe ('harbour bay') in Shetland. Whitehaven in Cumbria is also Scandinavian in origin.

75

hell

Although the various Gaelic terms for heaven do not appear in place-names, there are one or two apparent references to its opposite. The word for hell is *iutharn* (pronounced 'yoo-hurn') which seems to be a borrowing from Latin *infernus*. *Iutharn* possibly gives Loch Hourn in Knoydart and the Ben Iutharns in Perthshire; and it is true that each of these locations has its hellish aspect, especially in bad weather. (It has to be said that although doubt has been cast on these etymologies, the alternative meanings of 'berry-gap', 'furnace' and 'edge point' are somewhat feeble and lack a convincing basis in Gaelic; perhaps they also show a modern tendency to de-mythologise Scottish place-name study.) Hell's Glen in Argyll is given on the maps the alternative name of *Gleann Beag* ('little glen'); and although that glen too can have its fearsome aspect, the 'hell' bit looks like a misinterpretaion of an earlier name *Aifrinn*, meaning 'offering' (cf. Latin *offerenda)* or 'mass'. This word crops up frequently in Ireland, but its main location in Scotland seems to be Aberdeenshire, where we have Carnaveron ('mass cairn'), Tamnavrie ('mass hill') and Ardiffery ('mass point')—evidence of outdoor celebration of the sacraments.

The gloomy Loch Treig, traditional haunt of the kelpie, is said to mean 'loch of death', and this certainly corresponds with the later Gaelic word *treigte*, meaning 'forsaken, abondoned'. Romantic names are as a whole unusual in Scotland, but in this particular area there are two others—Glen Etive and Glen Salach. *Eiteag* was the name of a pagan goddess—it means literally 'little horrid one', and her traditional haunt was Glen Salach 'the foul glen'. The Gaelic word *teimheal* (pronounced 'tevvil') now means 'blackout' or 'swoon', but in a place-name signifies gloom or shade: Tummel comes from this word, no doubt on account of the thick woods which clothe the banks of this river.

Ben Wyvis is thought to come from the Gaelic *fhuathais*, meaning 'spectre'. Corpach near Fort William (it also occurs elsewhere in the north-west) means 'corpse place'—but not in any superstitious sense: it was the place where cadavers were kept overnight before island burial.

holm

The Old Norse word *holmr* means an islet, and is the origin of three places called Holm in the Northern Isles and in Lewis. The word is cognate with Old English *holm*, which could also have the meaning 'river meadow', and it is in this usage that it is most familiar in the Lowlands.

Holm is the basis of Langholm ('long meadow'), Denholm ('valley-field') and several others. Twynholm in Kirkcudbright appears to mean 'between the meadows'; Branxholme near Hawick is 'Branoc's mead'. There are however some southern 'holm' names to which this etymology cannot be ascribed: Yetholm, Smailholm and Smallholm are discussed under **ham**. 'Holm' in Aberdeenshire (pronounced 'howm') means 'smooth-sided hollow', as exemplified in Holmhead and Holmsburn.

Haugh is a Scots word meaning a river-meadow; it occurs on its own as a place-name at least four times, e.g. Haugh in Ayrshire, and in combination gives many place-names. Foxhall in Midlothian is really 'fox haugh', and indeed an earlier and less anglified form was *Tod Hauch* (tod being Scots for fox, and giving such names as Todhead, Todhills and Todrig). Sauchiehall Street in Glasgow was intended to be the Scots *saughie haugh* ('willow meadow') but got 'improved' somewhere along the line. Kelvinhaugh is on the river of that name; Philiphaugh is explained under **hope**.

hope

This ubiquitous word is found all over Scotland, in three different languages. Old Norse *hop* meant a landlocked bay or inlet; Hobkirk in Shetland is *hop kirkja* or 'kirk bay'. Usually the word becomes 'hope' in map-terminology: Longhope for example is 'long bay'. *Hop* to the Norseman also conveyed the sense of refuge and shelter, and it is possible that this idea lies behind the name of Ben Hope, the most northerly of our mountains.

Hop was borrowed into Gaelic in the form *ob* ; its diminutive is *oban*, and *an t-Oban Latharnach* means 'little bay of Lorn'—a neat description of the popular West-Highland resort of Oban. Opinan in Gairloch is 'little bays'.

The word 'hope' also occurs in southern Scotland, as in Kirkhope and Hobkirk, where the meaning is that of a valley. Philiphaugh near Selkirk, where Montrose was defeated in 1645 is a 'hope' name in disguise—it is literally 'foul hope haugh'—or 'meadow of the filthy valley'.

Anglo-Saxon *hop* is also found on the Scottish map, but with the meaning of 'hanging valley'; it is related to the Old Norse word, and indeed sometimes it is only the context that enables one to distinguish between the two. Hoptoun is clearly 'valley farm'; Dudhope in Dundee is 'Dudda's valley' Hopringle was the old name of a place in Stow, Midlothian; the *ringle* bit is just 'ring', and the meaning is a circular valley (it survives in the surname Pringle). Kershope in Liddesdale will be 'carse hope', *carse* being a reference to the flat land on the Scottish side of the Liddel Water. Hopetoun House near Edinburgh is ultimately from the same source, except that it comes directly from the surname of the family who acquired the marquessate of Hopetoun and earldom of Linlithgow.

I

inch

One of the Gaelic words for island is *innis*; it is pronounced 'insch' and of course recalls Yeats' poem on Innisfree ('heather isle'—see **fraoch**). (The circumstance whereby few of the thousands of Scottish islands incorporate this word is explained in the entry under **ey**). Innis also has the secondary meaning of 'meadowland by a river' and simply 'field'. The etymology possibly involves the reasoning that just as an island is something surrounded by water, so a field in early times was surrounded by moor, marsh or forest. *Innis* meaning island appears in Inchcape, the correct name for the Bell Rock; it is really 'inch skep', i.e. shaped like a beehive, and Inch Cailleach on Loch Lomond is 'nuns' isle'. Inchcolm in the Firth of Forth is yet another 'Columba isle'—the saint is widely commemorated in names—see **colm**. Nearby Inchgarvie is less hallowed: it means 'rough island', and performs the useful function of supporting a pier of the railway bridge.

In the sense of 'river meadow' we have the prime examples of the North and South Inch in Perth, large tracts of greensward by the Tay. In the lower Tay valley is a string of names embodying forms of the word *innis*—Megginch, Inchyra, Inchmartin, Inchmichael and Inchture. We know from geological evidence that these settlements were originally on islands in the marshes, but had probably become individual pastures by the time that they got their present names.

Finally, the many other examples of Inch, Insh and Insch probably always referred to fields or meadows. Inchinnan near Paisley is 'inch of Finnan', i.e. the bit of land enclosed by the Gryfe and the Cart. Inchaffray near Crieff is *innis aifronn*—'offering or mass enclosure'. Inchnadamph in Assynt is usually given the picturesque translation of 'island of the stag', but could equally well bear the meaning 'field of the ox'. Morangie, famous for its malt whisky (and pronounced, please, with the stress on the first syllable), is really *mor innse*—'at the big meadow'.

inver

This element has to be studied in conjunction with the Brittonic term **aber**, for *inbhir* is its Gaelic equivalent. The word *inbhir* is still used in Gaelic, meaning a creek or river mouth; it probably derives from an earlier Celtic form *eni-beron*, with the sense of 'in bring'.

The distribution of *inver*-names is much wider than that of *aber*, the latter being virtually confined to the Pictish areas of Scotland. In at least some recorded instances, the Gaelic term has replaced the earlier one. Inverbervie on the Angus coast was formerly *Aberbervie* (both mean 'mouth of the boiling stream'); and Invernethy coexists with Abernethy in Perthshire.

The term *inver* can stand on its own, and is the name of at least six places in the Highlands; but most often it is followed by the name of the river to which it refers. A typical case is Inverness—'mouth of the River Ness or Nesa' (from *nesta,* an ancient and possibly pre-Celtic river-name, thought to mean 'roaring or rushing one'). The river, as is always the case, was named many centuries before the settlement on its banks; Loch Ness also takes its name from the river. Inverleith and Inveresk are two settlements at the mouth of rivers, as are Inveraray and Inverurie, and the names of the rivers are clearly present, if etymologically obscure. The most southerly of the *inver* names has undergone anglicisation: the confluence of the Border river Leithen with the Tweed is called Innerleithen. Occasionally the term *inver* occurs at the end of a name. Lochinver is 'at the loch mouth', and Kilninver is *cill an inbhir*—'church at the confluence'.

It sometimes happens that an *inver* name outlasts the name of the stream which it describes. Where are the streams apparently referred to in Inverkip, Invergowrie and Inverdovat? No question arises in the case of Invergordon, which is a contrived name: the town was called after Sir Alexander Gordon, its proprietor in the eighteenth century. (Presumably there were already too many 'Gordon's-towns'—see **Gordon**).

Inverclyde was the name given in 1967 to the administrative district which encompasses the industrial centres of Greenock, Port Glasgow, Wemyss Bay and Kilmacolm; it is perpetuated in the reorganization of 1996. Although not a bad name as official coinages go, it doesn't sound right, and certainly fails to describe the topography which is that of a firth and not of a river mouth. Spontaneous names have an honesty about them that contrived ones lack: can one imagine a drunken reveller claiming that he 'belangs tae Inverclyde'?

Just as *inver* as explained above derives from an early Celtic form meaning 'in bring', another term, *con-beron* , means 'together bring'; this produces the Gaelic word *comar* which has only one meaning—a confluence of waters. Cumbernauld—an old name for a New Town—is *comar nan allt*—'meeting of the waters'. A derivative is *comrach,* meaning 'place of confluence': Comrie in Perthshire is situated at the junction of the Ruchil Water and the rivers Lednock and Earn, and there are two other Comries in the shire.

K

kil

Although St Columba may not have been the first to bring Christianity to Scotland (St Ninian had ministered to the southern Picts some centuries before), it was the Irish missionaries who left their mark on our place-names. St Columba, the most famous of them, has lent his name to at least fifty places on the modern map of Scotland—see under **colm**.

The Celtic church was monastic in character (unlike the diocesan church of Rome) and in its early days it spread by the establishment of cells—not unlike Communism in recent years. The Gaelic word for cell is *ceall*, in its dative form *cill*; and it is this word that appears as 'kil' in many hundreds of names in south-west Scotland.

The classic type of *kil* compound has a saint's name as its second element, most often the name of a Columban missionary. An entire book could be written about these saints: a few examples are Donan (commemorated in several Kildonans and of course Eilean Donan); Bride or Bridget (Kilbride —more than a dozen of them, including the New Town of East Kilbride); Brendan (Kilbirnie and Kilbrandon); Congan (Kilchoan); Syth (Kilsyth); Kiaran (Kilkerran); Finnen (Kilwinning) and Munna (Kilmun). Sometimes the Gaelic possessive pronoun is prefixed to the saint's name, as in Kilmacolm—'cell of my Columba', or Kilmarnock—'cell of my Ernon'. Kilconquhar in Fife is 'Conchar's or Conchobar's cell': the local pronunciation of 'Kinn-yucker' is probably aphetic (not to say downright sloppy). One of the commonest formations is Kilmuir and Kilmory—'St Mary's cell'; but Kilmore in Sleat is not St Mary's but 'great church'.

Occasionally the second part of a *kil*-name is descriptive of location: Kilcreggan is 'church of the little crag' and Killin (pronounced with the stress on the second syllable) is *cill fhion*—'at the white cell'.

The distribution of *kil* names is highly instructive. They are thickly spread over south-west Scotland, where the Irish missionaries may be supposed to have made their first impact; but the names extend right up the west coast as far as Skye and through the Great Glen to Easter Ross. They also extend across Lowland Scotland to Fife Ness, but are notably absent from Angus, east Perthshire and Aberdeenshire. The supposition is not that these latter areas were left unconverted by the missionaries but rather that the term *kil* had lost its force as a name-giving element by the time it reached them.

Kil became so firmly entrenched in the west that it attracted a number of analogic formations; or, to put it another way, a lot of names masquerade as *kil* names when they are in fact nothing of the sort. Kilbrennan, for example, is *caol Brennan*—'Brennan's kyle' (see **kyle**). Kildrummy is properly *Kindrummie*—'at the ridge end'; Killearn is documented as *cinn earrain*—'at the head of the land division' (see **kin**; but Killearnan properly commemorates St Ernan). Kilcoy is *cul coille*—'back of the wood' (see **cul**). Killiecrankie, like most *killie*-names is really **coille**—in this case *coille creitheannich*—'aspen wood' (but the battle is called in Gaelic 'Renrory'—*Raon Ruaaraidh*—'Rory's meadow').

kin

In Gaelic the word *ceann* means head, both in its literal and figurative senses: *ceann mor* is 'big head', more likely 'great king' in the case of Malcolm Canmore; and *cean cinnidh* is 'head of the family'. In place-names *ceann* sometimes becomes *ken,* and we have Kenmore—'big headland' and Kentra ('shore-head') in Ardnamurchan. (Kennoway in Fife however has traditionally been taken, without proper authority, to be a 'Kenneth' name).

But one of the problems is that place-names are rarely in the nominative case, and *ceann* usually appears in its dative form *cinn*, anglicised to *kin*. Thus Kinlochleven is 'at the head of Loch Leven'; Kinnaird, which is found in Perthshire, Angus and Stirling, as well as in Kinnairds Head near Fraserburgh, is *cinn na h'airde* 'at the end of the point of land'; Kinneil near Grangemouth was earlier *cinn fhail*—'at the end of the (Antonine) wall'. Kintail is *cinn t-saile*—'at the end of the salt-water', and Kintyre is 'at the end of the land'. Both are apt descriptions.

Where *kin* is followed by the letter 'g' it causes confusion because popular etymology is always tempted to read 'king' into the word. Although Kinghorn castle was at one time a royal possession, the name of the burgh has no kingly connection; it is *cinn gronn*—'at the headland of the mud or marsh'. Kingussie may have given rise to a mythical monarch called Gussie in the children's comic, but the name is really *cinn ghiuthsaich*—'at the head of the firs'—and there should be no 'ing' sound. Kinglassie (*cinn glassie*) is discussed under **glas**. The oddest example is *cinneadaradh*, which means 'at the head of the division'; this place in Aberdeenshire has been known for at least five centuries as 'King Edward'.

In fact there are few Scottish place-names that embody the English word 'king'. Kingsbarns, Kingskettle and King's Seat are minor examples, poor in comparison with the wealth of English place-names like King's Lynn and Lyme Regis. One could make an exception for Queensferry, named for

Margaret, the saintly wife of Malcolm Canmore, who commuted regularly by boat between Edinburgh and Dunfermline: in the fourteenth century it was literally 'the queen's ferry'.

In Gaelic the word for 'king' is *righ* (pronounced 'ree') and names incorporating that sound are often taken to refer to royalty. It is, however, hard to think of a single example that survives analysis. Portree is really *port righeadh*—'harbour of the slope'—the name predates the visit of James V; Kylerhea is *caol Rheithainn* (see **caol**). Rhiconich is *rudha coinnich*—'mossy cape'; and whereas Dalry may conceivably mean 'king's mead' it is just as likely to be 'heather mead' (*dal fhraoich*). In Scotland we tend to commemorate our sovereigns with street names, and practically every Scottish city boasts its quota, ranging from Queen Margaret Drive to Princes Street.

kirk

The Scots word *kirk* produces many place-names, of which Muirkirk, Falkirk (see p. 59) and Selkirk ('hall church') are obvious examples. Slightly more odd is Kirkcudbright, which is 'Kirk-Cuthbert'—an English saint commemorated in Scotland and, what is really puzzling, in a name whose word-order is Celtic. The Gaels nearly always put the generic first and the specific second, as in Kilcowan—'Comghan's church'. In fact there exist several parallel forms like Kilconnel and Kirkconnel, Kilcormack and Kirkcormack, Kilmichael and Kirkmichael, Kilpatrick and Kirkpatrick, and the probability is that the Gaelic *kil* has been replaced by the Scottish *kirk* without changing the order. Note, however, that names like Kirkden, Kirkland and Kirkhill have a normal Scottish (and English) word order, for in those cases *kirk* is the qualifying term: that is to say, Kirkden means 'church-den' and not 'den-church'.

The term *kirk* reached Scotland by two different routes however. As well as being the Scots and northern English form of 'church', the word also has the cognate form *kirkja* in Old Norse. It is a safe bet that Kirkwall is straight Norse, from *kirkju vagr*—'church bay'. Kirkness is 'church cape', and there are many others in the far north. It may even be that Kirkcudbright, Kirkmaidens and Kirkoswald show Norse rather than Scottish influence on an already established Gaelic name-giving pattern.

Kirk is a strong word, uniformly intelligible throughout Scotland, and it had a powerful effect on the obsolescent Brittonic word *caer* (meaning fort). *Caer* still flourishes in Wales (witness Caernarvon), but in Scotland it has been largely taken over by *kirk*. Kirkcaldy and Kirkintilloch are **caer** names.

The word *kirk* is still commonly found in the ubiquitous term 'kirkton', the name given to a settlement which grew up round an early church. The kirkton often existed in proximity to the 'castleton' (discussed under **castle**); Kirkton of Glamis and Castelton of Glamis for example were once two distinct places, which coalesced as they grew, and the terms 'kirkton' and 'castleton' were dropped as prefixes to plain 'Glamis'. In other cases, the castleton might grow at the expense of the kirkton, and the latter would become a farm name.

At one time there must have been hundreds of these kirkton names in the Lowlands and on the Highland fringe; the gazetteers now list around fifteen.

kyle

'There was a lad', wrote Robert Burns in autobiographical vein, 'was born in Kyle.' The district referred to is, of course, in Ayrshire and was named after the fifth century tribal ruler King Coel, who was celebrated in verse as 'a merry old soul'.

A completely different origin must be sought for the name Kyles of Bute. Ask any Scot where these are and you will probably get the right answer, but how many will know *what* the Kyles are? Yet it must be fairly obvious that they are the narrows of Bute; and indeed *kyle* is a rendering of the Gaelic *caol*, meaning slender or thin; the English spelling gives a good idea of the Gaelic pronunciation. *Caol an droma* is 'the small of the back', and it is in this figurative sense that *caol* and *caolas* are used in place-names.

There are at least fourteen different 'straits' in Scotland that are referred to as 'kyles'. Kyle of Lochalsh is the narrow entrance to Lochalsh (a name whose meaning remains obscure). Kyleakin is 'straits of Hakon'; he is said to have navigated them with his fleet after being defeated at the battle of Largs in 1263, and if this is correct it is a rare example of a place being named in consequence of an event in Scottish history. Kylerhea is called after Reathan, a hero of Fingalian romance, and Kylesku in Assynt seems to be *caolas cumhann*—'narrow strait'. *Caol* has undergone transformation in Kilchurn—'straits of the cairn'—on the narrow part of Loch Awe, and in Colintraive, which is *caol an t-snaimh*—'the swimming strait', where the drovers used to cross from Bute with their cattle.

Caolas appears terminally in the names Ballachulish (Gaelic *baile chaolais*—'village on the narrows') and Eddrachillis (Gaelic *eadar dha chaolais*—'between two channels'). These two are typical of Gaelic place-nomenclature, being straightforward topographical descriptions.

Oddly enough 'sound' which means much the same as 'kyle', is an English word found only on the maps of Scotland. It comes from the Old English word *sund* ('swimming'), and is found in such places as Sound of Bute, Sound of Mull, Sound of Jura. Although one would be disinclined to swim these straits, one sees what is meant. In Shetland there are two settlements called Sound, probably descriptive of the nearby voes or creeks.

L

lag

This little Gaelic word means 'hollow', and corresponds exactly to the Lowland word 'howe': in Gaelic the Howe of the Mearns is *Lag na Maoirne*. The similar Old Norse word *lagr*, related to the English 'low', was also productive of place-names. Lagg is the name of two settlements, one on Jura, the other on Arran, probably of Norse derivation; and Lag was the name of an old estate in Dumfriesshire. Lagavulin in Islay, home of a famous malt whisky, is 'hollow of the mill'. Laggish in Wigtonshire is *lag innis*—'field in the hollow'.

The diminutive of *lag* is *lagan*, and Loch Lagain in Sutherland is 'loch of the little hollow'. Loch Laggan in Inverness-shire took its name from the parish, but the meaning is the same.

In the locative case, *lag* becomes *lagaidh*, later *logaidh*, and the several Logies, ranging from Lothian to Ross, all mean 'at the hollow'. Loganlea in the Pentlands may well be *lagan liath*—'at the grey hollow' (now filled with water). In the dative, *lag* becomes *luig*: Carluke may be *caer luig*—'rock by the hollow', but this is by no means an established etymology.

Returning to the word *howe* we find that it yields a few place-names besides obvious ones like Howe of Fife ('hollow or low-lying part of Fife'). Howden in Roxburgh and Midlothian both mean 'den in the hollow', and Howgate in Midlothian will be 'road in the hollow'. Fogo in the Borders may be either Scots *fog howe*—'mossy hollow' or possibly *fog heugh* as in Kelso (see under **den**).

But watch out for the similar Old Norse word *haug*, meaning cairn: Maeshowe in Orkney is 'mighty cairn'.

lairig

This Gaelic term, meaning a pass between hills, is known to most people who frequent the Scottish mountains, and indeed tends to be used by them as a common noun. There are at least twenty passes in the Highlands which are known as *lairig* (pronounced 'lah-rig'), but only a few of these have found their way on to the maps.

The most celebrated pair are in the Cairngorms, and both take their name from the stream that drains them, namely the Druie and the Lui: they are the Lairig Ghru and the Lairig an Laoigh, more correctly *Lairig Laoigh*. (Bear in mind that the classic route of the Lairig Ghru is through Glen Dee and not Glen Luibeg, and that the Lairig an Laoigh begins or ends in Glen Lui). Druie is probably a pre-Celtic water-word meaning something like 'flowing'; the old-fashioned derivation from Gaelic *gruamach* ('gloomy') is a mistake. Lui is 'calf-one', as in Ben Lui; but the reference is mythical rather than practical and it is not necessarily to be inferred that the pass was ever a drove road.

The *Lairig an Lochain* runs between Loch Tay and Glen Lyon, but the map-makers turned things around and gave the name Lochan na Lairige to the tarn at its summit. The Lairig Gartain ('Gartain's Pass'—an Irish personal name found also in Strathgartney) runs from Glencoe to Glen Etive, between Buachaille Etive Mor and Beag (the 'Great and Small Herdsmen of Etive').

A word of similar appearance to *lairig*, but with no apparent linguistic connection, is *learg* (pronounced 'lerg') and meaning 'a sloping hill-face'. Such is the derivation of Largs (with an English plural 's') in Ayrshire. Largo in Fife and the two Larghills are similar, as are Largybeg and Largymore on Arran. But Lairg in Sutherland is different again: it is thought to be from *luirg*, the dative case of *lorg*—'a path'.

lanark

A Brittonic word *llanerch*, meaning 'glade' or 'clearing', gives us the name of what was, before regionalisation, the most populous of Scotland's counties. In pre-industrial times it is quite conceivable that the settlement of Lanark could have been situated in a forest glade. Barrlanark—'top clearing'—is the same word.

Scots speakers tend to metathesise words—that is, to transpose vowels and consonants to suit their own speech-mechanisms. Thus, grass becomes *girse* in broad Scots, bristle becomes *birsle*, board becomes *brod*, and so on. By the same process, *llanerch* sometimes becomes *lanrick*, and we arrive at the name of Lanrick, a village near Callander. Drumlanrig ('clearing ridge') near Dumfries and Caerlanrig on Teviot ('glade-fort') and the River Lendrick are similar formations. There is another village called Lanrick in

Perthshire, and two Lendricks further east. Lanrig near Whitburn, however, is probably the Scots *lang rig*—'long field' (see **rig**).

land

As might be expected, the English word 'land' turns up in countless place-names, and examples such as Newlands and Langlands require no explanation. Sometimes the reference is to measurement: Merkland was a parcel of land originally valued at one merk, or thirteen and a half pence in English currency, while Pennyland had a rental of one pence. (Ranfurlie near Bridge of Weir is even cheaper: *rann feorlin* is 'firlot part', a very small measure of grain.) Burntisland in Fife has been the subject of much speculation: the first syllable seems to refer to combustion, but the place is certainly not an island, and a possible derivation is to be found in the age-old practice of burning land prior to cultivating it (cf. Bruntlands in Aberdeenshire).

'Land' is also an Old Norse word, to be found in names such as the Pentland Firth (discussed under **firth**). The Lothian Pentlands may either incorporate the Brittonic word **pen** or possibly are in plain English 'penned lands'. The suggestion that this range of hills separated the Anglian kingdom from the Pictish 'Pettland' cannot be taken seriously. It is possible however that the modern form of Pentland may owe something by analogy to the northern firth.

The word 'land' tended to oust a much earlier Brittonic word *llan*, which survives in Welsh and means church—Llanberris is 'church of St Peris'; its Gaelic equivalent *lann* is to be found in Lanbryde in Morayshire ('St Brigid's church'). *Lann* later developed the wider meaning of enclosure or field; Lynchat in Badenoch is *lainn chat*—'cat's field', and Tarland in Aberdeenshire is *tarbh lann*—'bull field'.

In the Lowlands, *lann* undergoes some vowel distortion: Lumphanan in Aberdeenshire is 'St Finan's field', and Lumphinnans in Fife is no doubt the same. Longforgan near Dundee is thought to be *Lann for gronn*—'field above the bog' (nearby Monorgan being *moin fhorgrunn*—'bog of Forgan'). Lindifferon in Fife shows the same ending as Welsh Duffryn, and means something like 'field of the watercourse'.

lar

Lar in Gaelic means a floor, or ground, in place-names often a site. Lair in Glenshee stands on its own, but it is commoner in compounds. Ardlair is found thrice over in Aberdeenshire, and probably refers to an elevated site; its pronunciation ('Ardler') links it to the place of that name in Angus.

A derivative word *larach* is specifically the site of a building, usually a ruin. Arlary in Kinross will be much the same in meaning as Ardlair. Lary in Upper Deeside is 'at the ruin' and Aldlarie in Badenoch contains the element **allt**. Crianlarich is 'site of the aspen'.

law

The Old English name for a rounded hill, and between Forth and Cheviot the commonest hill-term to be found on the map. Strangely, 'law' does not appear south of the Border (usually no respecter of linguistic usage), where the fells and pikes come into evidence; and it is not merely a matter of topography, for there are numerous rounded hills in Northumbria at least.

Law near Carluke stands on its own, but the word usually appeared in tandem with a nearby place-name, like Largo Law and Berwick Law; it did not often attain the status of a proper noun (rather like 'hill' in this respect). Broad Law and Dollar Law (see **dale**) are notable summits in Tweeddale. Wardlaw is the name of several Border tops; it means 'watch-hill', as do others known as Wardhill. Notman's Law is interesting as preserving the name of the obsolete trade of 'nowt man' or cattleman, which became an occupational surname.

But the word *law* is ceasing to be understood, and pleonasms such as 'The Sidlaw Hills' and 'The Law Hill' (common Dundee usage) are increasingly frequent. (Sidlaw seems to be Gaelic *suidhe*—'a seat'—and one of the summits is called King's Seat). Greenlaw in the Borders is an example of a settlement named after a local green hill; at the other extreme of 'law' country, Rubislaw in Aberdeen seems to be 'Reuben's Law'. Uplawmoor in Lanark means what it says—'moor of the upper hill'. Law names do not appear in the Highlands.

letham

A puzzling name, which has been recorded in Scotland since at least 1200, and is familiar as that of a large village near Forfar and a small one in north Fife. It should properly be regarded as an element rather than a name; like Grange, it is often found in combination with other terms, some relating to a personal name (e.g. Lambieletham), others to an office (e.g. Priorletham). It comes from the Old Norse term *hlatha*, meaning 'at the barns'; borrowed into Anglo-Saxon, it gives several place-names such as Lathom in Lancashire and Layton and Laytham in Yorkshire.

The word *letham* must have been used by an English-speaking community, and in that sense it resembles another English name, Borland. The 'board-land' was that which was required to supply the culinary needs of the castle, and in some cases the term became a place-name; the difference is that it penetrated to the Highlands (Borlum on Loch Ness) which Letham never did. In Aberdeenshire, whose inhabitants were given to metathesis, it became Broadland.

Another semi-technical term of this kind is grange. A grange was originally a granary, and in France is still the ordinary word for a barn; it comes from Latin *granum*, meaning grain. It was formerly attached to a nearby abbey or monastery, but later came to be used for a group of farm buildings with barns. There are at least seven villages in the Lowlands with the name Grange, and several compounds such as Newtongrange ('new grange farm') and there is even a Letham Grange near Arbroath. The modern town of Grangemouth came about as a result of the Forth-Clyde Canal, begun in 1768; the name refers to the mouth of the Grange burn where it joins the River Carron. The burn takes its name from the nearby Abbot Grange.

letter

An approximate rendering of the Gaelic *leiter*, 'hillside' or 'long slope'. Lettermore in Argyll is 'the great slope', Letterewe is the slope above Loch Ewe, the earlier name for Loch Maree. Letterfearn on Loch Duich is 'alderslope' and Letterfinlay in Invernessshire is presumably 'Finlay's slope'. Dullatur is probably *dubh leiter*—'dark slope', and Findlater is certainly *fionn leiter*—'white slope'.

Ballater is something of a puzzle, because the name does not refer to the present site, and in any case was pronounced without the second 'a'; but the nearby Ballaterach is thought to be *baile leitreach*—'village of the slope'—with the stress on the *leit*.

leven

Loch Leven, still the mecca of anglers, is by far the largest expanse of fresh (or reasonably fresh) water in Lowland Scotland and must always have been of great significance to inhabitants of the Kinross area. Yet generations of scholars have believed that the name derived from the Gaelic *leamhan*—'an elm'. Is it conceivable, one must ask, that such a considerable sheet of water would be named after an elm, or even a stand of elms, on its banks? And consider the Highland Loch Leven, and ask if it is likely that elms would have flourished in such a situation a thousand years ago any more than they do today?

Perhaps a more acceptable explanation is that *leven* comes from a Celtic root, *limo*, meaning 'flood'. There is a Welsh form *llif*, and no doubt the word also passed through a Brittonic stage. Certainly a Brittonic origin for the Kinross Loch Leven is much more probable than a Gaelic one, for the area was undoubtedly settled in Pictish times. The 'elm' derivation looks rather like an example of the tendency of some earlier scholars to find a Gaelic origin at all costs.

Another significant point may be noted. Loch Leven is overlooked by the Lomond Hills in Fife. *Lomond* is from a Brittonic word *llumon*, meaning 'beacon' (as in Plynlimmon). The commanding position of the Lomond Hills (visible from Soutra in the south and Glenshee in the north—places which are about a hundred miles apart) would make them ideal sites for beacons. But there is a more famous 'beacon hill' to the west, namely Ben Lomond; and we are told by the eighth century writer Nennius that Loch Lomond was formerly known as Loch Leven—a probable enough statement, since the River Leven issues from its southern end.

It may be, as is so often the case, that the name Leven was originally applied to the river; but the Fife River Leven is a puny thing compared with the lake, and the Inverness-shire one is little more than a burn. It is therefore a reasonable proposition that both lochs Leven mean 'flood lake', that the three rivers Leven take their name from the lakes, and that the Vale of Leven and the town of Leven are called after the rivers.

As a footnote it might be added that the River Lyon appears to have the same root, as does the district of Lennox, which had the earlier spelling of 'Levenaux'.

linn

This word is familiar enough to Scots, if only because the Linn of Dee near Braemar is a favourite beauty spot. But the word refers properly to the pool or channel, not to the waterfall itself. *Llyn* was the Brittonic word for lake, and *linne* is Gaelic for pool; so, as we might expect, the word occurs in most areas of Scotland, excluding the south-east.

Linlithgow is probably *llyn llaith cau*—'wet hollow lake'. Lindores in Fife is *llyn dwr*—'water lake'—with an English plural, while Lincluden is the pool on the river Cluden. (Cluden is a pre-Celtic water word, unexplained but having an obvious affinity with Clyde). Linwood explains itself.

Turning to the *linne*-derivatives, Loch Linnhe is the obvious example; it is however a complicated name, and is discussed under **aber**. Dupplin near Perth is *dubh linne* —'dark pool', a description to be found also in Dublin.

There is even a theory that Lincoln derives from Celtic *lindo* and Latin *colonia*—'pool colony'. Be that as it may, one should not overlook another Latin word, *linum*, meaning flax: this underlies the meaning of Linton in

East Lothian and Peeblesshire, Linmill near Alloa and Linshader ('flax farm') in Shetland.

loan

A Scots dialect word meaning a grassy lane, or cattle track, often leading to a common grazing. It appears frequently in place-names, and there are at least four Loanheads in the Lowlands; reference would be to the end of a *loan*. Loanstone in Midlothian used to be Loanstane, and in either form means what it says. Auchterlonie in Angus, now more familiar as a sur-name, is probably 'at the top of the lane'.

The right of passage of animals over a loan was a *loaning,* preserved both in the song the *Flouers o the Forest* ('on ilka green loaning') and in the name of the village in Strathallan.

loch

As every tourist knows, *loch* is the Gaelic word for lake; the word has passed into Lowland Scots (and English) as a common noun—one of the relatively few loan-words from Gaelic to English. There are at least seven places called Lochend—probably relatively modern coinages by English-speakers.

Yet close examination of the word *loch* reveals problems: what is one to make of the name of a hill loch near Glen Tilt which appears on the map as Loch Loch? The answer that this particular lochan is shaped like a pair of spectacles and is therefore loch plus loch surely will not do. Why then such a bizarre name? For an explanation we must go back to an old Irish word *loch*, which meant black, and survives mainly in combination with the word *dia*, meaning, in this case, goddess. River names often embody the idea of water-gods, and the *loch dia*, or 'black goddess', figures prominently. Loch Lochy takes its name from the River Lochy which issues at Fort William and means 'black goddess river'. There is another River Lochy which flows into Loch Tay, and yet another which rises near Tyndrum; and the word appears also in three separate places called Lochty in Moray, Perthshire and Fife. The name of the lonely little Loch Loch, therefore, probably *means* simply 'black loch' but *refers* to something more sinister. Straloch and Stralochy in Perthshire and Aberdeenshire probably mean 'dark valley'.

Despite these complications, in ninety-nine cases out of a hundred the word loch may be taken to mean lake, even when it occurs terminally as in the Gare Loch (see under **fada**) and Benderloch ('hill between two lochs', namely Loch Creran and Loch Etive). When one considers the number of terms which Gaelic possesses to describe various shapes of hill or sizes of stream, it is perhaps strange that the word *loch* should be used indifferently to describe an inland lake and an arm of the sea.

One minor problem remains—why does the Lake of Menteith uniquely in Scotland enjoy that prefix? There is no completely satisfactory answer, but there may have been a confusion with 'the laigh of Menteith' (*laigh* being Scots for a stretch of low-lying ground). Apparently the lake was earlier known as the 'Loch of Inchmahome', a cumbersome title which dropped from everyday use. (The derivation is *Innis mo Cholmaig*—'isle of my St Colmoc' a childhood haunt of Mary, Queen of Scots).

long

When this word appears in Scottish place-names it rarely represents the English word 'long'. In the Scots dialect (and in Norse also) that word becomes *lang*, giving us Langholm—'long meadow', and Langavat—'long water'.

Long is in fact Gaelic for ship, and Loch Long is 'ship loch'; a borrowing of the word into Old Norse gives the occasional name such as Lunga—'ship isle'. An exception however is Longniddry which probably just involves prefixing the English word 'long' to an existing name *nuadh tref*—'new settlement church'.

The Gaelic term *longphort* means literally 'ship harbour'. In Ireland it was sometimes anglicised as Longford, but in Scotland it retains its Gaelic form but develops extended meanings such as an encampment, then a palace, then a hunting lodge. It appears in Longformacus (*longphort Maccus*—'Maccus's encampment'), and in strange forms such as Lungard and Luichart in Wester Ross. Luncarty in Perthshire is *longartaibh*—'at the harbour'—and is the traditional site of a victory over the Danes in the tenth century. Another Luncarty in Aberdeenshire will probably be 'field of the encampment'; Auchinlongford in Ayrshire will have a similar meaning, and Craiglockhart in Edinburgh may be of the same origin. But Leuchars in Fife and its namesake in Moray come from a different source: Gaelic *luachar*—'rushes', which is also the basis of Luthrie in Fife, the Lothrie burn in Kinross and Auchleuchries ('rushie field') in Aberdeenshire.

M

machar

Machair in Gaelic originally meant 'a plain': *a Mhachair Ghallda* was 'the

91

plain of strangers' or the Lowlands, and *a Mhachair Aonghais* was 'the plain of Angus' or Strathmore. Old and New Machar in Aberdeenshire have the meaning of 'plain', and Machermuir refers to 'links'. Machars in Wigtonshire is the same word with an English plural. Macharmore near Newton Stewart is just 'big plain', and Machrie in Arran seems to show a locative ending—'at the plain'.

But nowadays we think of a machar as a level grassy sea-shore or links, and the classic example is Machrihanish in Kintyre, which boasts an airfield and a golf course as well as having these other attributes. The name means 'machar of *sanas*' (thought to be a kind of grass).

maol

The Old Norse word *muli*, meaning 'headland', passed into Gaelic as *maol* (pronounced 'mul') appears in Mull of Kintyre and Mull of Galloway (but doubtfully in the Isle of Mull, which traditionally means 'mountainous' but whose etymology is hard to pin down). It is also found in Kisimul in Barra (*keis mul*—'bulky headland', the same word as appears in Kishorn).

In Gaelic *maol* acquired the more usual meaning of bald or bare. *Ceann maol* is bald head and *bo mhaol* is a hornless cow. The word occurs time and again in the hill-nomenclature of former Gaelic-speaking areas, including Galloway. Indeed, it survives in the Borders in a name such as Melrose—*moel ros* or 'bare moor'—a P-Celtic survival from the days before the Angles arrived there. A former barony in Aberdeenshire was called Meldrum—'bare ridge'—now better known as a surname. But note that with Glas Maol at the head of Glen Isla the map-makers made a mistake: while 'grey bald head' would be a very accurate description of the mountain it is in fact the very prosaic *glas meall* or 'grey lump', see **meall**. *Maol* is sometimes confused with **meall**, particularly in the West Highlands and the Islands where the former is quite a common term for a little conical hill.

The diminutive form of *maol* is *maolinn*, and means a bare round hillock; Moulin near Pitlochry has this sense, although the old guide-books used to derive it from *muileann*, a mill. Craigmailing is *creag mhaolinn*—'rock of the bare round hill'. Ballochmyle is 'bare pass'—see **bealach**.

Pursuing the idea of baldness, we find an extended use of *maol* meaning 'tonsured one' or 'servant'. *Maol Choluim* or Malcolm is a personal name which means 'devotee of St Columba'; Malise meant a follower of Jesus. One of the foremost saints of Gaeldom was Maol Rubha (642—722) a Celtic monk who founded the monastery of Applecross and was instrumental in taking the Christian message to the Picts. Greatly revered in later centuries, he leaves his mark on place names such as Loch Maree, Kilmarie in Skye (*Cill Maol Ruibhe*) and Amulree in Perthshire (*Ath Maol Ruibhe* or 'Maol Rubha's ford' over the Braan).

marc

There are several words for horse in Gaelic, and the one that is most productive of place-names is *marc*. There is a Glen Mark in Angus, and a Markinch ('horse-field') in Fife from the same source. *Marcaidh* seems to be 'horse-stream', and is the name of tributaries of the Spey, Feshie, and Deveron; there are several Glen Markies in various parts of the Highlands; A' Mharconaich, a mountain in Inverness-shire, is probably 'horse-ridge'. Rosemarkie is discussed under **ross.**

Another word for horse is *capall* (which obviously relates to the Late Latin *caballus*); from it we get Capel Fell in Selkirkshire ('horse hill') and the Capel Mounth, a pass over the eastern Grampians between Loch Muick and Glen Clova which must have seen horse traffic at one time. Kincaple near St Andrews will be 'horse headland' and Pitcaple is 'horse-place'.

But *marc* has the sense of 'steed', and *capall* was strictly a mare, and the everyday word for horse in Gaelic is *each* (pronounced 'ech' as in 'loch'); oddly, this has produced fewer place-names, the most notable examples being Loch Eck in Cowal and Ben Eighe in Torridon, together with a few hills and lochs.

may

It is a safe bet that nobody who has read this far remains incurious about the strangeness of certain place-names; so let us without more ado put under the onomastic microscope the example of Cambus o' May, a little Deeside village which was, before Beeching's mutilation of the rail system, arguably the most picturesque railway station in Britain.

The first part is discussed under **cambus**; the 'o' stands for 'of'; but what about *may*? Surely it does not refer to the month, or to the girl's name. In fact it is the Gaelic *magh* (the 'gh' is silent) meaning 'plain'; the full name in Gaelic is *Camas a Mhaigh*—'bend of the plain', and the situation of the village in fact corresponds with a bend on the River Dee. Rothiemay is *rath a mhaigh*—'fort on the plain'—and could just as easily have been anglicised as 'Roth o' May'.

Maybole in Ayrshire is thought to be *magh baoghail*—'plain of danger'. Magus Muir near St Andrews is really *magh gasg* (there is a nearby farm of Magask which preserves the sound of the original name) and means 'tongue of land on the plain'. Mawcarse near Stirling is 'carse plain' ('carse' being a word denoting alluvial land by a river, as in Carse of Gowrie).

Mauchline in Ayrshire is *magh linne* 'pool plain'.

Sometimes *magh* surrenders itself to another prefix, *mon* (see **monadh**) with which it has no connection. Monzie near Crieff (pronounced 'mon-ee') is really *magh eadha* ('corn plain'); nearby Monzievaird is 'bard's moss'. Likewise, Monzie Law in the Borders and Moonzie near Cupar in Fife are probably *magh* names.

The word *magh* in its dative form is *moigh*, which is pronounced 'moy' and gives us the district of Moy near Inverness, seat of the chiefs of the clan MacIntosh, together with four other places of the same name. Moyness near Forres shows the genitive form *muigh innis*—'plain meadow'—and is the same formation as Maginnis in County Down; all of which has taken us a long way from Cambus o' May.

meall

This is an all-pervasive word in Highland nomenclature; it just means a lump, and is pronounced like a cat's 'miaow' with a terminal 'l'. *Meall luaidhe* is a lump of lead, and *meall* is found countless times on the map as indicating a featureless and not very high hill. Add the familiar adjective *odhar* ('dun-coloured') or *reamhar* ('fat') and you get a fair description of some of the less interesting bits of the Scottish mountain landscape. There are very many hills called Meall Odhar, and some of them have very sensibly been anglicized. For example, two lower humps of Ben Lawers, both originally styled Meall Odhar, are known locally as 'the Mealour' and 'the East Mealour', as if Mealour (pronounced 'mailer') were a meaningful English common noun.

Meall combines with the usual adjectives of colour and size, and it should not require a dictionary to interpret Meall Glas, Meall Uaine, Meall Mor and Meall Beag. Nor Meall Garbh for that matter (see **garve**). Mealfourvounie above Loch Ness is more challenging: it is *Meall Fuarmhonaidh*, or 'lump of the cold mountain-range' (see **monadh**). But one sould not be dismissive about *meall*-type hills, for the biggest, Meall a Bhuiridh in Glencoe ('roaring hill'), is 3,636 feet in height.

mig

Perhaps the commonest 'bog'-word in Scottish toponymy is the P-Celtic *mig*, a term which survives in modern Welsh (see Introduction). P-Celtic names are found mainly in the eastern half of the country, and the distribution of *mig*-names conforms to this pattern. Migvie in Aberdeenshire is *migeaghaidh*, a bog beside a hill-face; the name occurs also in Angus, not far from two hills known as Craigie Meg and Craig Mekie, all referring to the boggy nature of the terrain. Meggernie in Glenlyon was once *migearnaidh*, ' boggy marsh'. Migdale in Sutherland does not mean 'midge dale', however appropriate that might be, but is the same as Meigle in Perthshire; both are *mig dol*—'water-meadow'. Strathmiglo in Fife incorporates an obsolete stream-name *Miglo* ('bog-loch') now the River Eden; the dampness of the landscape is confirmed by the adjacent Nethermyres ('lower marshes'). Megget Water in the Borders is of similar origin.

Given the annual rainfall in the Highlands, it is only to be expected that there will be many Gaelic words for bog; this is so, but they yield surprisingly few place-names. The Gaelic term for a mire is *feith* (pronounced 'fay'), which produces a few unimportant place-names—boggy land is not normally the site of major settlements. Finegand in Glenshee is *feith na ceann*—'bog of the heads', and the term *feith* appears all over the Cairngorm maps, where it usually means a bog-stream. The odd-looking-name Fafernie, on the high plateau between Angus and Mar, is *feith fearnach*—'alder-stream'; it has been transferred to a featureless summit which scarcely deserves a name to itself.

Lathach (pronounced 'la-huch') is a term meaning 'mire' and appears in selected localities; Lathallan, Lathockar, Lathones, Lathrisk are all in Fife and have obscure meanings; Latheron in Caithness relates to Larne in Ireland, and just means 'mire'.

Lon means a marsh, or in Scots a dub, and is apparently the basis of Lonmay in Aberdeenshire—*lon maigh* or 'marsh on the plain'; *lon dubh* ('dark marsh') is thought to be the source of the common name Lundie, of which there are are five examples, as well as Lundy in Inverness-shire. Lundin in Fife (an estate from which the modern village of Lundin Links gets its name) is probably *lon dun*—'marsh fort'—and it has been suggested that the English capital may be derived from the Brittonic equivalent of these two words.

A Gaelic word for soft is *maoth* (pronounced 'moo'); in a topographical context it means 'boggy', and it is thought to underlie such names as Methlick (*maoth tulich*—'wet hill') and Methil (*maoth coille*—'damp wood'). Muthill near Crieff (pronounced 'mew-thill') is *maothail*—'softening'.

In Gaelic the word *bog* itself is usually an adjective meaning 'soft, damp', borrowed into English as a noun meaning 'a mire' and found in Lowland place-names such as Bogmill, Bogbrae, Boghall, Boghill and Bogend, which are all self-explanatory. Ladybank in Fife was earlier *Lathy Bog*, a source of peat for the abbey of Lindores; the 'bog' bit is an adjective, the correct form being *leathad* ('slope') and *bog* ('moist').

95

The Scots dialect word for marshland—'mersh' or 'Merse'—gives the district name between the Lammermuirs and the Tweed. The English word mire however gives very few place-names, Myreside in Edinburgh and Hairmyres in Glasgow (see **har**) being two examples.

mill

Nearly all mills in mediaeval Scotland were powered by water, of which there was an abundant supply, then as now. Their rents provided a considerable revenue for the landowner, and mills for grinding corn were found on every large estate. Indeed there is not a parish in Scotland without its mill; very often the only remaining evidence is the farm name Milton, which was formerly prefixed to one or other of the local settlements. Apart from Miltons, there are dozens of 'mill' names on the map of the Lowlands, including Bogmill in the Carse of Gowrie, Waukmill ('fulling mill') on the Tay and Powmill (see **poll**). Millport is a modern name.

The word for mill is virtually the same in Latin (*molina*), Anglo-Saxon (*myln*), French (*moulin*) and German (*Mühle*), so it should come as no surprise that the Gaelic word is similar. If *muileannn* occurs with less frequency in the Highlands it is partly because there is much less arable land there than in the low country, but mainly because these names underwent mass translation to 'Mill of …' and 'Milton of …'. In upper Deeside alone there are well over a hundred place-names involving the word 'mill', all translations from the Gaelic. Nevertheless, *muileann* still appears with some frequency and more or less in its original form; examples are Loch a Mhuillin, Glen Muillin in Perthshire and Sgurr Voulin ('mill hill') near Achnasheen. Clovulin near Fort William is *cladh a mhuilinn* or 'mound of the mill' (but the better-known Clova in Angus remains an unsolved mystery). Evidence of the early presence of Gaelic in Fife is provided by names such as Pitmillie ('mill-place'). Corriemulzie in Mar is 'mill corrie'.

min

So pervasive nowadays is the term *mini* (as applied to cars, skirts and breaks) that one is tempted to see it lurking in place-names which contain this particular combination of letters. The temptation must be resisted.

It is true that the Gaelic *min* (pronounced 'mean') can mean small in the sense of pulverised or fine (see under **garve**), and that Minigaig, the pass leading from Atholl to Speyside, can be translated as 'little cleft'. (It clearly relates to the nearby Gaick pass, which traverses a more formidable gap.) And it is true that the Old Norse word *minne* means 'little' and is the basis of Minard ('small bay'). But it is not safe to go much further; for example,

Mingary is Old Norse *mikkin garthr*—'great enclosure' (cf. **gart**). Minnigaff in Kirkcudbright is even more treacherous: it is the Brittonic *minit y gof*—'smith's moor'. Minnishant in Ayrshire is either *moine seanta* ('holy moss'—see **moss**) or *muine seanta* ('holy shrubbery').

monadh

In the south-eastern Grampians two unpretentious summits have the grandiose names of Mount Blair and Mount Keen. They would not claim parity of consideration with Mount Everest or Mount Cook, and their prefixes are in fact renderings of the Gaelic *monadh*, which had the lowlier meaning of moorland or 'flat-topped ridge'. The collective name for the eastern Grampians was Mount (pronounced 'month'), and it is preserved also in the three tracks which cross the range—the Capel Mounth (see under **marc**), the Fir Mounth (the English 'fir') and the Tolmounth (from Glen Doll—see **dale**). The word also appears in the neighbouring hills of Monega, Mount Battock and Cairn o' Mount.

The range of mountains to the west of the Spey is still sometimes known as the Monadhliath—'the grey mountains'—to distinguish them from the Monadhruadh, the reddish hills of the southern Cairngorm range. The Gaels had no collective name for this massif as a whole; the name Cairngorm was used in the singular until it caught the popular imagination in modern times.

Monadh appears to be Brittonic in origin, and has its equivalent in the Welsh *mynydd*. It is often to be found in former Pictish areas, and examples are Moncrieff (*monadh chraobh*—'tree hill') and Mondyne (*monadh eadain*—'slope moor'). It frequently appears at the end of the word, as in Esslemont (unexplained, but possibly from a personal name) and Kininmonth ('at the end of the moor').

Remember however that the English word 'mount' has ultimately a common origin with *monadh*—namely the Latin *mons*, a hill, and where 'Mount' occurs in a Lowland place-name (as it frequently does) it may not have percolated through a Celtic language. Most of these 'mount' names are fancy, such as Mount Stuart (home of the Marquess of Bute). Mount Florida and Mount Vernon in Glasgow are grandiose modern creations. Others are descriptive, like The Mount near Cupar, the ancestral home of Sir David Lindsay, the celebrated seventeenth century poet.

more

Innocent as most Scots are of the Gaelic language, they will nevertheless know that Glen More means 'the great glen'. By an odd chance however, Glen More—that remarkable geographical feature which cuts a huge gash in the mainland of northern Scotland—is now usually referred to as the Caledonian Canal, and the name Glenmore has become familiar to us as applied to a national Forest Park in Rothiemurchus. This particular glen scarcely deserves the epithet, since it is an insignificant depression in the Cairngorm foothills. Some glens have greatness thrust upon them.

Combine the adjective *mor* with virtually any noun of Gaelic topography and you will get a Scottish place-name: Drummore, Kilmore, Ben More, Achmore, Ardmore, Kenmore, Balmore, Gartmore and many others. Aviemore is discussed under **bealach**. The opposite attribute is expressed by the Gaelic word *beag*, 'pronounced 'bake' and usually written *beg* on maps. Examples of 'small places' are Drumbeg, Glen Beg, Ardbeg, Inverbeg, Balbeggie and Ledbeg (*leathad* means 'slope'). The derivations of all these names can be worked out by referring to other entries in this book. If only all place-name study were as easy!

Unfortunately *mor* becomes confused with the English word 'moor'; Newtonmore is a comparatively modern coinage for 'new town on the moor'. Morton, common in the Lowlands, means 'moor farm', and the Border village of Morsham is 'moor village'. But moor in Scotland is often spelt 'muir', as in Boroughmuir, Tentsmuir and many others; in the Lowlands in fact *muir* is one of the commonest of all place-name elements, and occurs more than twenty-five times as a compound in settlement-names such as Muirhead and Muirton. (You would imagine from all this that Dalmuir near Dumbarton was 'field on the moor', but it isn't, for in this case the Scottish *muir* has got confused with the Gaelic *mor*, which takes us back to where we began.)

Even now we are not home and dry, for in Gaelic *muir* means sea; it deserves (and gets) an entry on its own—see **muir**.

moss

This is a Scots dialect word which refers not to lichens or plants but to a wetland, or a moor used for cutting peats. Moss-troopers were Border reivers. Like most Scots words it has its origin in Old English—in this case, *mos* meaning 'bog'; it has not however survived into modern English with this meaning. The term is commonest in the upper Forth Valley, where one finds Blairdrummond Moss, Drip Moss and Flanders Moss (said to be so called after the Flemish settlers). Further south are Airds Moss, Lochar Moss and Ironhirst Moss—all indicating a morass. At nearby Solway Moss there took place in 1542 a battle in which the army of James V suffered such a defeat at the hands of the English as to cause his death from depression three weeks later. (Solway is supposed to be from the Old Norse *söl vagr*—'muddy bay'.)

Mossgiel, the name of an unproductive farm tenanted by Robert Burns, is probably *moss ghyll*—'moor glen', and Mossmorran in Fife seems to be from a personal name. Mosshope Fell near Beattock is 'moor valley hill'. Mossburnford near Jedburgh is straightforward enough, as is Mossend near Motherwell. These are all Lowland names, and when Moss turns up in the Highlands it is usually a modern translation: Crinan Moss in Argyll is *Mhoin Mhor*—'the great bog'.

Moine is the Gaelic term for peat moss or peat bog, and despite a tendency to be confused with **monadh** it produces a whole range of place-names. Moinc between the Kyle of Tongue and Loch Hope shows the word in its purity. Very often it becomes 'mon', and examples are Monimail in Fife (*moine mil*—'moss on the hill'), Monifeith (*moine feithe*— 'marshy moss') and Monymusk (*moine musgach*—'muddy moss'). Corriemony is *coire mona*—'wet corrie', and Balnamoon in Angus is 'moss homestead'.

The water-table is similar in places designated *eanach* (pronounced 'ennoch')—a bog or moor. Loch Einich in the Cairngorms probably has the meaning of 'black marsh'. There are a few places called Enoch in the shires of Ayr, Kircudbright and Wigton, and there is an Annachie and an Annochie in Aberdeenshire; but St Enoch's in Glasgow is a reference to the mother of St Mungo.

muc

The Gaelic word *muc* (pig) is responsible for *Eilean nam Muc*, better known as Muck ('island of swine'), as well as Auchtermuchty (see under **auchter**). Muchalls on the Angus coast is from the extended word *mucail*—'place of swine'; the obsolete name *Mucross* ('boar promontory') near St Andrews is recalled by Boarhills. Muckhart near Dollar is 'boar's height' (see **ard**), Mugdrum in Fife is 'boar ridge' (see **drum**) and Pettymuck in Aberdeenshire is 'pig place'. Muckraw in West Lothian is 'swine fort' (see **rath**), and Loch Muick in Mar shows the word in the genitive form. For many years Ben Macdhui was thought to be a *muc* name (it was also supposed to be higher than Ben Nevis), but it is in fact 'Macduff's hill', after the clan which for centuries owned the terrain.

The specific Gaelic word for boar is *torc*, genitive *tuirc*; it yields surprisingly few place-names, but does account for Lynturk in Aberdeenshire (*leathad an tuirc*—'slope of the boar'). An Turc, a rounded hill in the Pass of Drumochter is more usually known as The Boar of Badenoch; its southerly neighbour is The Sow of Atholl. But Brig o' Turk in the Trossachs is a tourism-inspired name.

A young pig is *banbh*, which gives Banff on the Moray Firth, Banff Hill near Inverbervie, Bamff near Alyth, Banavie in Lochaber, Banvie in Atholl and Benvie near Dundee. Some of these were originally river-names (a class of name frequently taken from animals—cf. Buckie, which means the same as 'Bucksburn'); but another theory derives Banff in particular from *Banba*, a poetic name for Ireland (see **Erin**).

It must not be thought however that the foregoing names necessarily refer to the practical business of pig-rearing (although Auchtermuchty—like Swinton—probably does). More likely is a reference to the nature of the animal. Indeed, a much older name is *orc*, the Brittonic word for boar; the island of the Orcs, a tribe called after this animal, is mentioned by a Roman geographer of the first century AD and is known to us as Orkney.

muir

Muir looks like a Scots dialect word meaning moor, which indeed it is; but it is also a very common Gaelic term for sea. Related to the Old English *mere* and the French *mer*, in its early Celtic form it was *mori*. Combined with **tref** this gives us *mori tref* or Moray—'sea settlement'. Morvern is *mor bhearn*—'sea gap'—a reference no doubt to the great cleft of Loch Sunart. *Mur gheal* means 'sea-white' and is the basis of the girl's name Muriel. Ardnamurchan may come originally from the personal name Murchol, but as it stands it is 'point of the sea hounds' (i.e. otters).

Muir is found in combination with some unlikely words, one of which is **balg**, which as we saw means 'bulge'. In sea-terminology it is metathesised to *bhlag*; *murbhlag* therefore means 'sea-bag' or bay, and is found in its diminutive form as Murlagan, of which there are two in Lochaber, one on Loch Long and one on Loch Ness. The term occurs quite commonly inland, and appears on Loch Lomond and Loch Earn as Ardvorlich and Ben Vorlich (discussed under **ard**). *Mur magh* is 'sea plain', and underlies the names Morvich in Kintail, Murroch in Dunbartonshire and Morroch in Wigton.

mullach

This everyday Gaelic word means top or summit; *mullach an tighe* is 'roof'. We find it in such places as Balmullo in Fife ('top village'), but it is most familiar in mountain-terminology. However, although there are over a dozen Cairngorm tops described on the map as *mullach*, the word has never entered the active vocabulary of the hillwalker. The most noteworthy and spectacular 'mullachs' are Mullach nan Coirean ('top of the corries') in the Mamores; Mullach Coire Mhic Fhearchar ('top of MacFarquhar's corrie', near Kinlochewe); and Mullach an Rathain (highest point of Liathach massif); the meaning of the latter is obscure, but *rathan* looks like 'teeth'.

N

nemed

Lowland Scotland was colonised largely by Anglian traders and adventurers, who left their mark on commercial settlement-names which are still recognisably in the English language. The West Highlands on the other hand were first colonised by Irish missionaries, and the place-name evidence of this is heavily ecclesiastical in character. The elements **kil** (cell) and **annat** (church) are discussed separately, but another term which is almost as common is the Old Irish *nemed*, a sacred place or sanctuary, very often of pagan origin but sanctified by the expanding church. *Nemed* is a somewhat obscure term, which, although related to *neamh* (Heaven) does not appear in the Gaelic dictionary. The 'm' of *nemed* very often aspirates to a 'v' sound or disappears altogether; thus Duneaves near Fortingall in Perthshire is *tigh neamhidh*—'sanctuary house'—with an English plural 's', and Rosneath on the Gare Loch is *ros neimhidh*—'promontory of the sanctuary'. Navitie near Loch Leven in Kinross, and Navity in Easter Ross have the same origin, as do Navar and Nevay in Angus; the last-named gives the surname Neaves. Newmore in Easter Ross is a *nemed* name, as is Finavon in Angus, originally *Fothneven* and probably meaning 'wood-sanctuary'.

ness

This is another word of Germanic origin that has come to Scotland via two routes, from the Old English *naes* and the Old Norse *nes*, both meaning a point or headland. The connection with Latin *nasus*, a nose, will be obvious.

Names like Fife Ness, Tarbat Ness and Bo'ness may be taken to embody the *naes* form: they are the northern equivalents of English names like Skegness and Skipness. Bo'ness is Borrowstounness—'headland of Beornward's town'. The various projections of the 'divided' island of Skye mainly involve the Gaelicised -*nish* ending: Trotternish is 'Thrond's Ness' (cf. Trondheim in Norway), Waternish is easy, and Minginish is thought to be 'main ness'. Callanish of the standing stones is from the personal name Cala, which crops up several times in Lewis.

Caithness is 'cape of the *cataibh* or cat-men', the name given to the

Pictish tribe which occupied these parts. Stenness is 'stone cape'. Stromness is Old Norse *straumr nes*—'cape in the current'. (The word *straumr* also gives Kylestrome in Sutherland, a Gaelic-Norse compound meaning 'current narrows', while Strome Ferry is a Norse-English synthesis.) Inverness however comes from a totally different source (see **inver**).

Gaelic-speakers used a different word for *ness*: this is their own word for nose, which is *sron*. It appears in place-names as Strone (there is a village of that name near Dunoon) and it is a common hill name in Aberdeenshire. Strontian on Loch Sunart gave its name to strontium; the mineral was first found there in 1790. Stranraer is *sron reamhar* or 'thick nose'.

Another similar name comes from the Gaelic word *soc* meaning 'snout'; 'The Socach' is a common name for snout-like hills in the Grampian range, and Succoth in Aberdeenshire provides another example.

Troon comes either from *an t-sron* ('the nose') or from the Brittonic equivalent *trwn*, also meaning nose or point. The usual Brittonic term for cape however is *ryhn*, as in Rhinns of Galloway, Rhynd on the Tay, and Renfrew (*rhyn frwd*, meaning 'current point'). In other parts of Scotland the term 'head' is used—e.g. Peterhead (name of the patron saint of the parish of Inverugie). 'Cape' seems to occur only once—in Cape Wrath (Old Norse *hvarf*, cognate with 'wharf'). Names incorporating 'cape' and 'head' are probably relatively modern.

neuk

Neuk is the Scots version of the English 'nook', and is preserved in the useful expression 'The East Neuk of Fife'. It occurs terminally in a few other names such as Craigneuk and is a popular element in house-names.

More productive of names is the equivalent Old Gaelic word *cuil* (pronounced 'cool'). It can occur on its own, as in Coull in Badenoch and Strathearn, or in obvious combinations such as Loch Glencoul in Sutherland and Colquhoun (thought to be *cuil cumhann*—'narrow corner'). Less obvious are Cullen ('little nook') and Culzean ('bird corner'—but pronounced 'Cull*ane*'). The Cuillins of Skye and Rum are however something quite different: they are thought to commemorate *cu Chulainn*, 'the hound of Culann', an Ossianic hero.

An obsolete Gaelic word for nook or gusset is *gasc*, which appears in place-names as Gask. There are three different places called Gask, in the shires of Perth, Inverness and Aberdeen. Fingask in Gowrie will be 'white nook' and Findo Gask in Strathearn is possibly the same. Drumgask in Laggan is 'ridge hollow'.

The opposite of a nook or gusset is a projection: there are two words which express this on the maps—shank and tongue. Shank is a favourite Scots term for a projecting hill slope in Angus and Aberdeenshire (it means literally 'a leg'); Shankhead near Hawick is a settlement-name of the same type, while the surname Cruickshank probably comes from an obsolete and unidentified place-name rather than being a reference to the bow-leggedness of the bearer. Tongue is found in the Lowlands to indicate a slip of land, e.g. Tongland in Kirkcudbright; but the Caithness village of Tongue will be from the Gaelic cognate *teanga*.

new

The Pont Neuf is the oldest and loveliest of the bridges in Paris. When it opened in 1604 it was literally the 'new bridge', and these words only gradually acquired capital letters; (they also survived a linguistic change whereby *neuf* became *nouveau*). This is normally how place-names come into existence, not by referring to past events nor anticipating future developments, but simply describing what is there at the time.

The same thing happened over and over again in Scotland, and 'new' is one of the commonest prefixes to Lowland place-names. When a group of new houses was built the result might be called Newbigging: there are still eight hamlets of this name. A castle-restoration might be called Newark ('new work'), and the name would persist long after the castle had become a venerable ruin; four of these survive.

Newburgh in Fife was brought into existence in 1266 by a charter of Alexander III, permitting the monks of Lindores to erect their town into a 'new burgh'; it is likely that Newburgh in Aberdeenshire is not much younger. Newton is one of the commonest farm names (see under **ton**), and with a qualifying suffix becomes a village and later suburban name—Newton Mearns is an example. (The Mearns bit, which is also the name of a district in Angus, is in Gaelic *an Mhaoirne* or 'The Stewartry', a district administered by a steward). Newton St Boswells is discussed under **saint**. Newport-on-Tay is later than Ferryport-on-Craig (Tayport), and is the most recent crossing of the Tay before the advent of the bridges. The Newhaven which links with Dieppe is roughly coeval with the one near Leith, built as a royal dockyard in the early 1500s.

It was a similar motive which made the Scots settlers devise the term Nova Scotia, which remains one of the happiest 'new' names.

O

ochil

The Brittonic word *uchel* means high, and is to be found in the name Ochil Hills (not, one admits, of any great height) which run across central Scotland from Stirling to Perth and beyond. Ochiltree in Ayrshire is *uchel tref*—'high stead'—and occurs in almost identical form in the Welsh name Ucheldref. Ogilvie, which was an Angus place-name long before it became a familiar surname, is *uchel fa*—'high plain'. Glen Ogil near Lochearnhead is 'high valley' and Achilty near Dingwall is *uchel* with a locative ending. Even farther north, the River Oykell embodies the same word: the second century geographer Ptolemy called it *ripa alta*—'high bank'.

The wide distribution of these *uchel* names serves as a reminder of the extent to which the Brittonic language was spoken in Scotland in pre-Gaelic times (see Introduction). *Uchel* did pass into Gaelic in the form *uasle* meaning 'of high birth': a *duine uasail* is a perfect gentleman. Scott uses the term in *Waverley*, in his own inimitable spelling of 'duinhe wassel' (not, certainly, a bad phonetic rendering).

ord

Ord is the Gaelic for hammer; *ord-mor* is sledge-hammer; but in place-names the reference seems to be to a round throwing-hammer, and on the map Ord usually means a hammer-shaped hill. There are places called Ord in Sleat on Skye and in Aberdeenshire and Banffshire; Muir of Ord near Beauly comes from a nearby property named Ord, and there is a hill called Ord Bain ('white hammer') near Kingussie. Ordhead in Aberdeenshire is a Gaelic-English hybrid. The Ord of Caithness also refers to rounded contours, and Loch Ordie near Dunkeld probably has a similar source.

The word for a smith's fire or forge is *teallach* (pronounced 't-ya-lach'); An Teallach is the name of a spectacular mountain in Dundonnel, Wester Ross; it has been suggested that the mist which often surrounds its summits recalls the steam in a smiddy. Poltalloch in Argyll appears to be 'forge pool'.

Ceap (pronounced 'key-up') is the word for a shoemaker's last, or a block, and it seems to have been intended to describe certain block-like landscape-features. Kippie Law is a hill near Dalkeith; Kipford in Kirkcudbright involves the same word. So does Inverkip, but in a somewhat obscure way (see **inver**). Edinkip in the Borders and Edinchip near

104

Lochearnhead are both *aodann an chip*—'hill-face of the block'. In its diminutive form *ceapan* it has the sense of 'little stump', and such is the derivation of Kippen (both of them). East and West Kip in the Pentlands are probably similar. But Keppoch is from a different word, *ceapach* meaning 'tillage plot'.

Gobhal (pronounced 'go-ull') is Gaelic for fork, and is responsible for Craigowl (the highest summit of the Sidlaws) and for Glenhowl in Galloway. Gylen in Kerrara has the same origin, as have the various places called Gyle and Gyles, not to speak of Glengyle in Perthshire and Loch Gyle in Mull.

Tools of trade are seldom commemorated in Gaelic place-names. *Gilb* is the word for chisel, and Loch Gilp has just that shape. There are a few implements of a more domestic nature: *cuach*, a cup (in Scots—'quaich'), gives Glen Quaich near Aberfeldy, and the Quaich Water which enters Loch Leven in Kinross. One might assume that Glen Quoich in Mar is named after the cup-shaped potholes in the river, but this has been disputed.

Another word for a drinking vessel is *meadar*: Madderty near Crieff is thought to be *meadar Ethernain* or 'St Ithernan's milk-pail'. And *cuineag* also is a pail or stoup, which is the meaning of the oddly-shaped hill called Quinag in Assynt.

Iall in Gaelic is a leash or thong or leather strap, thought to be the origin of Loch Eil near Fort William (possibly from its shape). Old Norse *kamr* means 'comb', which in place-names usually refers to the crest or ridge of a hill; the origin of the six places called Kaimes and the three called Kames is however probably the Scots version of comb which is *kame*. Kemnay in Aberdeenshire is thought to be named for a conspicuous ridge which intersects the parish; Kaimhill in the same county is similar. The final item in this tool-kit is *snathad*, the Gaelic word for needle, which gives Inversnaid on Loch Lomond.

P

pan

The Gaelic and Old English terms for a valley have been discussed under **glen** and **den** respectively; a Brittonic word with approximately the same meaning is *pan*, modern Welsh *pant*, which on the Scottish scene usually just means a hollow. The word is confined to a small area of Eastern Scotland, part of which was formerly Pictland. In Angus one finds Panmure, which is *pant mawr* or 'big hollow'; Panbride ('Bridget's hollow') is nearby, and the farm of Panlathie ('clay hollow') not far off. Pannanich Wells near Ballater is possibly of the same derivation.

peel

A Scots word for a defensive palisade (cf. Mediaeval Latin *pela*, a stake), latterly a fortified house or tower. In place-names the word quite often became *pil*. Pilmore Links in St Andrews and Pilmuir in East Lothian indicate a piece of common land enclosed by a fence. Pilton in Edinburgh will be *peel toun* (many districts have their farm which is simply known as 'The Peel'). Pilrig is 'peel-ridge', and there are a Peel Fell and a Peel Burn in the Borders. Names of this type are not found in England: Peel on the Isle of Man referred originally to the castle only; its use as the town name is relatively modern. The English villages called Pilton are from a proper name.

peffer

A P-Celtic word (see Introduction) which survives in modern Welsh as *pefr* and means radiant or beautiful. In Scottish place-name terminology it was mainly applied to a stream, and the most obvious example is Strathpeffer in Easter Ross—'vale of the radiant stream'. Peffery in Aberdeenshire is now appropriately rendered 'Silverburn'. Innerpeffray near Crieff is where the Peffray joins the Earn, and Peffermill near Edinburgh must originally have been a water-driven mill on the Braid burn (nothing to do with pepper). There are various other watercourses of the same origin, eg. the Paphrie burn in Angus and the two Peffers in East Lothian.

The nearest Gaelic equivalent is probably *geal*, pronounced 'gyal' and meaning white, clear, bright. Carngeal, a common Highland name, means 'white hill' and Dalziel (pronounced 'Dalyell') is 'white dale'. As a water name *geal* usually becomes *geallaidh*, in modern parlance 'gelly': there are Gelly burns near Perth and Dundee, and a Lochgelly in Fife (strange how the dreariest places can have the prettiest names). Glen Geldie in the Cairngorms takes its name from the 'shining stream', as do Abergeldie and the two Gelder streams in Aberdeenshire.

Another Gaelic adjective of this kind is *alainn* (pronounced 'alin'), which means handsome or beautiful. It is the source of Loch Aline in Morvern (but not of the various Allan river-names which are discussed under **all**).

pen

This P-Celtic term (see Introduction) means 'hill' or 'end', and is commonly found in the west of England from Penzance to Penrith, with heavy concentrations in Wales. In Scotland it is found in the south (the old kingdom of Strathclyde) but not in Pictland (north of the Forth-Clyde line) nor in Galloway or Ayrshire, which all became Gaelic-speaking at an early date. Penicuik in Midlothian is *pen y gog* 'cuckoo-hill'; Cockpen is probably *coch pen* 'red head', and Penpont in Dumfries is 'bridge-end'. Pennel in Renfrewshire is *pen allt*—'head cliff', and Pencaitland in East Lothian is 'hill of the copse'. Dozens of other *pen*-names (so to speak) are to be found on the maps of the Borders, and others became obsolete before getting that far.

Perth

The ancient city of Perth surprisingly shares the same linguistic ancestry as le Perche in north-west France, the beautiful district where Percheron horses come from. The parent word is the Continental Celtic *pert*, meaning wood or thicket, which is still current in modern Welsh as *perth*, and appears in names like Aberpert in Wales.

A parish near Montrose is called Logie Pert—'copse hollow'—and there is a Perter Burn near Dumfries. Pappert Law and Pappert Hill (in Dunbartonshire and Lanarkshire respectively) must once, from their etymology, have been wooded. Larbert near Stirling is apparently *lled perth*—'half wood'—but what can have been meant by that is not readily understandable. Partick in Glasgow is probably from the same source— 'thicket place'.

The city of Perth was better known in late mediaeval times as St Johnstoun, taking its name from the fifteenth century church of St John the Baptist, which still graces the centre of the city. The name survives only in the surname Johnston and in the St Johnstone football team.

Perth in Western Australia is now more than ten times the size of its Scottish eponym. The original thicket has become a vast forest.

pit

This insignificant little word has been the subject of more intensive and scholarly study than almost any other place-name element in Scotland. More than three hundred names with this prefix occur, and all are located in areas known from historical and archaeological evidence to have been settled by the Picts. It will not do however to characterise these names as Pictish, for the second element is almost always Gaelic. Scholars have come up with the following theory: the word *pit*, which has the cognate form *petia* in Continental Celtic and Low Latin, meant part or share and passed into French and English as 'piece'. This term must have been used as a Pictish settlement-description, and was taken over by Gaelic-speakers, who added their own qualifying epithet—much in the same way that American settlers took over the French word *prairie* and made it their own. The likelihood is that *pit* names were coined during the bilingual period when Gaelic-speaking settlers were occupying Pictish lands in the ninth and tenth centuries.

Geographers have analysed in some detail a number of *pit* names and have reported interesting results. These names tend to occur at some distance from the immediate coastal areas, and predominate in elevated, south-facing sites away from marshes and adverse exposures. In other words, the early settlers bagged the best sites and left the others to later Gaelic-speaking incomers who were by that time using the term **bal** to denote their settlements.

The second element of a *pit* name is also instructive. It often refers to a person's name: Pitcatmick in Strathardle is 'Cormac's share'; Pitkeathly is 'Cathalan's share'; Pitkennedy in Angus is 'Cennetigh's share' and so on. Pitfour is 'pasture part', and Pitblado is 'flour part'. Sometimes the actual terrain is described, as in Pitcairn—'cairn part'—and Pitlochry (*cloichreach* means 'stony'), whereas Pitkerro and Pitcoig refer to quarter and fifth shares respectively. Pittenweem is *pit na h-uamha*—'cave place'. Animals are referred to in Pitcaple (see under **marc**) Pettymuch (see under **muc**) and Pitgobar (see under **wedder**), and trees appear in Pittencrieff—see **crieff**).

Sometimes *pit* is in the locative case: Petty near Inverness is 'at the place', and Pettycurr looks like 'at the place of the wet plain'.

If one were to analyse every *pit* name on the map one would have a vivid and unique picture of the settlement of eastern Scotland in the early mediaeval period.

poll

The Gaelic word *poll* is pronounced 'pool' and means just that, as well sometimes as a hollow or pit. It always occurs at the beginning of a place-name: Ullapool for example is something different—see *boll* under **ster**. Polmaise in Stirlingshire is 'pool of the plain', *maes* being the Brittonic form of the Gaelic *magh* (see under **may**). Polmadie near Glasgow may look as though it involves *madaidh* (dog), but the earlier spelling of 'Polmacde' shows the true derivation to be 'hollow of the sons of Daigh'.

Balgownie is the name of a bridge over the Don at Aberdeen, and clearly refers to a large pool in the river; its earlier and correct form is *Pol gobhainn* ('smith's pool') or even *Pol gamhainn* ('stirk's pool').

The diminutive form of *poll* is *pollaidh* which gives Stac Polly ('peak of the little pool') near Loch Broom and Pollock in the Lowlands. Pollokshaws and Pollokshields are similar formations, and are discussed under **shaw** and **tigh** respectively.

The word passed into Lowland Scots in the form *pow*, which usually means 'a slow-moving, ditch-like stream', and occurs mainly in the carses of the great rivers. Powgavie ('marsh stream') is on the Tay; nearby Carpow means 'ditch-fort'. Powfoot is on the Solway, and Powmill in Kinrossshire. But sometimes *pow* is spelt 'pol' in the Lowlands, making it difficult to determine which language is involved: Polmont near Stirling is probably Gaelic, with the meaning of 'hill-pool'; but if the components were Scots, it would mean 'pool-hill', each language having its distinctive word-order. Beware however that Polwarth, being in Berwickshire is less likely to be Gaelic: in fact, as its earlier spelling 'Paulewurthe' shows, it is 'Paul's farm' (see **worth**). Also note that there is a separate Scots term *pow*, meaning 'head', a version of 'poll', as in 'poll-tax'.

port

A very familiar English place-name element—think of Portland and Portsmouth—with an obvious meaning. From its Latin source *portus*, a haven, it passed into Gaelic with much the same meaning, although not always with a marine connection. The obvious seaports include Portpatrick, on the Rhinns of Galloway, pointing to Ireland and referring to its patron saint; and Port Askaig and Port Ellen on Islay (both from personal names). Port a' Churaich on Iona is 'harbour of the curricle', where St Columba is said to have landed from Ireland; opposite it on Mull is Fionnphort—'fair' or 'holy' port. Portknockie and Portsoy on the Moray Forth are respectively 'port of the knocks' or hillocks, and 'port of the sage' or wise man. Portree is discussed under **kin**.

Inland 'ports' include Portmore in Lothian, where there are the well-preserved remains of an ancient fort (which probably represents the 'haven' element). Port of Menteith clearly refers to a stronghold of some kind; as does Portmoak ('St Madoc's port') near Loch Leven. Loch Awe, one of the largest inland stretches of water in Scotland, has four different settlements on its shores which are known as 'port', although they are little more than landing-stages. Portobello near Leith was named around 1750 to celebrate Admiral Vernon's earlier victory at Darien.

preas

Preas in Gaelic (pronounced 'press') is a shrub or thicket; this word provided the suffix in Dumfries (discused under **dun**), and there are dozens of forgotten farm-names in the north-east which contain the syllable 'press'. (Pressley in Moray was just one example; and since *preas* was originally a Brittonic word, occurring also in England, it may well provide the etymology of the name of the celebrated pop-star, i.e. 'bush place'). In Aberdeenshire the word is metathesised to Birse.

Raineach in Gaelic means 'fern' or 'bracken', and the district of Rannoch means 'bracken place'. So does Ranachan in Wester Ross. Drumrannie near Girvan is 'bracken ridge'. There is a beauty-spot near Alyth in Angus known as the 'Slug of Auchrannie', where the River Isla plunges through a spectacular gorge; Auchrannie will be 'fern or bracken field', and Slug is discussed with *slugan* under the heading **drum**.

Dris is a bramble, and *driseag* (pronounced 'drish-ag') a little thorn; Ardrishaig in Argyll and Drumdrishaig in Knapdale mean respectively 'thorn point' and 'thorn ridge'. Tiendrish in Lochaber is discussed under **tir**.

Caorann (pronounced 'cu-run') is a mountain ash or rowan. It seems to be the basis of Tullochcurran ('rowan hillock') near Kirkmichael in Perthshire and Pitchirn ('rowan place') in Badenoch; but although rowan trees were held to be valuable in warding off Satanic impulses, the name does not often appear on the map. It also tends to get confused with *caora*, the word for sheep.

Holly is *cuilionn*, which gives Pitcullen ('holly-place') in Aberdeenshire; and Culross in Fife (pronounced '*coo*-russ') is *cuileann ros*—'holly wood or point'). The shrub called broom (which was used in the manufacture of besoms or brushes) gives rise to a number of place-names with very obvious meanings. There are several Broomhills, a Broomielaw (which means the same) and at least two Broomhalls. What makes these names seem markedly Scottish is the fact that their southern counterparts use the term in its Old English form, giving Bromwich, Bromley and Brompton.

Airne means a sloe-tree or damson, and *airneach* is the adjectival form. Balerno is *baile airneach*, which was also the original form of Balernach in Angus and Balernoch in Argyll; all mean 'sloe settlements'.

The rivers Truim and Tromie in Badenoch both take their names from the Gaelic *troman*, a dwarf elder or, in Scots, *bourtree* ('bower-tree'). Glen Truim is 'elder glen' and Glen Tromie is 'elder-place glen'; it should not be surprising how often one finds neighbouring places sharing the same or similar names (see Introduction).

One would not expect to find many place names derived from plants

110

and herbs; but Luss on Loch Lomond seems to be from Gaelic *lus* a plant, as does Lossiemouth, a newish (1698) settlement at the mouth of a river with an ancient name, probably pre-Gaelic. Kinloss is similar (see **kin**). Liff near Dundee is possibly *luibh*, meaning herbs.

priest

In the mediaeval Scottish church, priest was the title given to any member of the clergy; it comes from Old English *preost*, cf. Latin *presbyterus*. The priesthood was not normally celibate, and priests could be persons of some temporal importance. The word is found in Lowland place-names with astonishing frequency.

Prestwick (in Ayrshire and Berwickshire) is 'priest's dwelling' and of course corresponds with Prestwich in Manchester. Preston, as well as being part of a large Lancashire conurbation is the name of at least a dozen villages, hamlets or farms in Scotland. Indeed, places like Preston in East Lothian would start life simply as 'priest's farm'.

Preston also formed compounds such as Prestongrange (see **grange**), and Prestonpans, where salt was made by the monks of Newbattle Abbey. Preston was a territorial designation in Scotland from the twelfth century, and became the surname of a landed family some time later. The surname in turn gave rise to further place-names such as Prestonfield in Edinburgh.

The Old Norse word for priest (*pap*) is equally productive of place-names, although not showing the same settlement-pattern. There are four islands called Pabbay and eight called Papa—all are *pap ey* and mean 'priest isle'.

R

rath

Rath (pronounced 'ra') meant a circular fort, originally a dwelling surrounded by an earthen rampart; these were apparently very widespread in the area to the north of the Clyde/Forth line once known as Pictland. Most of them did not survive as settlement-names, but there is a cluster of *rath*-names in Fife: Rathillet is 'Ulsterman's fort', and Rathelpie (now part of St Andrews) is 'Alpin's rath'.

Radernie looks like 'Irish rath' and nearby Rumgally looks like 'strangers' rath' (see **gall**). Ramornie is *rath Morganaigh*—'rath of Morgan's people'. Craigrothie will be 'rath crag'.

Rattray in Perthshire and Aberdeenshire are both *rath tref*—'rath stance', or 'fort place'. Rothiemay is discussed under **may**, and Rothiemurchus is 'rath of Muirgus', whoever he may have been. Rohallion in Perthshire is 'rath of the Caledonians' (cf. Schiehallion). Logierait in Strathtay is another *rath* name (see **lag**). Further north, Reay is thought to be a *rath* word; Raigmore near Inverness is 'big fort'; and Dounreay in Caithness (*dun rath* or 'hill fort') has gained worldwide fame.

The Lowland names of Raitt and Raith show the unqualified term, as does Ratho, which lies well south of the historical Pictland. It appears that in these outlying parts, *rath* came to mean an enclosure or garden: Romanno near Peebles is *rath manach*—'monks' rath'. Redgorton near Perth is possibly *rath Gartain*, from a personal name that crops up with some frequency, or it may be *rath gortain* ('enclosure fort'—see **gar**).

As a place-name element, *rath* must often have succumbed to the much more vigorous **strath**, and it is very likely that many Lowland strath-names really refer to raths. Where there is neither a substantial river in the vicinity, nor a broad flat valley, it is a fair bet that there is a hidden rath. To give a few Fife examples, Strathkinness and Strathtyrum are probably 'Kenneth's fort' and 'dry fort' respectively. Nearby Stravithie, which also occupies no obvious strath, is less easy to explain.

Rest and Be Thankful

is the inscription on a stone erected by Cope's soldiers in 1740 at the summit of the military road leading from Dumbarton to Inveraray; it has given its name to the whole section of the road that flanks Ben Ime. The poet Keats relates in a letter how, when on a walking tour in Argyll, he had hoped to breakfast at the Rest and Be Thankful, under the impression that it was a wayside inn. All part of a poet's education.

This title has been chosen as the heading of a section devoted to what might be called Scotland's Comic and Curious Place-Names. Let us therefore rest from serious etymologising and be thankful that there are not more of these fancy names to detain us.

Several of them owe their odd appearance to the fact that they are phonetic transliterations from Gaelic. In Aberdeenshire and north Angus it seems to have been the jokey habit to turn misunderstood Gaelic terms into personal names: thus **magh** becomes Maggie, as in Maggienockater (from *mag an fhucadair*—or 'fuller's field', a tolerable representation of the sound); **tom** becomes Tam, as in Naked Tam (*tom nochta*, or 'bare hill'); **meall** becomes Mally, as in Mally Watt (*meall fhad*, or 'long hill). Shambelly

112

is a phonetic attempt at *sean baile*—'old town'; Seanbhaile occurs as a place-name in parts of Ireland.

Sometimes it is mistranslation that produces a silly name: The Study, a rocky outcrop in the gorge of Glencoe is a mis-rendering of an old Scots term *stithy* or *studdie*, which means 'anvil'.

Religious enthusiasm is responsible for a number of ill-fitting names. Joppa near Edinburgh is a version of Jaffa; the county of Angus has three biblical names in close proximity—Padanaram, Zoar and Jericho, all naturalised and having function without meaning. Post-Napoleonic smugness accounts for both the Lowland villages called Waterloo: not many names give such precise dating as do these two.

Gloweroi um seems to be a self-conscious attempt at humour, and it is found twice in the gazetteers: it means 'stare down at them', presumably from a vantage point. Titaboutie, of which there were four examples in Aberdeenshire, reaches the limits of silliness: it is Scots 'teet aboot ye' or 'look about you'. The farm-name Unthank, which occurs more than once, is a reference to the unrewarding nature of the land; an early spelling, Wnthank, was misread as Winthank, the name of a farm near Cupar.

The much-visited John o' Groats (by no means the most northerly settlement in Scotland) was traditionally the name of an octagonal house with a table of corresponding shape and eight windows. John of Groat of Duncansby was a historical character who was employed in the early sixteenth century as 'baillie to the earl in these pairts', but whose subsequent celebrity has greatly outstripped his contemporary usefulness.

Lamancha near Peebles is an oddity of Iberian origin. Admiral Cochran, of the Grange of Romanno, renamed his property in 1736 after his previous home in Lamancha, a province in Spain. Patna, a former mining community in Ayrshire, was so named by its founder in recollection of his birthplace in India.

A few names appear unusual only because of their modernity: Stanley on the Tay was named for Lady Amelia Stanley, later marchioness of Atholl. Maryhill in Glasgow takes its name from a previous owner, Mary Hill of Garbraid. Alexandria was called after Alexander Smollett, MP for Bonhill in the 1760s.

A name that seems to exert some fascination is Picktillum or Pickletillem; it exists in both versions, the former as the name of at least six farms in the Aberdeen hinterland, the latter as a solitary hamlet in Fife. It is thought to be from an archaic legal term *pictellum* meaning a small hedged parcel of land; the term found its way into Old English, but how it came to pop up in rural Scotland is anybody's guess.

rig

The Scots word *rig* has several different if allied meanings, all deriving from its origin in the English word ridge (which originally meant 'back' in the anatomical sense, cf. Gaelic **drum** and German *Rücken*). First, an elongated field: this is what Burns means in his song *Corn Rigs and Barley Rigs*. Secondly, a ridge of high ground, sometimes expressed by the word 'rigging'; 'The Riggin' was the name given to parts of the Grampian range, and 'The Riggin o' Fife' was the term used to describe the high part of the Kingdom between Forth and Tay. Thirdly, a strip of building land in a burgh.

The precise sense of the term is not always clear in place-names: Rigg and Eastriggs in Dumfries clearly refer to fields, as does Riggend near Airdrie; Rigside at Douglas Water could be 'ridge side'; Bonnyrigg in Midlothian is discussed under **bon**. Trochry in Strathbran has been explained as *droch rig*—'bad field', which would be a rather unusual Gaelic-Scots hybrid.

A much older term for ridge is the Brittonic *cefn*, which gives two different places called Giffen. Giffnock may be simply a diminutive, but looks like a combination of *cefn* with the Scots *knock*, the result being 'ridge-knoll'.

ross

In Gaelic *ros* means a promontory, often a wooded one; the word has its cognate in P-Celtic (see Introduction), and *rhos* is a common place-name element in Wales and Cornwall, usually with the slightly different meaning of 'moor'. In Scottish place-names it is not always possible to say which of the two languages is relevant and which meaning is correct: the district, formerly county, of Ross could be either, but the Ross of Mull appears on the map as an extended promontory. The Pembrokeshire name Rosemarket is probably the same as Rosemarkie in the Black Isle (both of them involving the word *marc* or horse), but the Welsh one is a moor while the Scottish one is a point.

Usually a smallish feature is described; Rossdhu on Loch Lomond is 'black point', and Durris (Aberdeenshire) and Dores (on Loch Ness) are probably the same, but with an inverted word-order; the attempted derivation from the modern Gaelic *doruis*, a door, is mistaken. Rosneath is 'sanctuary point' (see under **nemed**), and Ardross is 'height of the cape'. Kinross is 'head of the cape' (where it projects into Loch Leven), and Montrose was originally *monadh rois* or 'moor cape'. Rosehearty near Fraserburgh is 'Abhartach's cape'; and Rosyth, which would originally be on a promontory, invites comparison with Kilsyth (see under **kil**). Roseisle on the Moray Firth is probably another description of the promontory which now contains Burghead.

Melrose (discussed under *maol*) involves *ros* meaning moor, and the same may be said for Restenneth and Rescobie in Angus, Rosehaugh in the Black Isle and Roslin and Restalrig in the Lothians.

An extension of the word is *rosach*—'wooded part'—exemplified in places called Rossie. Rossie near Montrose and Rossie Priory near Dundee are two among many.

ruadh

Ruadh, pronounced 'roo-a', is the Gaelic word for reddish (but bright red is *dearg*). The name Ruthven, which crops up in the shires of Inverness, Perth, Angus and several others, is thought to be *ruadh mhaighinn* ('red place') but since it is almost invariably the site of a fort an alternative etymology is possible (see **rath**); Aberuthven in Strathearn (pronounced with the elision as 'Abriven') must be *aber ruadh abhuinn* ('mouth of the red river'), and Rutherglen's earlier spelling indicates the derivation *ruadh gleann*. Ruchill in Glasgow is thought to be *ruadh coille*—'red wood'. *Ruadh* is not dissimilar to our word 'ruddy', but very often transliterates into English as 'roy'. Rob Roy was 'Ruddy Robert' (on account of his hair-colouring), and Glen Roy, discussed under **glen**, is the same.

But beware the usual pitfalls, because the 'ruth' combination of letters can have a non-Gaelic origin. Rutherford near Kelso embodies the Old English word *hryther* meaning cattle (cf. Rotherhithe and Rotherham); Ruthrieston in Aberdeen is just 'Ruari's croft', and Ruthwell in Dumfries is properly 'rood-well' or 'cross well'.

Dearg (pronounced 'jerrag') is less descriptive of landscape and so produces fewer place-names. Dreghorn in Ayrshire is said to be one. There are several mountains called Ben Dearg; but the most appropriate use of the word is in *saighdear dearg*—the Gaelic term for 'redcoat'.

rubha

Rudha (pronounced 'roo-a', like the previous entry) is an interesting little Gaelic word. It basically means a 'turn', as in *cuiridh so rudha seachad*—'this will do its turn'. In place-names (where for some reason it is now spelt *rubha*), it means a point of land in the sea—presumably something to be 'turned' by a navigator.

There are no fewer than sixty-nine Rubha names on the map of the north-west Highlands, but not one of them will be familiar to the general reader.

There are three reasons for this: first, the word never caught on in English, as did loch, glen, corrie and even lairig, no doubt because its pronunciation is not immediately obvious; secondly, the type of minor promontory described by the word *rubha* is of very little importance in terms of human geography; and thirdly because *rubha* territory tends to be very thinly populated.

Very occasionally *rubha* is simplified, as in Rhue, near Ullapool; and Rhu on the Gare Loch is a tolerably familiar example. Rhubodach on Bute may be mentioned for its picturesque quality—it means 'promontory of the old man', or even 'goblin'. Rowardennan on Loch Lomond is 'Adamnan's cape' (see under **Colm**).

S

saint

Scotsmen and women in the early mediaeval period were deeply preoccupied with saints, of whom there were large numbers, especially in the Gaelic-speaking parts of the country. The name Brigid for example was borne by no fewer than fifteen saints, and is commemorated in the numerous churches and monuments styled 'St Bride's'. Many **kil-** and **kirk**-names contain the name of a saint; but in this section we shall be concerned only with the more important place-names which actually incorporate the term 'Saint'.

Of these the most notable must be St Andrews. The cult of the Apostle Andrew spread from Constantinople to Italy, France and Britain, arriving in Pictland some time during the tenth century. According to legend, of which there exist two separate versions, several of the saint's bones were brought to a little settlement known as *Cill rimhinn* on the coast of Fife, where a church of St Andrew was formed along with a reliquary. The town of St Andrews was founded in the twelfth century, the building of the great cathedral started at about the same time, and the University began to take shape two centuries later. (Since the modern form of the name derives from the vernacular *Sanct Androis* an apostrophe at the end is wrong). It was during the Wars of Independence that the cult of St Andrew first became of great national importance; his saltire cross provided the motif for a patriotic flag, and his adoption as the patron saint of Scotland led in due course to the establishment of a 'St Andrew's Church' in most towns in Scotland,

England and the Commonwealth.

On a much smaller scale this scenario is repeated all over Scotland. Moinnen, who died about 571, was first bishop of Clonfert in Ireland; his relics were brought to Fife, and the church of St Monan was founded in his honour. Nearby Kilrenny is named for another Irish saint, Ethernan.

Fergus was a Pict who for many years was a bishop in Ireland; after many wanderings in Scotland he settled in Buchan; St Fergus is only one of many places named in his honour. Fechan was an Irish monk who died of the plague in the seventh century; the Latinised form of his name gives us St Vigeans near Arbroath; he has already been noted under **eccles** and **lios**, where he inspired the names Ecclefechan and Lesmahagow. Ninian, a Rome-trained Briton, was traditionally resonsible for bringing the gospel to the southern Picts; his principal foundation was *Candida Casa* in Dumfries, now known in its Old English form of Whithorn ('white house'), but he is commemorated by name in St Ninians near Stirling.

St Abbs Head takes its name from Aebba, sister of King Oswald of Northumbria and first abbess of Coldingham in the seventh century. St Boswells comes from Boisil, prior of Melrose at the same period; the -*well* ending is a vernacular version of Norman *ville*, and the name has nothing to do with Dr Johnson's biographer (who was of course no saint).

Fillan succeeded St Mund as abbot at the Holy Loch; he gives his name to St Fillans and also to Strathfillan in Perthshire.

Our place-names record some completely bogus saints however. The name St Kilda is a nonsense, for there was and is no such person; a recent suggestion in *The Scots Magazine* that the name may be a corruption of the Scandinavian words *sunt kilde* ('source of fresh water') is intriguing. Hirta, the largest islet of the archipelago, may mean 'deadly' (an accurate enough description of its dangerous coast). St Fort in Fife is a grandiose and silly version of 'sand ford'. Canonisation must have been a painless process in these parts, for the nearby St Michaels is named after a disreputable Irish-man, Michael Kelly, and in St Andrews the street known as St Gregory's commemorates the inventor of Gregory's Mixture.

sal

There is an abundance of water in Gaeldom, in the form of sea-lochs, in-land lochs, rivers, streams and marshes, not to speak of precipitation. Being a poetic language, the Gaelic word for salt-water (*sal, sail, saile*) is also one of the many words for the sea; (the word for fresh water is *burn*—what comes out of the cold tap is *burn fuar*). Kintail is *cinn t-saile* 'at the end of the salt water' or 'at the head of the sea', which comes to much the same thing.

A derivative is *sailean*—'little sea-inlet'—which is the meaning of the two places in the north-west called Salen. But Saline near Dunfermline is 'salt-pit', from the Latin *salina* (which itself has the same etymology as the Gaelic word). Saltcoats is probably a bit more recent: it means 'salt-workers' huts'.

The correct name for outer Loch Linnhe was *Linne Sheileach*—'the brackish pool'; the inner part was *an Linne Dhubh*—'the black pool'—see also under **linn**.

sand

Although the word is the same in Old Norse as in English it is not difficult to determine the origin of the many place-names in which it appears. In the far north there are two places called Sand, one in Shetland and the other on Gruinard Bay. Sanda and the two Sandays all mean 'sand isle', Sandaig and the four Sandwicks all mean 'sandy bay' (compare Sandwich in Kent). Sandbister is 'sand farm' (see **bol**), Sand Fiold in Orkney is 'sandhill' (see **fell**), Sannox in Arran is just 'sandy place', and Sandness and Sandsound in Shetland have obvious meanings; all these names are of Scandinavian origin. Handa is an aspirated version of Sanda.

Sandford near Strathaven was devised by English-speakers; St Fort in Fife is a perversion of the same name. Sandend on the Moray Firth is English, as is Sandfordhill at Buchan Ness. Sandbank in Argyll seems to be modern.

The Gaelic word for sand, *gainmheach* (pronounced 'ganvich') is curiously unproductive of place-names; apart from Gannochy in Glenesk, Ganavan near Oban and various little sand-fringed lochs called Gaineamhaich or Ganvich there is little to be found on the maps.

setr

Names ending in -*setter* illustrate some of the problems of Scandinavian place-nomenclature (see Introduction). *Setr* was the late Old Norse term for a pastoral dwelling, sometimes a shieling, and formed part of the naming-vocabulary of Viking immigrants of the later ninth century. *Setr* often becomes *setter* or *shader* on modern maps, except when it becomes *ster*, thus causing confusion with the more common Old Norse term *bolstadr* (see **ster**). Inkster in Orkney for example is *eng setr*—'farm meadow'.

There are dozens of *setr* names in the Northern Isles and Hebrides, but in the nature of things they represent places of no importance, quite unfamiliar to most readers, and therefore out of place in a book of this kind. Even the less recherché ones like Gunnister in Shetland ('Gunni's farm') and Grimshader ('Grim's stead') in Lewis are of limited interest, while purely topographic references such as Uigshader in Sky ('bay stead'), Earshader in Lewis ('west farm'), and Flashader in Skye ('flat shieling') do not add much to our knowledge either of the area or the period. In Sutherland these -ster endings, having been gaelicised to sheder, tend to become anglicised to side, producing names such as Linside ('pool place') and Culside ('back place').

sgurr

This Gaelic word describes a peak or cliff or sharp point, and is a term familiar to mountaineers in Scotland. An alternative spelling in Gaelic is sgorr, which also means a 'buck-tooth'—the metaphor is picturesque and appealing.

Sgurr, to give it the commoner spelling, never quite became a common noun, as did ben, although The Scorrie in Glen Doll and the Sgurr of Eigg are surely steps in this direction. On the maps, perhaps because of the nature of the terrain, the word sgurr appears more often in the rugged north-west than in the more rounded Grampians. Sgurr nan Gillean is a familiar Cuillin peak, replicated on Rum; it is 'the lads' peak'. Nearby Sgurr Alasdair is a modern name, in honour of Sheriff Alexander Nicolson of Skye; indeed, most of the Cuillin hills are 'sgurrs' and one should add Sgurr Dearg ('red peak', of the Inaccessible Pinnacle), and Sgurr a Mhadaidh ('dogs' peak'). An Teallach in Wester Ross has Sgurr Fiona as one of its peaks, while Sgurr a Mhaim above Glen Nevis and Sgurr na Ciche in Glen Dessary both refer to the female breast. Glencoe has Sgurr na Feine ('peak of the Fingalians'). There is a Sgorr an Fhuarain in Invernessshire, and another in Ross and Cromarty which is phonetically rendered Sgurr Ouran; both mean 'peak of the springs' (see spring). Perhaps the most poetic sgurr name is one to the east of Loch Broom—Sgurr Eideadh nan Clach Geala— 'Peak of the Garment of White Stones'; for those who wish to say this mouthful in Gaelic, it sounds like 'skoor eja nan clach gyala'.

The Scots word scaur, meaning a steep hill or precipice, has a different etymology—from Old Norse sker (cf. 'skerry'). It appears in Scots guise in The Scores in St Andrews ('the cliffs') and also gives the prefix of Scarborough (but Skara Brae in Shetland is from the personal name Skari). The Gaelic equivalent sgeir is very common in the Hebrides, but the word seldom appears in the form 'skerry'.

shade

In Scots, the verb 'to shed' means to separate (as might be, the sheep from

119

the goats). A shed is a parting of the hair, a watershed of the waters. (But a garden shed is from a different word, viz. shade meaning shelter). A distinct and separate piece of land was a shed, or more usually in place-names a 'shade'.

Bandshed in Kintore was 'top land'; Broadshade, also in Aberdeenshire, Chapelshade in Dundee and Middleshade near St Andrews all related to land-divisions; some have now become suburbs.

Remaining with Scots dialect terms, the word for an enclosed meadowland was 'ward'. Ward is the name of four places in East Aberdeenshire, and is very common in farm names in that area. In compound names the term is invariably misunderstood: Backward in Aberdeenshire means 'rear meadow' and Largoward in Fife means 'Largo-field'; neither name refers to a direction.

shaw

Shaw (from Old English *sceaga*) is an archaic word meaning a wood or thicket; it is different from the Scots dialect word 'shaw' e.g. the part of the 'tattie' that 'shaws' above the ground. There are two places in England called Shaw, plus a Shawford and a Shawhead, all referring to copses. Shawwood in Ayrshire (unless it embodies the personal name Shaw) says the same thing twice. Shawlands in Glasgow will be 'woodlands' and Hangingshaw is descriptive of a wooded steep. Pollokshaws is presumably the wooded part of the Pollock estate; Wishaw seems to be the wood of someone called Wice, and Shawhead near Dumfries is obvious enough. Note however that Shawbost in Lewis is *sjar bolstadr*—'beach-place' (see **ster**) and Schawpark near Alloa was traditionally the site of a *wappenschaw* ('weapon-show') or military review.

shee

When the early Celts settled in Ireland they found burial mounds belonging to an earlier occupancy; they called these *side* (pronounced 'shee') and peopled them with their own deities. In Scottish Gaelic the word *sithean* means a conical hill associated with fairies and other supernatural beings. Schiehallion is 'the fairy hill of the Caledonians' (a term introduced by Ptolemy to identify the tribe that occupied the central Highlands during the period of the Roman occupation). Ben Tee and Ben an t-Sithean in Strathyre both involve the element *shee*. Strontian may have given its name to strontium 90, but the etymology has pleasanter associations—*sron t-sithean* or 'promontory of the fairy hills'

Usually *shees* are smaller hills, like the Shee of Ardtalnaig which looks

120

across Loch Tay to Ben Lawers (*talnaig* is an unexplained stream-name); they can even be hillocks or mounds. The name of the Campsies is often taken to be from the Gaelic *cam sith*—'crooked hill', to which an English plural has been added. Glenshee is probably called after one of the *shee*-type hills which abound in the vicinity (they are actually moraines). But since *sithe* also means peace in Gaelic (the fairies were 'the people of peace'), a more romantic derivation of the name is not impossible. Until the last century there was certainly a strong local tradition that Glenshee meant 'glen of fairies'.

Sligo

One has to go to Ireland to find Sligo, but it provides the most obvious example of the use of the Gaelic word *slige* meaning 'shell', more commonly found in its adjectival form of *sligeach* or 'shelly' (pronounced 'shlig-uch'). In Aberdeenshire we have Pitsligo, meaning 'shelly place' (shell sand was dug for lime in these parts); and Sligachan in Skye has much the same meaning. An Sligearneach is a hill in the Forest of Atholl—not an obvious place for shells.

The Vikings had a similar word for shell; Skelbo in Easter Ross, Shelibost in Harris and Skelister in Shetland all mean 'shell farm', and Skelwick in Orkney is 'shell bay'.

The Lowland counties have their quota of places with names like Shell Bay and Shelly Point, probably of fairly recent origin; and the word appears very infrequently in English place-names.

spittal

A Scots word meaning a hospice for travellers, especially in mountainous country. Examples are to be found in most of the Grampian passes, sometimes at either end: the Spittal of Glenshee was matched by Seanspittal ('old hospice') on the Mar side, and there was a Spittal on each side of the Cairn o' Mount pass. The Spittal of Glenmuick was a house that served the Capel Mounth, and Dalnaspidal (*dail na spideal* or 'hospice field') is at the southern end of the Drumochter pass. The term is of Late Latin origin (*hospitium*—hence our hospital) and was borrowed into Gaelic; Lowland names such as Spittalfield in Perthshire and Spittalhaugh in Aberdeenshire must have referred to similar establishments, now long forgotten.

spring

It must be obvious after a moment's thought that when this word occurs in a place-name the reference is not to the season but to the water-supply. (Further thought will of course reach the conclusion that the two usages have the same origin, in the idea of rising). There are at least three Springfields in the Lowlands, each meaning a field with an outflow of water; Springburn in Glasgow has the same sense and the word figures in several other place-names in Scotland (but very few in England).

The Gaelic equivalent is *fuaran*, as in Meall nam Fuaran ('spring hill') in Glen Almond and Pitfirran ('place of springs') in Fife. Foveran near Ellon in an older form was *Fobharan*, and comes from the same word, the spring being still identifiable; so does The Wirren. Very often the initial letter is aspirated, giving an anglicised spelling of 'ouran'; Sgurr nan Fhuaran and Sgur Ouran, the simplified version, occur many times and mean 'peak of the springs'. (But Fuaran na Sgor near Braemar means 'spring of the peaks'). The word was common in place-names which are now obsolete: the Wells of Dee on Braeriach were formerly known as *Fuaran Dhe*.

sruth

This Gaelic word (pronounced 'sroo') means a stream or current. It has several derivative forms including *sruthach* ('current-place') and *struthaigh* ('at the stream')—which give us Struie and Pathstruie in Perthshire, Struan in Atholl and Struy in Strathglass. The diminutive of *sruth* gives Struan, 'streamlet', the name of a little place on Loch Bracadale in Skye; different still is the form *sruthail* which provides the origin of Loch Trool in Galloway.

The Lowland name Struther, as in Strutherhill near Larkhall and Bellstruther Bog in Berwickshire, is more problematical; it may derive from *sruthair* (yet another version of *sruth*) but on the whole is perhaps more likely to represent the Scots dialect word *strother*, meaning a marshy piece of land. This would link it with Stroud in the Cotswolds, which comes from the Old English *strod*, itself the origin of *strother*. Anstruther in Fife, because it seems to contain the Gaelic definite article *an*, has commonly been derived from *sruth*; but the presence of Westruther across the Firth of Forth must surely point to an Old English origin for both names.

staff

The Old Norse word *stafr* means staff, and gives us the names Staffa and Staffin (the columnar basaltic rocks presumably resembling staves); Dunstaffnage was *dun stafr nes*—'fort on the staff ness').

The Gaelic word for a shaft or handle is *cas*; it can also mean foot, and the dative form *cois* is seen in *cois a mheall*—'at the foot of the hill'—an apt description of the Strathtay hamlet of Coshieville.

122

A related Gaelic word is *sgonn* which means a lump of wood. This is the reputed origin of Scone (pronounced 'skoon') near Perth, but it is not known how the coronation-place of the Scottish kings came to have so mundane an origin. The parish of Scoonie near Leven is thought to be the same, as is Skene in Aberdeenshire. The Gaelic word for wood in the sense of timber is *fiodh* (pronounced 'few'). Fiddes is the name of an old Barony in Kincardineshire, which became Fettes when transplanted to genteel Edinburgh; the derivation is *fiodhas*—'wood stance'. Glenfiddich in Banff is probably 'wooded glen', and Feddinch in St Andrews looks like 'wood enclosure' (see **inch**).

ster

The visitor to Orkney and Shetland cannot fail to notice the large number of place-names with the curious ending *ster*. This is usually a reduction of the Old Norse *bolstadr*: if we dissect the word we get *bol*, which means lot or share, and is comparable with the Brittonic **pit**, meaning the same thing. The *stadr* part is a word meaning farm, cognate with English 'stead' and German *Stadt*. The distribution of the element *bolstadr* is almost co-extensive with what we know historically of the Scandinavian settlement of north-west Scotland, although the word, when Gaelic-speakers took over, underwent severe mutilation.

Kirkbister and Swanbister—'church farm' and 'Sven's farm'—show the word almost complete; there is some compression in Lybster ('lee farm') and Scrabster ('skerry farm'). In Breabost ('broad township'), Carbost ('copse farm') and Shawbost and Skeabost ('beach part') only the first syllable remains, and it is even more truncated in Embo—'Eyvind's place' and Skibo—'ship place'. A measure of anglicisation has taken place in Ullapool—'Olaf's *bolstadr*' and Unapool (pronounced 'Unnapool' and meaning 'Uni's farm'). Eriboll in Sutherland is Old Norse *eyri boll*—'place on the gravel bank'—and Torboll in the same county is 'Thor's estate'.

stone

The Old English word **stan** ('stone') has been a very powerful agent in the production of names: one has only to point to the numerous Stanleys, Stansteds and Stantons south of the Border. In Scotland it would normally become 'stane', and indeed we have Stane in Lanarkshire as well as Stenton and Stenhousemuir ('moor of the stone house'). But it has to be said that the modern English form of the word is even commoner: Stonefield, Stonehaugh, Stonehouse, Stoneybridge, Stoneyburn and Stoneywood are scattered all over the Lowlands, and there is even a Stonybeck in Orkney.

(The name Stonehaven is discussed under **haven;** the local version, *Steenhive*, is supported by early spellings: 'steen' would be the normal local pronunciation of 'stone', but the ending is problematical). Very often the 'stone' bit comes at the end of the compound: Greystone is one of the commonest farm-names in the north-east. All these names have obvious meanings.

In Gaelic the everyday word for a stone is *clach*; *clach mhile* is a milestone and *clach mhuillin* a millstone. Scotland being a stony place, one would expect to find a lot of place-names incorporating this word; but this is not really so, for most of the 'stone' names have either undergone translation or were never strictly speaking place-names in the first instance. Examples are *Clach nan Taillear* in Glen Dee and *Clach Dhion* by Loch A'an, known to habitués of the Cairngorms as 'The Tailors' Stone' and 'The Shelter Stone'; the Gaelic names no longer appear on modern maps. In a different case is Clachnaben, a curious rock-formation at the summit of the Cairn o' Mount pass: it must mean something like 'mounth-rock' (see **monadh**), but there is no translated version. The best-known 'stone' name is Clackmannan, which means 'Manau stone', that being the old term for the district at the upper end of the Firth of Forth. (Slamannan involves the same word, preceded by *sliabh*—thus 'Moor of Manau').

Clachnacuddin means 'stone of the tubs' and marks the spot where the women of Inverness are said to have rested their pitchers after filling them with water from the river. Also near Inverness is Clachnaharry, in Gaelic probably *Clach na h-Aithrige*—'stone of repentance'.

An older term is *clachan*, which meant originally a stone cell or church, later a village. There are four places called Clachan in various parts of Scotland; they are the Gaelic equivalent of 'Kirkton'. Clachaig, of which there are three examples, is thought to mean 'rocky'. In the genitive case, *clach* becomes *cloich*, as in Fasnacloich (see **fas**). Pitlochry is in modern Gaelic *Baile Chloichrigh* and probably means 'place of stepping-stones' (see under **pit**).

A flat stone in Gaelic is *leac* (pronounced 'lechk'); Auchinleck in Ayrshire is *achadh nan leac*—'field of the flagstones'—and the same formation is found in a shortened form in Affleck in Angus and Aberdeenshire.

More obscure is the Old Gaelic term *coirthe* which meant 'standing stone'. There are at least six farms in the north-east called Auchorthie, and one Auchnagorth: these names seem to involve the word in the genitive plural, and invite the translation 'field of the stone-circle'. Other examples are Craigforthie in Aberdeenshire, Pitforthie in Angus and the Mearns and Pitcorthy in Fife. All refer to places where there are or were standing stones.

124

strath

The Gaelic term *srath* (pronounced 'sra') denotes a broad valley, usually smoother and less steep than a glen; this is neatly illustrated by comparing the lower Dee valley (Strath Dee) with the mountainous source of the river (Glen Dee). In general, straths take their name from that of the river which flows through them, and if they are less common in the north-west Highlands the cause is usually topographical rather than linguistic. Occasionally however the two terms have been combined in the one place-name, as in the pleonastic Glen Strathfarrar.

All the major watercourses in Celtic Scotland have the *strath* prefix—Strathtay, Strathspey and Strathcarn. (The name Strathclyde in mediaeval times referred quite properly to the valley of the river Clyde; after the reorganisation of the 1970s it became the name of a region stretching from Oban to Girvan, a senseless and confusing nomenclature). Other broad valleys have been correctly named—Strathmore (great valley), Strathfillan (named after the saint of that name), and Strathgartney ('Gartney's strath' in the Loch Katrine basin).

Some *strath*-names are however more problematical: Strathcathro is discussed under **caer**, and probably relates to a fort; since however it does not describe a recognizable valley it may be a **rath** name. Strathmartine near Dundee may also be similar ('St Martin's fort'). Strathblane looks like a genuine strath, but it was originally *Strathblachan*, and does not apparently come from St Blane (as does Dunblane—see under **dun**).

The diminutive of strath is *srathan*, which accounts for the village name Strachan in Kincardineshire (and of course for the more famous surname). The obsolete name The Straans at Crathie has the same meaning and gives the correct pronunciation.

stuc

The Gaelic language has a bewildering number of words to describe configurations of the landscape, especially hill-shapes. Although *stuc* does not occur as often as **beinn**, **meall** and **sgurr** it deserves a mention as being the prefix of one of the most southerly and conspicuous of Scottish munros—Stuc a Chroin, the neighbour of Perthshire's Ben Vorlich. *Stuc*, plural *stuic*, is just a borrowing of the Scots word 'stook'; for those too young to remember, a stook was a gathering of corn-sheaves, usually twelve in number, set up in a field to ripen. *Cron* is a croon or dirge. So Stuc a Chroin is literally 'croon-stook', or more poetically 'peak of the dirges'—an illustration of the fact that Gaelic is not such an alien language to Lowlanders as might be thought. Near the summit of Ben Lawers there is a protuberance called on the maps An Stuc: why didn't the map-makers simply call it The Stook, which is what it both means and resembles? On the Lochnagar summit ridge we have another feature called An Stuic, to which the same considerations might apply. Again, why was the Perthshire place *An Stuiceannan* anglicised to Stix instead of Stooks?

A similar but unrelated word is *stac*, which is a borrowing either from the Old Norse *stakkr* or the English stack. It means what you think, and appears in such names as Stac Polly in Wester Ross ('stack of the pools') and Ben Stack in Sutherland. More lowly examples are to be found in the Stack of Handa and others.

For completeness one must mention a third term—*stob*—another Gaelic borrowing with the same meaning in that language as in English i.e. stob, post or stick. Stob Coire nan Lochan in Glencoe is literally 'stob of the corrie of the little loch', which hardly does justice to its spectacular shape when seen from below. Stob Gabhar in the Black Mount looks like 'goat-stob', while the nearby Stob Coir' an Albannaich refers to the 'corrie of the men of Alba', or the Irish (see Introduction).

Stob is in fact more familiar as a Lowland place-name element. Stobo, a hamlet on the Tweed near Peebles, is from the Old English *stubb-holh*, meaning just 'post-hole', and Stobs in Roxburgh has the same origin. Stobhall and Stobhill clearly have a similar derivation, Stobcross is self-explanatory, and the Dundee district of Stobsmuir must at one time have been a moor with posts.

T

tarbert

Tairbeart is not necessarily a proper noun in Gaelic, being the usual word for isthmus. The word is interesting in itself, since its origin is the older term *tairm-beart*, literally 'over-bringing' or porterage. As a place where ships could be carried over, it would have considerable strategic importance; and indeed in popular history an eleventh century Norwegian king annexed Kintyre by having his ship dragged across the isthmus between the two Lochs Tarbert with himself at the helm. Although this is the most famous Tarbert, there are several others in the West Highlands, including one on Harris and one in Sutherland. Tarbet is the name of a strip of land separating Loch Long from the inland Loch Lomond; another Tarbet is to be found in North Morar. Torridon is thought to incorporate the word *tarbert*. Tarbat Ness is the name of the promontory of Easter Ross, not such an obvious place for boat-dragging; and the so-called 'tarbat' connecting the mainland with the islet of Fidra in the Firth of Forth seems to have disappeared from modern maps.

tarff

Tarbh is Gaelic for bull, and has obvious connections with Latin *taurus*. In place-names it was usually applied to a stream, where the allusion is not to any particular animal but to the mythic qualities of the breed—impetuous, rushing, roaring. It may be noted that bulls were a favourite motif on Pictish carved stones. The Old Norse word for a bull is similar—*tarfr*—and it is not always possible to say which language is the basis of certain names; Tarradale on the River Beauly and Tarvie in Strathpeffer are clearly of Viking origin.

The Tarff, which empties into Loch Ness near Fort Augustus, answers to this description, as do the Water of Tarff in Atholl and its namesake in Glenesk. There are other names involving *tarff* which do not refer to streams: Tarvit in Fife, Tarves and Pittentarrow all mean 'bull place'. Tarland in Aberdeenshire means 'bull field' (see **land**).

Where the Gaelic word for cow (*bo*) appears in place-names, it is because droving was an important occupation and cattle at one time represented the local currency; Bealach nam Bo appears both in Applecross and on the map of the Trossachs; in the latter case it refers to the gap through which Rob Roy is said to have driven the cattle which he 'lifted' from the Lowlands; the name is however probably an invention of Sir Walter Scott who set *The Lady of the Lake* in the vicinity. More genuine is Loch Ba ('loch of the cattle') on Rannoch Moor and Carnbo in Kinross-shire; the name crops up in several other places.

The name for a calf—*laogh*—is also well represented on the map. It is found in the Cairngorm pass of Lairig an Laoigh (see **lairig**). Glen Loy in Lochaber is really *Glen Laoigh*; there is another in Cowal. Its anglicised spelling of 'lui' gives the approximate pronunciation, and the term is to be found in Ben Lui, in Ardlui ('calf point') on Loch Lomond and Glen Lui in Mar.

Stirk in Gaelic is *gamhain*, giving Pitgaveny ('stirk place') near Elgin, Gamrie in Aberdeenshire and Loch Gamhna in Rothiemurchus. Ox is *damh*, as in Inchnadamph (see under **inch**), Dava in Moray (see under **ford**) and Ben Damph in Torridon. The generic term for cattle in Gaelic is *crodh*, found rather infrequently: the only example that comes to mind is Badachro in Gairloch ('cattle thicket'—see *bad* under **coille**).

An older Brittonic term for cow is *buwch*, thought to be the origin of Buchan (the part of Aberdeenshire north of the Ythan), and also of Buchanty in Glen Almond and Buchany in Kilmadock parish (but the old district name of Buchanan near Loch Lomond is different—see *both* under **tigh**).

Nor must we overlook the Old English word for cattle, which was *neat*. Although it became *nowt* in Scots, the name Neidpath near Peebles preserves the older form and probably means 'cattle track'.

Thurso was originally *thorsa*, from an earlier Celtic form meaning 'bull river'. It was translated into Gaelic and re-interpreted as 'Thor's River'. The town name comes from the river.

Tay

Reference was made in the Introduction to the difficulties posed by pre-Celtic names such as Tay, which cannot be identified as belonging to any particular language. Other examples in this class are Tain (the burgh takes its name from the river), the Tanar in Aberdeenshire, the Teviot and the Midlothian Tyne (which clearly relates to its big brother in Northumberland). All that these names appear to have in common is that they refer to watercourses and that they derive from a 't' sound which must mean something basic like 'flow'.

If antiquity is the reason for the opacity of these names, there are others more modern which are scarcely any easier. Cupar in Fife has a wide variety of recorded spellings, none of which has led to a definitive etymology. The name corresponds with the abbey town of Coupar Angus, which in the Middle Ages was no less important than the Fife burgh, and one might well look for a common source. The Gaelic words *cul barr* ('back of the hill') fail to ring true either linguistically or topographically, and one is left with the near homonym Coburty in Aberdeenshire, which might conceivably derive from *comh pairt* or 'common land'.

Elie in Fife has been explained as Gaelic *Ealadh*—'at the tomb'—on the analogy of a place on Iona where the dead were landed before burial; but the survival in Fife of such a Gaelic term in all its purity would perhaps be unlikely. The fact that the existing isthmus at Elie was once an island has led to the speculation that the Gaelic word *eilean* might be involved; but this word occurs nowhere else in the east, the characteristic term for island being **inch**. Looking to the Cambridgeshire Ely for guidance one gets the Old English etymology *el ige*—'isle of eels' which is by no means impossible for the Fife resort.

Airlie in Angus and Errol in Perthshire look like twins, and a suggested etymology is the Brittonic *ar ol*—'on the ravine'. But this is quite impossible to reconcile with the flat carse-land on which Errol is situated. The Buchan name Errol is imported from Gowrie.

Erskine near Glasgow has been explained as Brittonic form *yr ysgyn*—'green ascent', which will have to serve until we find a better.

teine

The Gaelic word for fire is *teine*, pronounced something like 'chinny'; it figures in place-names in many parts of Scotland. Carntyne in Glasgow is 'cairn of fire', and Glen Tennet in Angus is of similar origin. The derivative *teineadh* ('fiery') is responsible for Restenneth near Forfar (originally *Rostinoth*—'fire moor'). Tinto and Tintock are from *teinteach* ('place of fire').

But beware that some similar-looking names in fact involve a completely different word: Craigentinny near Edinburgh is *Creag an-t Sionnaigh*—'fox crag'; Ardentinny is probably 'fox-height', and Auchendinny in Lothian probably 'fox haugh'.

temple

'The Poor Knights of Christ and of the Temple of Solomon', usually known as 'the Templars', were a religious order established in the early twelfth century initially to provide military protection for the Crusaders against marauding Muslims. Helped by the patronage of St Bernard of Clairvaulx, their numbers and prestige grew, and they acquired vast wealth and a diversity of purposes. Their extensive property-holdings throughout Europe were extended to Scotland through the influence of the Templar family of the Sinclairs of Rosslyn. The Templars soon however became a political and military and even economic threat to the European establishment, and the order was suppressed by the Pope in 1312; its members went underground, and the order survived only in unofficial and picturesque forms inspired by some of the ideals of Freemasonry.

The Templars left their mark on Scottish place-nomenclature, as witnessed by the number of settlements which incorporate the word 'temple'. There is a Temple in Midlothian and another in Govan, a Templand in Dumfries and another near Rhynie, a Temple Hall near Berwick, together with numerous farms called Templeton. There is an intriguing road-sign on the A94 just short of Stonehaven which reads 'Temple of Fiddes'; Fiddes (discussed under **staff**) will be a former Templar farm: sightseers should not expect a Scottish Taj Mahal.

It should be noted however that the Gaelic word *teampull* can just mean 'church', and the existence of a place-name such as Teampuill Chaon ('St

Comgan's church') in Sleat cannot be taken as evidence of Templar penetration so far north; conversely there is many a Templar property in Scotland whose current name no longer records the connection: for example, the Templars built a chapel in Strath Dee in 1487 to St Mary, the patron of their Order; the place is now called Maryculter. Temple names are also quite common in England.

tigh

This is one of the first words that the Gaelic-learner comes across: it means house and is pronounced with a short vowel somewhere between 'tie' and 'toy'. It is not very productive of place-names, but Tyndrum (accented on the second syllable) is 'house on the ridge'; Tighnabruaich is 'house on the bank'; Tayvallich is *tigh bhalaich*—'house of the pass', and Taychreggan is *tigh a' chreagan*—'house of the little crag'.

If common *house* names are hard to find in Gaelic, they are not much more common in English. There are three places called Stonehouse, as well as Stenhousemuir—'moor of the stone house'. Fauldhouse is 'house on the fallow land'. Easthouse and Easterhouse are to be taken literally; Grantshouse near Berwick-on-Tweed was a station-name devised by the North British Railway Company to replace the rather more down-to-earth 'Tammy Grant's Inn'. Corehouse is not a *house* name, but contains *coireach*—'place of corries' (see **corrie**). Likewise Auldhouse is *allt fhuathais*—'stream of the spectre'—and the same word occurs in Auchterhouse near Dundee (see **auchter**).

A humbler abode than a house is a shieling, or hut, usually situated on high summer pastures: Shillinglaw is 'shieling hill'. The word came from the Old Norse *skali*, which also supplies the first syllable of the English word shelter. Scalloway is 'shieling bay', and Galashiels recalls long-disappeared 'huts by the Gala Water', probably for fishermen. Pollokshields were the 'huts at Pollock', a name discussed under **poll**; and the meaning of Cauldshields is all too obvious.

Not far removed in meaning is another Old Norse word, *skjoldr*, which occurs in the name Shieldaig—'shield bay'. Shieldhill in the Lowlands probably has a similar sense, that of 'shielding', or 'sheltering' hill.

Another type of abode is a hut, for which there are three similar Gaelic nouns—*both*, *bothan* and *bothag*: the last of these gives the Scots word 'bothy' and the second the Irish 'bothan' or 'shebeen'. These words have acquired a somewhat disreputable flavour in English, but in Gaelic place-names *both* is quite respectable. Indeed Balmoral, as indicated by earlier spellings, had its origin as a 'hut in the big clearing'. Balnaboth ('bothy-township') is the name of the estate in Glen Prosen where Scott planned his Antarctic expedition; Buchanan (now much more familiar as a surname) is 'canon's hut'; Buchlyvie is *both sleibhe*—'house on the moor', and Bohuntine may be *bothan teine*—'fire house'. In Aberdeenshire the element *both* often gets confused with *bog*: Bogengarrie could be either 'dyke bothy' or 'dyke bog', and Boggieshalloch could be either 'willow hut' or 'willow bog'.

tir

Tir nan Og, as most readers will know, means 'Land of Youth', the 'blessed land' of Fingal and his Celtic warriors; but *tir* (pronounced 'teer') is used also in a much more mundane way: *tir-mor* for example is the mainland. The word is found in Tiree, but the ending of that name is the subject of much speculation. Tirinie near Coshieville is *tir-ingnigh*—'land of the claw-place'—a reference to the configuration of the terrain. Tirnadrish or Tiendrish in Lochaber is 'land of thorns'; the word *dris* is found also in Ardrishaig (discussed under **preas**). Tervin on Loch Awe is 'land of meal', and Terpersie near Alford is 'copse-place'.

Blantyre, birthplace of David Livingstone, is 'edge land'; Altyre in Moray is 'river land', and Tyrie in Aberdeenshire and Fife seems to mean 'corn land'.

tobar

In the days when Scottish history used to be taught in our schools, every youngster in the land had heard of the Battle of Tippermuir, after which Montrose's victorious army could have (and probably did) walk all the way to Perth on the bodies of slain Covenanters. The name Tippermuir is not to be found on the map nowadays, but the pleasant little hamlet of Tibbermore lies just south of the main Perth-Crieff road near Methven.

Tobar is the Gaelic word for a well or source, and at Tibbermore there is a fine spring beside the ancient church. The name is usually explained as *tobar mor*—'big well'. But the locals usually call the spring the Lady Well, which suggests a different etymology. There are dozens of Ladywells to be found, and the reference is usually to the Virgin Mary. Now, *Mairi* is the familiar Gaelic version of Mary, but that is really a loan-word from the French: the older Gaelic word for Mary (especially the Virgin Mary) is *Moire*. Tibbermore could therefore equally be *tobar Moire*—'Mary's well'—which is in fact the derivation of Tobermory.

Tipperlinn is the name of a road in Edinburgh, called after a village which once existed in the vicinity. It must mean 'well by the pool' (see

linn). There are several examples of Tipperty, meaning 'well-place'; but the best known of all is Tipperary, which being in Ireland is outside the scope of this book.

Tobar tends to be a domestic type of well, and with the coming of mains water-supplies most of them are now forgotten. An exception is *Tobar nan ceann* in the Great Glen—'the well of the heads'—where in 1645 the severed heads of nine malefactors were washed before being dispatched to the Privy Council as evidence of an act of rough justice which the MacDonalds had perpetrated.

The Gaelic word for a natural spring is *fuaran* (see under **spring**); and there are of course dozens of Scottish place-names incorporating the English word 'well'. Most of these (e.g. Wellwood, Wellbank) are too transparent to require analysis; others, like Motherwell, Marywell and Ladywell, usually refer to the Virgin. (But as usual there are exceptions: e.g. Ladybank, which is discussed under **mig**). Possil in Glasgow seems to be 'post well'.

toll

This word means a tax in English and a hole in Gaelic, and it is not very difficult to distinguish the two meanings as they appear on the map. A tolbooth was originally a place where the money was collected, and Tollcross in Edinburgh and Glasgow obviously refer to former checkpoints. In the Highlands the word is often applied to a hole in a stone, as in *Clach Toll*, since such things had magical associations. Toward in Cowal is really *toll-aird*—'hole point'—a reference to the hole-filled limestone of which it is composed.

In mountain terminology, *toll* can be a hollow. Tollomuick in Ross and Cromarty is from *Toll a Mhuic* ('swine hollow'), and nearby Tol an Lochain is 'hollow of the lochans'. But Tolmount, a Munro summit on the high plateau between Angus and Aberdeenshire, now refers to the track from Glen Doll to Glen Callater; it clearly takes its name from the former glen (see **dal**).

Gaelic words involving *-oll*, when taken over by Lowland Scots, usually become *-ow;* thus, *coll* ('hazel') is rendered Cowie (a place near Bannockburn). The Gaelic word *tollaig* ('at the hole-place') becomes Towie. Towie Barclay, Towie Hill and Towiemore all have this sense.

The old-fashioned Scots word for ploughing was 'drilling', and a furrow was a 'dreel' (possibly the origin of the name of the Dreel Burn which joins the North Sea at Anstruther). Terms like drill and furrow one would not expect to be productive of place-names; but the Gaelic equivalent, *clais*, is surprisingly well represented on the map, often with the wider meaning of hollow or gully or even ravine. *Clais* (pronounced 'clash') is one of the commonest place-name elements in Highland Aberdeenshire, producing easily-recognisable forms such as Clais Mhadaidh ('fox or wolf hollow'), Clais an Toul ('barn hollow'), Clais Meirleach ('thieves hollow') and dozens more. Across the Highland line the word tends to become *clash* and is often accompanied by the definite article, as in The Clashmach (a furrowed hill near Huntly) and the Clash Brae at Kincardine o' Neil. Although *clash* is not listed in the Scottish dictionaries (except with the meaning of 'gossip') one suspects that it must have survived locally for a short time after the disappearance of Gaelic.

ton

This is a characteristically English place-name ending—think of Kensington, Islington, Leamington, etc. It is originally an Anglo-Saxon term meaning homestead, and it occurs in southern Scotland in settlements such as Symington ('Simon's stead'), and Haddington ('Hadda's stead'). Other examples are Livingston ('Leving's farm'), Elphinstone ('Alpin's farm'), Merchiston ('Markham's toun'), Stevenston and Uddingston ('Oda's farm').

The Old Norse personal name *Ormr* appears to have enjoyed some popularity, for there are two Ormistons in Roxburghshire, another two in Lothian and an Ormistoun near Peebles. *Ormr* seems to have been cognate with 'worm' (in the sense of serpent), which probably underlies the similar names of Wormiston and Wormit on Tay.

The foregoing examples (and there are dozens more) all derive from personal names. Others are however occupational, such as Fullarton—'fowler's toun'; and other groups of *ton* names are discussed under **castle** and **mill**. The most frequent use in Scotland of *ton* was in the late-mediaeval period when it became the almost universal term for a farm-stead. *Toun* or *ton* in combination with a few other words produces a fascinating list of farm-names, most of which have never outgrown this status, although a few have become hamlets and even suburbs.

The original estate or domain of a farm would probably be known as 'The Mains' (*demesne*), usually in combination with a parish name—such as 'Mains of Fintry'. The new farm would be called Newton (of Fintry, or whatever); the farm occupied by the husbandman or even the laird (if he didn't occupy the Mains) was the 'hall-toun' or Hatton; a humbler settlement inhabited by cottars would be known as the 'cot-toun' or Cotton. The upper farm was the Hilton or Overton, the lower the Netherton. It would be possible to base an interesting study of the whole process of the Scottish agricultural revolution on these farm-names, which are found all over the Lowlands.

The prevalence of *ton* as a place-name ending gave rise to a number of analogical formations. Edderton on the Dornoch Firth is an example—it should be *eader dun*—'between the hillocks'. Earlston in the Borders is not 'earl's town' but *Ercildoune* (of Thomas the Rhymer fame); the name probably contains the personal name Earcil, followed by **dun**. Plockton is an odd-looking name for Lochalsh; in Gaelic it was *Am Ploc* ('the lump'—immediately recognisable when you are there) and the popular *ton* ending was added for good measure.

Names ending in *town* as distinct from *ton* are usually modern. Grantown-on-Spey was a model village created by the laird of Grant in 1766; Campbeltown was created a burgh in 1667 and named after Archibald Campbell, earl of Argyle [sic]. Gardenstown, also from a surname, is another planned village, and Pultneytown was a creation of the British Fisheries Commission. As these are artificially created names they are not subject to the normal laws of onomatology. Prize examples of contrived names are to be found in the North Sea oilfields—Auk, Claymore, Cormorant, Piper, Tartan and Brent. One wonders what place-name scholars of the future will make of these curious board-room creations.

tor

This is a word that one associates with Devon and Cornwall rather than Scotland. But a Brittonic language was spoken in south-west England until the Middle Ages, and *tor* was Cornish for hill. The word also exists in Gaelic, with a double 'r' and with a slightly less elevated meaning of lump, mound or heap. In colloquial speech it can just mean 'a lot': *thachair torr bho 'n de*—'a lot has happened since yesterday'.

Tormore, which occurs twice, is 'big tor'; Kintore is literally 'Hillhead'; Torness near Dunbar means 'cape, mound'. Torduff and Torphin are black and white tor respectively. Torlundie in the north-west is 'marsh tor'. Torpichen is sometimes given the picturesque derivation of *torr phigheainn*—'magpie hillock', but the second element is a borrowing from Middle English 'pie', and somewhat suspect as a Gaelic compound; in any case magpies were not very common in West Lothian.

Torry in Strathbogie and Torry, part of Aberdeen, are just 'at the mound', and it is likely that Turriff is a variant of the same, although the ending is problematical. Sometimes *tor* becomes *tar* in the Lowlands, as exemplified in Tarbolton in Ayrshire ('Bolton's tor') and Tarbrax near Forfar (*tor breac* or 'speckled knoll'). The diminutive form *toran* ('little mound'), with an added English plural, gives Torrance, the name of a place near Glasgow and of another at East Kilbride.

In the far north and west, however, *tor* is usually a reference to the Norse god of thunder. Torboll in Sutherland is 'Thor's place', Torosay off Mull is 'Thor's isle', and Torrisdale is 'Thor's dale'. But Thurso is different and so is Torridon: they are discussed under **tarff** and **tarbert** respectively.

traigh

This Gaelic word is pronounced 'tray' and means shore; it is a very uncomplicated term which appears in numerous place-names, all in the west. The most familiar is Ballantrae in Ayrshire, 'village on the shore'; Kintra in Mull ('shorehead') is another example. Not so familiar are Traigh Bhagh in Tiree ('strand bay'), Traigh Ban in Colonsay ('white sands'), and Traigh House in Arisaig.

The equivalent term in Old Norse would be *eyrr*, a gravel beach. Erradale near Gairloch means 'beach dale' and Eriboll in Sutherland is 'gravel or shingle place'.

tref

The commonest place-name element in any language you care to think of is the one that means simply settlement or village or homestead. In English this element is *ham* (as in Nottingham and Birmingham) or **ton** (Darlington, Swinton); in France it is *ville* (Abbeville, Deauville), in Germany *heim* (Mannheim, Hildesheim) and so on. In Gaelic it is *baile* (see **bal**) and in Old Norse *stadr* (see **ster**) and **by**. In Brittonic it is *tref*, as is evidenced by the number of Welsh and Cornish villages (e.g. Tregair, Tremaine) which are named in this fashion.

The Scottish name which comes nearest to embodying this combination of letters is Threave in Ayrshire, but the number of *tref*-derived names is considerable. The word is usually reduced to *tra*, and in this form it is found in Tranent, originally *tref yr neint*, meaning 'village of the streams'. Traquair is 'hamlet on the River Quair' (which probably involves another Brittonic word, *gwer*, meaning green). Trabrown is *tref yr bryn*—'hill village' —and Traprain is *tref pren*—'tree house'. These names would be immediately intelligible to a Welsh speaker, for all the elements are Brittonic. There are many more, but these are the best known.

A group of *tref* names which has caused some problems is one which has the generic element at the end. This is quite uncharacteristic of Celtic place-nomenclature: we never talk of 'Macdhui ben' or 'Leven loch'. Whatever the explanation may be, the following names all end in a form of *tref*:

Rattray (see **rath**), Fintry (*fionn tref*—'white stead'); Menstrie (*maes tref*—'plain dwelling'); Soutra (*sulw tref*—'outlook place') and Niddrie and Longniddry ('new dwelling').

Names beginning with *tref*-forms are nearly all to be found within the boundaries of the ancient kingdom of Strathclyde, where a Cumbrian dialect of Brittonic was spoken. The remainder belong mainly to what might be termed Pictland, and the distribution is comparable to that of *pit* names (see **pit**).

tulloch

The mediaeval Scottish landscape was very different from today's: marshes have been drained, moors cultivated, forests levelled and gullies filled. The old place-names remind us of the topographical features that formerly were of such importance to early settlers. For example, a ridge or knoll might be the only negotiable part of a marshy territory: the common Gaelic term for this is *tulach*, meaning an eminence. This has passed into place-nomenclature as Tulloch, and there is a village of that name near Dingwall. But there are hundreds of other names which contain this element. Tullochgorum is *tulach gorm*—'blue-green hill'. The 'ch' ending disapears as often as not, and we have Tullibardine (*tulach bardainn*—'warning knoll') and Tullibole ('hill of danger'—cf. Maybole). Tullybelton in Perthshire is 'hill of Beltane', the Celtic version of May Day, and Tullibody is 'hill of the bothy or hut'.

In Aberdeenshire the word occurs particularly frequently in the form *tillie*: there are at least eleven such instances around the city alone: Tilliecairn is 'cairnhill' and Tilliedrone is 'lump hill'. The same pattern is to be seen farther west in Tillicoultry, which is *tulach cul tir*—'back-land knoll'. An even more mangled version of *tulach* occurs in Tough, near Alford.

Sometimes *tulach* occurs terminally, as in Kirkintilloch (see **kirk**), in Mortlach and in Loch Morlich (*mor tulach*—'big hillock'), and apparently in Murthly. Newtyle in Angus is thought to have a *tulach* ending.

A more conical type of hillock was called *tom* in Gaelic, giving Tomintoul in Banffshire (*tom an t-sabhail*—'little barn hill'), Tomatin near Inverness (*tom aitionn*—'juniper knoll'), Ballintuim in Strathardle (*baile an tuim*—'village on the knoll') and Tomnahurich (*tom na h-iubhraich*—'yew-tree knoll'). These places are all in the Central Highlands; the word appears to have been used less in the north and west, and not in the sense of 'knoll': in colloquial Gaelic, *tom* tends to mean dunghill.

The Gaelic word *cnoc*, meaning 'round hillock', passed into the Scottish vernacular speech as *knock*, and many a little hill in the Lowlands is referred to as 'The Knock'; the one in Crieff is a good example. (The same word is the basis of the surname Knox). Knockando is *cnoc cheannachd*—'market knoll'. Cnoc as a place-name element is concentrated in the extreme north-east and south-west of the former Gaelic-speaking territories.

The nearest English equivalent of these words is mound. The Mound near Golspie is an embankment designed by Telford and built in 1816 to carry the road over the tidal River Fleet. The Mound in Edinburgh is nearly contemporary and was created for not dissimilar purposes.

A landscape-protuberance can be described by the Scots word *knap*, Old Norse *nabbi*, Gaelic *cnap*, all of which are cognate with the German word *Knopf* (button) and English knob. Knapdale in Argyll is the best example, but others are to be found in Nab near Lerwick and The Knapp near Dundee.

But the smallest type of elevation must be that described by the Gaelic word *guireag*—'a pimple', which is the name of the rounded hill on the Clyde estuary known to the world as Gourock (and an excellent phonetic rendering of the original).

U

uaimh

This Gaelic word is not regarded in anglophone circles as user-friendly, and consequently tends to appear on the maps in its English translation as 'cave'. *Uaimh a Phrionnsa* in Balmacara Bay is now called 'Prince Charlie's Cave' (which indeed it traditionally was). *Uaimh Chrom* near Oban means 'the curved cave', and provided a hiding place for a MacDougall chief after the affair of 1715, but it is apparently no longer considered map-worthy. The term is preserved in Loch nan Uamh ('loch of the caves') in Arisaig, where Charles Edward landed on the Scottish mainland in August 1745 and departed for France a year later; there is another Loch nan Uamh on Sleat in Skye.

The problem of course is the pronounciation, which is 'oo-av' in Gaelic, but usually changed to 'weem' in English. This gives us Weem ('at the cave') near Aberfeldy and Wemyss in Fife and Ayrshire (in both of which an English plural has been substituted). Pittenweem in Fife is *peit na h-uamh* ('place of the cave')

The Vikings no doubt had their own term for cave, but the word which appears on the map is *smuga*, 'a narrow cleft', from *smjuga* to creep (cf. the old Scots word *smook*); such is the derivation of Smoo, the most spectacular cavern in Scotland.

W

water

There appear on the map of Scotland expressions such as 'Water of Leith', 'Water of Unich' and 'Water of Ken', usually with reference to something between a large burn and a small river, and mainly to be found in the south-west and north-east. These terms reflect a Gaelic word-order in an anglophone milieu, which may account for their quaintness; although they must at one time have been part of oral tradition, they are now seldom used colloquially. Similarly, expressions such as Bervie Water and Ruchill Water describe the same feature, are even more common, and are always shorn of their suffix in normal speech ('The Ruchill'). But why do the maps refer to Turret *Water* in the same breath as *River* Lednock, which are in the same small area of east Perthshire and are of almost identical size? On the other hand, terms like Blackwater and West Water, which drain Glenshee and Glen Lethnot respectively, and which must be relatively modern, enjoy popular usage.

The everyday Gaelic word for water, *uisge* (whence 'whisky'), very seldom appears as a generic in place-names. The only examples that come to mind are Baluss in Aberdeenshire and Balass in Fife (both *baile uisg* or 'water-stead'). In its earlier form of *easg* however it gives us the two Rivers Esk in Angus, the Midlothian Esk and the Dumfries Esk, not to speak of various lochans and burns in the Highlands. It may appear strange that there are two River Esks which enter the North Sea within half a dozen miles of one another, but in fact it was quite common to name rivers in pairs: the Devon and the Black Devon, the Blackadder and the Whitadder are other examples. The explanation may well be that all these names— Esk, Devon, Adder and a few others—are in fact ancient and primitive Celtic words, with simple meanings such as 'watercourse' or referring to a water-deity, and so were originally intended as common nouns and not proper names. All have parallels in English and continental river-systems; Esk in particular is related to the English Exe and the Welsh Usk.

way

This is usually an anglicisation of the Old Norse word *vagr*, meaning bay; another form is *voe*, as in Sullum Voe ('solan' or 'gannet bay').

Stornoway was either *stjorn vagr*—'steerage bay' or *stjarna vagr*—'star bay'; Scalloway is 'shieling bay'. (Note, however, that Galloway is not a *vagr* name: it is discussed under **gall**). Sometimes the intractable word *vagr* has become modified to *wall*, as in Kirkwall and Osmondwall.

The Vikings had a vested and proprietary interest in bays, and in addition to the words **vagr** and *vic* (see **wick**) they also used the word *hop*, which is discussed under **hope**.

wedder

Sheep-names are common in the Lowlands, whereas in the Highlands it is cattle-names that abound (see under **tarff**). The reasons are historical, sheep having made a late appearance in the north as a result of the Clearances.

The Gaelic word for sheep is *caora*, plural *caorach* (pronounced 'curach') and there are a few names such as Loch Caorach and Meall na Caora, but no important settlement-names. A further reason may be that the word *caorach* was difficult for Lowland tongues, and often underwent translation: Sheep Isle is a user-friendly version of *Eilean nan Caorach*.

The Vikings had their sheep also: the various islands called Soay (Old Norse *sauthr*) must have been used for grazing sheep, and indeed one of them has given its name to a breed of sheep. Fair Isle is also associated with the animal through the Old Norse word *faer*.

The most ubiquitous sheep-names involve the Scots word *wedder*, English wether, as in Wetherby. We have Wedderburn near Duns, Wedderlairs and Wedderlie in Lauderdale, Wedderlaw in Dumfries and Wether Hill.

Goat names tend to be commoner in the Highlands. The Gaelic word is *gobhar*, pronounced 'go-ur', and usually appears on the maps as 'gower'. There are numerous Craigowers ('goat crag') all over the Highlands. The river Gowrie in Wester Ross is from *gobhar* and Gowrie on Tayside is possibly from the same, although the derivation through Gabran, king of Dalriada, is more likely (see under **erin**). Pitgobar in Aberdeenshire is 'goat-place'.

wick

This word appears in the Scottish place-name vocabulary in two completely different forms, which must not be confused. The first and less common form is the Old Norse word *vik*, meaning bay or creek; it appears in Wick, Lerwick (*leir vik*—'mud bay') and Brodick—'broad bay'. The Gaels took over the word and gave it their own pronunciation and orthography: examples are Uig, which just means bay, Arisaig—'Aros bay', Boreraig— 'fort bay', Diabaig—'deep bay', Ostaig—'east bay', Scavaig—'claw bay', and Mallaig (*mar vik* or 'seagull bay'). These places are all found in the extreme north-west. Nigg near Aberdeen (there is another in Easter Ross) may be the same word, but preserving the Gaelic definite article—thus, *an uig*.

The other form is the Anglo-Saxon *wic*, meaning a settlement or encampment, and later, a farm. Paradoxically, the word Viking probably comes from this source—'camp men'. The term *wic* is found mainly in the southeast; examples are Hawick ('hedge settlement'), Borthwick ('home farm') and Darnick ('hidden place'). Some outlying *wic* names are thought to be of later origin: Prestwick ('priest farm') and Fenwick ('marsh place') are in Ayrshire, a district rich in Gaelic names; and Angus has the names Hedderwick ('heather place') and Handwick ('cock farm'). Wigton is *wictun*—'farm stead'. There are no *wic* names in the Highlands.

National boundaries do not always coincide with linguistic ones, and thus we find *wic* in the north of England, notably in Berwick ('bere' or 'barley farm') and Alnwick ('dwellings by the River Aln'). Similar names occur farther south also, but the characteristically northern hard 'ck' sound is softened to 'ch': thus, Bromwich, Droitwich and Greenwich.

witch

Throughout Scotland a belief in witchcraft was almost universally held, and between the 1550s and the 1690s its practitioners were zealously persecuted. Yet hardly a trace remains on the map to reflect this national peculiarity: even the names of Witch Lake (a rock-pool at St Andrews used for the ducking of sorceresses) and nearby Witch Hill (where they were burned) have been forgotten by that enlightened community. To find out the reason, we have to look a bit further than the term 'witch'.

The Old Norse word *karl* just means a male, and gives us the English word churl and the name Charles. The word survived in the Scots term *carl*—a fellow—and in its female form of *carline*. Carl has jolly rather than sinister overtones, but carline very often meant a witch. Carlingcraig and Carlingden are in Aberdeenshire, one of the counties noted for witch-hunting in the early seventeenth century. Carlinheugh ('witch ravine') is probably legendary rather than historical in origin; Carlin Tooth (a Cheviot top) is merely derogatory. The village of Carlops in the Pentlands was not founded until 1784, but it comes from *Kerlin lippis* ('carlin's loups') the name of a nearby burn; Carlops is taken to mean 'witch's leaps'.

If the derivation of *carlin* is straightforward, that of its Gaelic equivalent *cailleach* is complicated. *Cailleach* originally meant a nun, and its ultimate origin is Latin *pallium*, a hood, cloak or veil. The Brittonic *pall* becomes the Gaelic *caille*—'veiled one' (note the change from P-Celtic *pall* to Q-Celtic *caille*). In common speech *cailleach* became an old woman, usually of the hag-like variety, and in place-names the references are various. Inch Cailleach on Loch Lomond is 'nun's isle', but Leum na Cailliche (the

140

name of a bad step in the Arran hills) is definitely 'witch's leap'. Alltcailleach, a state forest near Ballater, is 'stream of the nuns, witches or old women' according to choice. There are very many *Cailleachs* in the West Highlands and Hebrides referring to hills or rocks; but the word, possibly because of difficulties in pronunciation ('kel-yuch') never quite made it into the vocabulary of tourism.

The male equivalent, *bodach*, is just as common in everyday speech, but gives no familiar place-names other, possibly, than Rhubodach (see **rubha**). Despite a few spectral overtones, the word is usually affectionate in usage.

worth

A common English place-name element meaning 'enclosure' or 'fenced village', cf. Wandsworth—'Wanda's enclosure'. It occurs only infrequently in Scotland, and not outside the south-eastern counties, where Anglian influence was strongest. Polwarth in Berwickshire is probably 'Paul's enclosure', and Cessford in Roxburgh is that of Cessa; but note that 'worth' has given way to the better-understood 'ford'. The most notable and interesting name in this category is Jedburgh, whose earlier form was Jedworth (even earlier, *Gedwirth*), and which means 'enclosed village on the River Jed'. The earlier forms are recalled both by the local pronunciation of 'Jeddart' and the neighbouring Bonjedward (itself a confused reference to the 'foot of the river', see under **bon**.

The river-name Jed may come from the Brittonic source *gwd* meaning 'turn' or 'twist'.

Postscript

...correct a wrong pronunciation when you hear it...

Aviemore virtually started life as a small L.M.S. village and in the course of half a century became an international resort. As a result the pronunciation of the name has undergone a transformation from Avie*more* to *Avie*more—an example of the great sound shift which Standard English is imposing on our Scottish place-names.

The reason is this. Most English place-names carry the stress on the first syllable: *Col*chester, *Scar*borough, *Bir*mingham, *Ber*wick. This is correct, because the first syllable is specific (often a reference to an Anglo-Saxon personal name) and the last syllable is generic (*caster, burgh, ham,* and *wic* are all settlement terms). But normal Gaelic word order is quite different, with the unstressed generic term coming at the beginning (*inver, bal,* etc.) and the specific noun or qualifying adjective coming at the end. Brae*mar* stresses the second syllable to link it with Brae*moray* and Bread*albane* (the 'upper part' of Mar, Moray and Albyn); this is totally lost if the stress is wrong. So *Avie*more is semantic nonsense, and so are *Mon*ifieth and *Cairn*gorm. *Mont*rose is just plain daft. How long will it be before we have to become accustomed to *Inver*ness and *Aber*deen? Some Scots seem to think it smart to follow this trend. Yet it is hardly conceivable that the mispronunciations

Liver*pool* and Black*burn* would for long remain uncorrected.

We have become reconciled to loss of meaning in Scottish place-names; it is inevitable because of the disappearance of Old Norse and Brittonic and the gradual decline of Gaelic. But in the long run the loss of the music and rhythm of our names would be just as damaging—and less excusable because avoidable. So the message is this: correct a wrong pronunciation when you hear it, demolish a false etymology when you can, and resist further attempts to anglicise these peculiar but splendid old names.

Reading List

For the general reader, books on place-names usually suffer from one of two defects—either they are so scholarly and densely written that they tend to repel the non-specialist, or they are so oversimplified as to be misleading.

Into the first category come W. J. Watson's classic *The History of the Celtic Place-Names of Scotland* (Blackwood, 1926, reprinted 1993) and W. F. H. Nicolaisen's *Scottish Place Names* (Batsford, 1976). Everything that these two authors have written repays study, and their occasional articles, scattered through numerous periodicals, are often more approachable than their *magna opera*.

Into the second category come J. B. Johnston's *Place-names of Scotland* (John Murray, 1934, reprinted 1970) and Isaac Taylor's *Words and Places* (Everyman, 1911). Johnston's book has enjoyed some popularity and is useful in giving the oldest forms of the many names discussed; but some of the etymologising (with its determination to find a Gaelic source at all costs) goes somewhat astray. Taylor's book (originally issued in 1864) has been unkindly classed as fiction, but it is a wonderfully stimulating introduction to onomastics.

Regional studies worth consulting are A. MacBain's *Place Names of the Highlands and Islands of Scotland* (Eneas Mackay, 1922) and W. M. Alexander's *The Place-names of Aberdeenshire* (Spalding Club, 1952). Restricted in scope, but a model of its kind, is Allan and Watson's *The Place Names of Upper Deeside* (AUP, 1984).

A dictionary of Scottish place-names has been long in the making. In the meantime the enthusiast must be content with the foregoing titles, several of which are unfortunately out of print.

A useful tool for the beginner is a booklet published by the Ordnance Survey in 1973. It is a glossary of the most common Gaelic and Scandinavian elements used on maps of Scotland. The section on Welsh elements is an added bonus even for those readers whose interest is mainly Scottish.

Index

Note: non-Scottish names are italicised

A

A'an, Ben, Loch 21
Aare, River 23
Abbeville 135
Aberarder 51
Abercrombie 45
Aberdeen 15
Aberdour 15, 51
Aberfeldy 15
Aberfoyle 15
Abergeldie 106
Abernethy 15
Aberpert 107
Aberuthven 115
Abervrack 15
Aboyne 63
Achallader 35
Acharacle 63
Acharn 16
Achiltibuie 69
Achilty 104
Achlean 16
Achmore 16, 98
Achnacarry 16
Achnahannet 18
Achnasheen 16
Achnashellach 44
Achray 42, 43
Advie 26
Affleck 124
Affric, Glen, Loch, River 31

Airdrie 19
Airds Moss 19, 98
Airlie 128
Airth, Airthrie 19, 21
Aldclune 38
Alder, Ben 51
Aldlarie 87
Ale Water 17
Alexandria 3, 113
Alford 63
Aline, Loch 106
Allan Water 17, 106
Allander 17
Alligin
Alloa 16
Alloway 16
Alltcailleach 141
Almond, Glen, River 23, 70
Alne, River 17
Alness, River 17
Alnwick 140
Altnabreac 31
Altnaharra 45
Altyre 131
Alva 17
Alvie 17
Amulree 63, 93
Ancrum 45
Andet 18
Angus 56
Annan, Annandale 47
Annat, Annot 18

Annochie 99
Anstruther 122
Aonach Beag, Buidhe, Dubh 18
Aonach Eagach, Mor, Shasuinn 18
Appin 55
Applecross 5, 46
Arbroath 15
Ardarie 21
Ardbeg 98
Ardchyle 38
Ardeer 19
Ardelve 19
Ardentinny 129
Ardeonaig 40
Ardersier 19
Ardgay 67
Ardgour 19
Ardiffery 76
Ardlair 86
Ardler 86
Ardlui 127
Ardmore 98
Ardnamurchan 19, 100
Ardoch 19
Ardoyne 38
Ardrishaig 110
Ardross 110
Ardrossan 19
Ardtalnaig 120
Ardtornish 19
Arduaine 38
Ardvorlich 24
Ardvreck 31
Argyll 66
Arisaig 139
Arivurichardich 21
Arlarie 87
Armadale 48
Arnamul 57
Arnaval 57
Arnbrae 20
Arnclerich 20
Arngask 20
Arnish 57

Arnisort 57
Arnprior 20
Arnvicar 20
Arran 57, 58
Arrochar 50
Arthur, Ben, Loch 20
Arthurlee 21
Arthur's Fountain 20
Arthur's Seat 20
Arthurstone 21
Ashestiel 44
Atholl 56, 63
Attadale 59
Attow, Ben 59
Auchencruive 43
Auchendinnie 129
Auchendryne 7
Auchenharvie 45
Auchenleuchries 91
Auchenshuggle 1, 16
Auchinleck 6, 124
Auchinlongford 91
Auchnafree 64
Auchnagorth 124
Auchorthie 124
Auchrannie 110
Auchterarder 51
Auchterderran 22
Auchterhouse 130
Auchterless 68
Auchterlonie 90
Auchtermuchty 1, 22, 99, 100
Auldbar 17
Auldearn 17
Auldhouse 130
Aultbea 17, 43
Aviemore 26, 98, 142
Avoch 23
Aven, River 22
Avon, Ben, Loch, River 22
Avranches 15
Awe, Loch, River 23
Ayr 6, 23

B

Ba, Loch 127
Bacca, Bachd, Back, Bakki 31
Backward 120
Badachro 39, 127
Badanden 39
Badbea 39, 43
Badcall 39
Baddidarach 39
Baddybae 43
Balass 138
Balbeggie 98
Balblair, Balblairs 29
Balerno, Balernach 110
Balfour 24
Balgay 67
Balgie, Bridge of 24
Balgowan 24, 72
Balgownie 72, 108
Balharie, Balharvie 45
Ballachulish 24, 38
Ballantrae 6, 24, 135
Ballater 24, 88
Ballaterach 88
Ballencrieff 43
Ballendollo 48
Ballinbreich 30
Ballindalloch 48
Ballinluig 24
Ballintuim 136
Ballo, Hill, Reservoir 26
Balloch 24, 26
Ballochbuie 25
Ballochmyle 92
Balmoral 130
Balmore 98
Balmullo 100
Balnaboth 130
Balnagowan 24, 72
Balnamoon 99
Balquhidder 24
Baluss 138
Balvaig, River 65

Bamff 100
Banavie 100
Banchor, Glen 28
Banchory 28
Bandshed 120
Banff 100
Bangor 28
Bangour 28
Bankend 30
Bankfoot 30
Bankhead 30
Banknock 30
Bannockburn 28
Banvie 100
Barassie 59
Barcaldine 25, 44
Bargeddie 25
Barlinnie 25
Barmekin, The 26
Barr 25
Barra 25
Barrhead 25
Barrie 25
Barrlanark 85
Bathgate 5, 39
Bawkie Bay 24
Bealach a Mhargaidh 25
Bealach nam Bo 25, 127
Beanncharain, Loch 28
Bearsden 49
Beath 43
Beattock 43
Beaufort 26
Beauly 26
Bedcow 39
Beinn—*see* Ben
Belhaven 75
Bellshill 24
Bellstruther 122
Belmont 27
Belses 27
Benarty Hill 21
Benbecula 28
Ben a Chlachair 72

Ben a' Ghlo 25
Ben an t-Sithean 120
Ben Attow 59
Ben Bhraggie 31
Ben Bhreac 31
Ben Cleugh
Ben Dearg 115
Benderloch 90
Ben Eighe 93
Ben Fhada 59
Ben Glas 69
Ben Ledi 61
Ben Loyal 60
Ben Macdhui 99
Bennachie 52
Ben na Ciochan 52
Benvie 100
Ben Vorlich 24
Ben Vrackie 31
Berneray 58
Berriedale 48
Berwick 140
Bettyhill 3
Bidean nam Bian 28
Birgham 74
Birkhill 43
Birks of Abergeldie 43
Birmingham 74
Birse 110
Bishopbriggs 32
Blackadder 28, 29
Blackcraig 28
Blackford 28
Black Isle 28
Blacklaw 28
Blacklunans 29
Black Mount 28
Blackness 28
Blackwater 28
Blackwood 28, 40
Blair 29
Blairadam 29
Blair Atholl 29
Blairbeg 29

Blairdrummond Moss 98
Blairgowrie 29
Blairingone 29
Blair Logie 29
Blairmore 29
Blantyre 131
Blaven 60
Blawrainy 29
Boarhills 99
Boat of Garten 67
Bodiebae 43
Bogbrae 95
Bogie, River, Strath 24
Bogend 95
Bogengarrie 131
Boggieshalloch 131
Boghall 95
Boghill 95
Bogmill 95, 96
Bohuntine 131
Bolton 75
Bonaly 29
Bonar Bridge 29, 32
Bonawe 23, 29
Bo'ness 101
Bonjedward 29, 141
Bonnington 30
Bonnybridge 30
Bonnyrigg 30, 114
Bonnyton 30
Bonskeid 29, 38
Bootle 74
Boreraig, 32, 139
Boreray 32, 58
Borgue 32, 60
Borland, Borlum 87, 88
Boroughmuir 98
Borrodale 48
Borthwick 140
Borve 32
Bracco, Braco 31
Braclinn 31
Brae, Braes 30
Braehead 30

Braemar 7, 30, 37
Braemoray 30
Braeriach 30
Braid Hills 30
Braigh Coire Chruinn-bhalgain 25
Branxholme 77
Breabost 123
Breadalbane 30
Breich 30
Breakachy 16, 31
Brechin 31
Brecon 31
Bridgefoot 31
Bridgend 31
Bridge of Gaur 65
Bridge of Orchy 32
Brig o' Turk 99
Brigton 31
Broadford 62
Broadland 88
Broad Law 87
Broadshade 120
Brodick 139
Bromley, Brompton, Bromwich 110
Broomfaulds 59
Broomhall, Broomhill 110
Broomielaw 110
Brough 32
Broughton 32
Bruachladdich 30
Bruntlands 82
Buachaille Etive 85
Buccleuch 49, 50
Buchan 128
Buchanan 128, 131
Buchanty, Buchany 128
Buchlyvie 131
Buckhaven 75
Buckie 100
Bucksburn 100
Builg, The 24
Buittle 74
Bulg 24
Bunchrew 29, 43

Bunessan 29, 54
Bunrannoch 29
Burdiehouse 27
Burghead 32
Burnmouth 18
Burn of Sorrow 18
Burntdales 48
Burntisland 86
Burra 32

C

Caerlanrig 85
Caerlaverock 34
Caernarvon 34, 82
Cairn 35
Cairney 35
Cairngorm 35, 69, 97
Cairngressie 72
Cairn o' Mount 35, 97
Cairnryan 34, 35
Cairntoul 35
Cairnwell 24
Caithness 41, 101
Caldcleugh 50
Calder 35
Calgary 67
Callander 35
Callanish 101
Callater 35
Cambus 36
Cambusbarron 36
Cambuskenneth 36
Cambuslang 36
Cambusnethan 36
Cambus o' May 31, 93
Campbeltown 154
Campsie 60, 121
Camusericht 36
Canisbay 33
Canonbie 33
Caorach, Loch 139
Capel Fell 93
Capel Mount 93, 97

Cape Wrath 102
Carbost 123
Cardenden 36
Cardney 35
Cardno 36
Carfrae 34
Carlingcraig, Carlingden 140
Carlinheugh 140
Carlin Tooth 140
Carlops 140
Carluke 34, 84
Carmunnock 34
Carmyle, Carmyllie 34
Carn Aosda 35
Carnaveron 76
Carnbo 127
Carnegie 34
Carn Elrick 72
Carngeal 106
Carnoustie 35
Carntyne 35, 129
Carnwath 35
Carpow 109
Carradale 37
Carrbridge 37
Carrick 36
Carrickfergus 36
Carron, Loch, River 37
Carr Rocks 17, 137
Carse of Gowrie 93
Castlebay 38
Castlecary 38
Castle Douglas 38
Castle Haven 75
Castlehill, Castle Law 38
Castleton, Castletown 7, 37
Caterthun 34
Cathcart 34
Catlaw 41
Catterline 34
Cauldcleuch 50
Cauldshields 130
Cawdor 35
Cessford 141

Champfleurie 27
Chapelshade 120
Chesthill 5
Chester 34
Chroisg, Loch a' 46
Clachaig 124
Clachan 124
Clachnaben 124
Clachnacuddin 124
Clachnaharry 45, 124
Clais an Toul 133
Clais Meirleach 133
Clais Mhadaidh 133
Clackmannan 124
Clash Brae 133
Clashmach, The 133
Cleugh, Ben 60
Clova, Clovulin 96
Cluanie 38
Cluden 89
Clunes 38
Clunie, Cluny 38
Clyde 89
Clydebank 30
Coatbridge 32
Coburty 128
Cockpen 107
Coigach 50
Coilacriech 38
Coilantogle 38
Coille Bhrochan 38
Coire Cas, Coire na Ciste 42
Colchester 142
Coldingham 74
Colinton 39
Colintraive 83
Collafirth 39
Collieston, Colliston 39
Collin 39
Colquhoun 102
Comrie 79
Conavel 60
Conglass, Glen 41
Conon, Strath, Water 41

Connish 41
Cora Linn 42
Corehouse 130
Corgarff 42
Corpach 76
Corriemony 99
Corriemulzie 96
Corrieshalloch 42
Corrievreckan 31, 42
Corrour 42
Corsby 46
Corse 46
Corseford 46
Corsehill 46
Corsemill 46
Corsewall 46
Corstorphine 46
Coruisk 42
Coshievillc 122
Cotton 133
Coull 102
Coulter 47
Coultra, Coultrie 47
Coupar Angus 128
Cowal 56
Cowden 44
Cowdenbeath 43, 44
Cowdenknowes 44
Cowgate 69
Cowie 132
Coyles of Muick 39
Craichie 42
Craigannet 18
Craigcllachie 17, 37
Craigendarroch 44
Craigendoran 51
Craigentinny 129
Craigforthie 124
Craigie 37
Craigievar 7
Craiglockhart 37, 91
Craigmailing 92
Craigneuk 102
Craignure 44

Craigower 139
Craigowl 105
Craig Phadrick 37
Craigrothie 112
Craik 37
Crail 17
Cramond 34
Crathes 42
Crathie 42, 43
Cray 42
Creag a Bhinnean 37
Creag an Fhitheach 59
Creag an Leth-Choin 41
Creag an t-Seabhag 51
Creag Dubh 37
Creag Mhadaidh 41
Creag Righ Harailt 37
Creich 44
Crianlarich 87
Crichie 44
Crichton 44
Crieff 43
Crimond 44
Crinan Moss 99
Cromalt 45
Cromar 7
Cromarty 45
Crombie 45
Cromdale 45
Cromlet 45
Cromlix 45
Cromrig 45
Crosbie 46
Crose, Cross 46
Crossbost 46
Crossburn 46
Crossford 46
Crossgates 46, 69
Crosshill 46
Crossipoll 46
Crosslee 46
Crossmichael 46
Crossmyloof 46
Crossnish 46

Crossraguel 46
Cruachan, Ben 52
Cuillin 102
Culbin 47
Cullen 102
Culloden 47
Culreach 47
Culross 47, 100
Culside 119
Cults 39
Cultoquhey 39
Cultybraggan 39
Culzean 102
Cumbernauld 79
Cumbrae 57
Cupar 128
Currie 42

D

Dalgarnock 65
Dalbeathie, Dalbeattie 43, 48
Dalbreck 48
Dalgrassick 72
Dalguise 43
Dalkeith 39, 59
Dallas 7, 59
Dalmally 48
Dalmarnock 48
Dalmore 48
Dalmuir 98
Dalnaspidal 48, 121
Dalness 54
Dalreoch 48
Dalry 82
Dalwhinnie 48
Dalziel 106
Damph, Ben 127
Dargavel 40
Darlington 135
Darnick 140
Daugh, The 50
Dava 43, 127
Dawlish 70

Dearg, Ben 115
Deauville 135
Dee, Linn of 89
Deerness 48
Denby 49
Denhead 49
Denholm 76
Denny, Dennyloanhead 49
Denork 5
Derby 33
Derry, Glen, Loch 40
Dessary, Glen 21
Deveron, River 23, 56, 61
Devon, Glen, River 29, 70
Diabaig 139
Dingwall 16
Dirnanean 56
Dochart, Glen, Loch 50
Dochfour 50
Dochgarroch 50
Doll, Glen, River 48
Dollar 48
Dollar Law 87
Don, River 54
Doon 54
Doran, Ben 51
Dores 114
Dornie, Dorniegills 52
Dornoch 52
Douglas 61, 69
Doune 53
Dounreay 112
Dover 51
Dowally 17
Dreel Burn 132
Dreghorn 115
Drem 51
Drip Moss 98
Droitwich 150
Dron 54
Druie, River 85
Druim Fada 59
Drumbeg 51, 98
Drumbowie, Drumboy, Drumbuie 52

Drumchapel 51
Drumchardine 36
Drumdrishaig 110
Drumdurno 52
Drumgask 102
Drumgoldrum 52
Drumindarroch 44
Drumlanrig 85
Drummond 52
Drummore 51, 98
Drumnadrochit 32, 52
Drumochter 22
Drumrannie 110
Drumsheugh 52
Drunkie, Loch 54
Dryden 49
Drymen 52
Dublin 89
Dudhope 77
Duffryn 86
Duffus 59
Duirnish 48
Dulais 70
Dull 48
Dullatur 88
Dumbarton 53
Dumfries 54, 100
Dumyat 54
Dunalasair 53
Dunan 53
Dunbar 25
Dunblane 53, 125
Dunbog 5, 25
Duncansby 33
Dundas 53
Dundee 53
Duneaves 101
Dunfermline 53
Dunedin 55
Dunira 63
Dunkeld 53
Dunkerque 53
Dunnichen 3, 53
Dunning 53

Dunoon 53
Dunotttar 60
Dunrobin 52, 54
Duns 53
Dunshalt 72
Dunsinane 53
Dunstaffnage 122
Duntroon, Duntrune 53
Dunure 44
Dupplin 89
Dura Den 49, 51
Durie 51
Durness 48
Durno 52
Durris 114

E

Eaglesham 55
Earshader 119
Earlston 134
Earn 23, 56
Eassie 54
East Haven 75
Easthouse, Easterhouse 130
East Neuk of Fife 102
Eastriggs 114
Ecclefechan 1, 117
Eccles 55
Ecclesgreig 55
Ecclesmachan 55
Eck, Loch 93
Edderton 134
Eddrachillis 83
Edinample 55
Edinbane 55
Edinburgh 32, 55
Edinchip, Edinkip 55, 104
Edindurno 52
Edinglassie 55
Edinkillie 55
Ednam 74
Edzell 48
Eigg 58

Eildons 17
Eilean Donan 58, 70
Eilean Mhunna 58
Eil, Loch 105
Einich, Loch 99
Elcho 17
Elderslie 43
Eldbottle 74
Elgin 56
Ely 128
Ellick 72
Elphinstone 133
Elrick 72
Elie 128
Embo 123
Enoch 99
Enochdhu 18
Erchless 70
Eriboll 128, 135
Ericht, Loch, River 19
Eriskay 57
Erracht 19
Erradale 135
Errochty, Glen 19
Errol 128
Erskine 129
Esk, River 138
Essich, Essie 54
Esslemont 97
Ethie 63
Etive, Glen, Loch 76
Eun, Loch nan 56
Evan Water 22
Exe, River 138

F

Fada, Ben, Loch 58
Fafernie 95
Fair Isle 139
Fala 59
Falkirk 5, 59, 82
Falkland 59, 72
Falloch, Glen 59

Falmouth 59
Falside 59
Fasnacloich 59, 124
Fasnakyle 59
Fassifern 59
Fauldhouse 130
Fearn, Fearnan 43
Fedderat 60
Feddinch 123
Fender, Glen 51
Fenwick 140
Ferindonald 20
Ferintosh 20
Fernate, Glen 43
Fern, Fernie, Ferniehurst 43
Fetterangus 60
Fettercairn 36, 60
Fetteresso 54, 60
Fhada, Ben 59
Fhitheach, Craig an 57
Fiddes 123
Fiddich, Glen 71, 123
Fife Ness 101
Finavon 101
Fincastle 61
Findhorn 23, 56, 61
Findlater 88
Findochty 50
Findo Gask 102
Findon 61
Finegand 95
Fingask 102
Finglas, Glen 61
Finlarig 61
Finlas, Glen, River 61
Finnart 61
Fintray, Fintry 61, 136
Fionn Loch 61
Fionnphort 61, 109
Fir Mounth 97
Fishcross 46
Fiunary 21
Flanders Moss 98
Flashader 119

Flodigarry 67
Floors 27
Fodderty 60
Fogla 57
Fogo 84
Foinaven 61
Forfar 60
Forgandenny 49
Formartin 20
Forres 22
Forsa, River 54
Forse 54
Forsinard 54
Fort Augustus 64
Forter 64
Forteviot 60, 64
Fort George 64
Fortingall 64
Fortrose 22, 64
Fortune 62
Fort William 63
Foss, Braes of 59
Foula, Fula 57
Foulden 49
Foulis Castle 22
Fountainbleau 26
Foveran 122
Fowlis 22
Foxhall, Foxton 77
Foyers 60
Fraoch, Fraoch Eilean 64
Fraserburgh 33
Freuchie, Freugh 64
Frew, Fords of 62
Friockheim 64
Fuaran, Meall nam 122
Fuaran na Sgorr 122
Fuaran, Sgurr nan 122
Fugla Field 60
Fullarton 133

Gaineamhach, Loch 118
Gair, Loch 59
Gairloch, Gairlochy 59
Galashiels 130
Galla Ford 62
Gallatown 66
Galloway 66, 138
Galloway, Mull, Rhinns of 102
Gallowflat 66
Gallowgate 66
Gallow Hill 66
Galston 127
Gamhna, Loch 127
Gamrie 127
Ganavan 118
Ganvich, Loch 118
Gannochy 118
Gardenstown 134
Gare Loch 90
Gargunnock 67
Garioch 67
Garmouth 59
Garnock 65
Garonne 68
Garrachory 68
Garry, Glen, Loch 67, 68
Garscadden 67
Garscube 67
Gartcosh 67
Gartcraog 67
Garth 67
Gartloch 67
Gartly 67
Gartmore 98
Gartnavel 67
Gartness 67
Gartocharn 67
Gartsherrie 67
Garvalt 68
Garve 67
Garvellach 67
Gask 102
Gateshead 69
Gateside 69

Gatwick 69
Gaur, Bridge of 65
Gelder, Glen 106
Geldie, Glen 106
Gellyburn 106
Geusachan, Glen 43
Giffen 114
Giffnock 114
Gigha 58
Gight, Bog of 67
Gilliesfaulds 59
Gilp, Loch 105
Girnaig, Girnock, Glen 65
Girvan 59
Giubhasach, Glen 43
Glamis 26
Glas, Ben 69
Glasgow 69
Glas Maol 69, 92
Glassary 21, 92
Glassford 63
Glass, Strath 70
Glas Tulachan 69
Glasven 69
Glen Banchor 28
Glen Beg 98
Glencoe 70
Glencoul, Loch 102
Glencorse 46
Glen Dee 125
Glen Derry 39
Gleneagles 55, 56, 71
Glenelg 56
Glen Falloch 59
Glen Fiddich 71, 123
Glenfinnan 62, 71
Glen Garry 47, 68
Glen Geusachan 43
Glengyle 105
Glenhowl 105
Glenmore 70, 97, 98
Glen Moriston 54
Glen Muick 99
Glenrothes 50, 71

Glen Roy 70, 115
Glenshee 121
Glen Strathfarrar 125
Glenure 44
Glowerorum 112
Goatfell 60, 67
Goil, Loch 66
Golspie 33
Gordon, Gordonstone, Gordonstoun 71
Gourdon 71
Gourock 137
Gowanbank 72
Gowanhill 72
Gowrie 56, 139
Grampians 73
Grandtully 67
Grange 88
Grangemouth 88
Grantown-on-Spey 134
Grantshouse 130
Greenhill 38
Greenlaw 38, 87
Greenloaning 38, 90
Greenock 38
Greenwich 150
Gressiehill 72
Gretna 50
Greystone 124
Grimshader 119
Guardbridge 68
Guay 67
Guisachan 43
Gulabin, Ben 52
Gullane 52
Gunnister 118
Guthrie 66
Gyle, Glen, Loch 105
Gylen 105
Gyles 105

H

Haddington 133
Haddo 50

Hairmyres 75, 96
Halladale, Strath 74
Halbeath 73
Halkirk 73
Hallival 73
Hamna Voe 75
Handa 118
Handwick 140
Hangingshaw 120
Harburn 75
Hare Cairn 75
Hare Stane, Harestanes 75
Harewood 75
Harlaw 75
Harris 58
Hartfell 49
Harthill 49
Hartlaw 49
Hartree 75
Hatton 73, 133
Haugh 77
Hawick 140
Hawkhill 57
Heatherwick 65
Hebrides 66
Hedderwick 65, 140
Helensburgh 3, 33
Hell's Glen 76
Helmsdale 48
High Force 54
Hildesheim 135
Hilton 133
Hindside 49
Hirtal 17
Hobkirk 77
Hollywood 74
Holm, Holmhead, Holmsburn 76, 77
Holy Island 74
Holy Loch 74
Holyrood 74
Holytown 74
Hope, Ben 77
Hopeman 27
Hopetoun House, 77

Hopringle 77
Hoptoun 77
Hourn, Loch 76
Howden 84
Howe of the Mearns 84
Howgate 84
Hoy 58
Humbie 33
Hunthill 72
Huntingdon 71
Huntingtower 72
Huntly 71
Huntly Bank, Huntlywood 71
Hyndland 49

I

Inch 78
Inchaffray 78
Inch Cailleach 78, 140
Inchcape 78
Inchcolm 40, 78
Inchgarvie 78
Inchinnan 78
Inchkeith 39
Inchmahome 91
Inchmartin 78
Inchmichael 78
Inchnadamph 49, 78, 127
Inchture 78
Inchyra 78
Inkster 118
Innellan 58
Innerleithen 79
Innerpeffray 106
Innisfree 78
Insch, Insh 78
Inver 79
Inveraray 79
Inverawe 23
Inverbeg 98
Inverbervie 79
Inverbrothock 15
Invercauld 35

Inverclyde 79
Inverdovat 79
Inveresk 79
Invergarry 61
Invergordon 71, 79
Invergowrie 79
Inverkeillor 35
Inverkeithing 39
Inverkip 79, 104
Inverleith 79
Inverness 79, 102
Invernethy 79
Inveroran 51
Inversnaid 105
Inveruglas 70
Inverurie 79
Iolaire, Carn, Creag 57
Iona 40, 58
Irongath 67
Irongray 20
Ironhirst 20
Irvine 23
Islay 56
Islington 133
Iubhair, Loch 44
Iutharn, Ben 76

J

Jedburgh 32, 144
Jericho 113
John o' Groats 113
Johnshaven 75
Joppa 113
Jura 48, 57
Jura, Sound of 84

K

Kaimes, Kames 105
Kaimhill 105
Keir 34
Keith 39
Keithock 39

Kelso 50
Keltie, Kelty 35
Kelvin, River 23
Kelvingrove 23
Kelvinhaugh 23, 77
Kelvinside 23
Kemnay 105
Kenmore 81, 98
Kennoway 81
Kensington 133
Kentra 81
Keppoch 105
Kershope 77
Kettla Ness 42
Kettlebridge 42
Kettleshiel 42
Kettleston 42
Kettletoft 42
Kilbirnie 80
Kilbrandon 80
Kilbrennan 81
Kilbride 80
Kilchoan 80
Kilchurn 83
Kilconnel 82
Kilconquhar 80
Kilcormack 82
Kilcowan 82
Kilcoy 81
Kilcreggan 80
Kildonan 80
Kildrummy 81
Kilkerran 80
Killearn 81
Killearnan 81
Killeonan 40
Killiecrankie 81
Killin 80
Kilmacolm 40, 80
Kilmally 48
Kilmarie 92
Kilmarnock 80
Kilmichael 82
Kilmore 80, 98

Kilmory, Kilmuir 80
Kilmun 80
Kilninver 79
Kilpatrick 82
Kilrenny 117
Kilsyth 80, 115
Kilwinning 80
Kinaldie, Kinaldy 17
Kincaple 93
Kincraig 37
Kindallachan 48
Kincardine 36
Kindrochit 132
Kingarth 67
King Edward 81
Kinghorn 81
Kinglass, Glen 41, 70
Kinglassie 70, 81
Kingoldrum 52
Kingsbarns 81
Kingskettle 42
King's Lynn 81
King's Seat 81
Kingussie 5, 43, 81
Kininmonth 97
Kinkell 39
Kinlochleven 81
Kinloss 111
Kinnaird, Kinnairds Head 81
Kinneil 81
Kinnell 17
Kinnoull 17
Kinross 114
Kintail 81, 117
Kintore 134
Kintra 135
Kintyre 81
Kintyre, Mull of 92
Kip, East, West 105
Kipford 104
Kippen 105
Kippie Law 104
Kirkbister 123
Kirkby 33

Kirkcaldy 34, 82
Kirkconnel 82
Kirkcormack 82
Kirkcudbright 82
Kirkden 49, 82
Kirkforthar 64
Kirkhill 82
Kirkhope 77
Kirkintilloch 34, 82, 136
Kirkland 82
Kirkmaidens 82
Kirkmichael 82
Kirkness 82
Kirkoswald 82
Kirkpatrick 82
Kirkton 83
Kirkwall 82, 139
Kirriemuir 50
Kishorn 92
Kisimul 92
Knapdale 48, 137
Knapp 137
Knockando, Knock, The 136
Knoydart 62
Kyle 83
Kyleakin 83
Kyle of Lochalsh 83
Kylerhea 82, 83
Kylesku 83
Kyles of Bute 82
Kylestrome 102

L

Ladybank 95, 132
Ladywell 132
Lag, Lagg 84
Lagain, Loch 84
Lagavulin 84
Laggan, Loch 84
Laggish 84
Lair 86
Lairg 85
Lairig an Laoigh 25, 85

Lairig an Lochain 85
Lairig Gartain 85
Lairig Ghru 25, 85
Lamancha 113
Lambieletham 87
Lamlash 74
Lanark 85
Lanbryde 86
Langavat 91
Langholm 76, 91
Lanrick 86
Lanrig 85
Larbert 107
Larghill 85
Largo 85
Largoward 120
Largs 85
Largybeg, Largymore 85
Larkhall 73
Larne 95
Lasswade 63
Lathallan 95
Latheron 95
Lathockar 95
Lathom 87
Lathones 95
Lathrisk 95
Law 87
Lawers 65
Laxadale, Laxdale 31
Laxay 31
Lax Firth 31
Laxford 31, 62
Laxo 31
Laytham, Layton 87
Leamington 133
Ledaig 61
Ledard 61
Ledbeg 61, 98
Ledcrieff 61
Ledi, Ben 61
Ledmore 61
Lednock, Glen 61
Lendrick 85

Lennox 89
Lerwick 139
Leslie 68
Lesmahagow 68, 177
Letham 87
Lethnot 61
Letterewe 88
Letterfearn 88
Letterfinlay 88
Lettermore 88
Lettoch 50
Leuchars 91
Leum na Cailliche 140
Leven, Loch, River 88
Lewis 58
Leys 68
Liddesdale 47
Liff 111
Lightnot 61
Lincluden 89
Lincoln 89
Lindifferon 86
Lindores 89
Linga 64
Linlithgow 89
Linmill 90
Linnhe, Loch 15, 89, 118
Linn of Dee 89
Linshader 90
Linside 119
Linton 89
Linwood 89
Lismore 68
Liverpool 142
Livingston 133
Llanberris 86
Loanhead 90
Loanstone 90
Lochaber 15
Loch a Chroisgn 46
Lochalsh, Kyle of 82
Loch a Mhuillin 96
Lochan a Chait 42
Lochan na Lairige 85

Loch an Eilean 58
Lochan Uaine 38
Lochar Moss 98
Loch a Vealloch 26
Loch Carron 37
Loch Eil 105
Lochend 90
Loch Gair 59
Loch Garry 67, 68
Lochgelly 106
Loch Gilp 105
Lochinver 79
Loch Iubhar 44
Loch Loch 90
Loch Long 59, 91
Lochmaddy 41
Loch Maree 92
Loch Muick 99
Lochnagar 65
Loch nan Eoin, Eun 56
Loch nan Uamh 137
Loch Rosque 46
Lochty 90
Lochy, Loch, River 90
Lockerbie 33
Loganlee 84
Logie 84
Logie Mar 7
Logie Pert 107
Logierait 112
Lomond, Ben, Loch 89
Lomond Hills 89
London 95
Longannet 18
Longford 91
Longforgan 86
Longformacus 91
Long Haven 75
Longhope 77
Longniddry 91, 136
Lonmay 95
Lorn 56
Lossiemouth 111
Lothrie 91

Loy, Glen 127
Loyal, Ben 60
Luban 45
Lubnaig, Loch 46
Luib 45
Luichart, Loch 91
Lui, Ben, Glen 85, 127
Lumphanan, Lumphinnans 86
Luncarty 91
Lundie, Lundy 95
Lundin Links 95
Lunga 91
Lungard, Loch 91
Lurcher's Crag 41
Luss 111
Luthrie 91
Lybster 123
Lyme Regis 81
Lynchat 86
Lynturk 99
Lynwilg 24
Lyon, Glen, Loch, River 70, 89

M

Machar, Macharmore 92
Machermuir 92
Madderty 105
Machrie 92
Machrihanish 92
Maeshowe 84
Magask 93
Maggienockater 112
Maginnis 94
Magask 93
Magus 93
Maiden Paps 53
Mains 133
Mallaig 139
Mally Watt 112
Mambeg 52
Mamore 57
Mam Ratagan 52
Mannheim 135

Marcaonach 18, 93
Maree, Loch 92
Mark, Glen, Water of 93
Markie, Glen 93
Markinch 93
Marsco 57
Maryculter 130
Maryhill 113
Marywell 132
Mauchline 94
Maud, Old 17, 141
Mawcarse 93
Maybole 93
May, Isle of 58
Mealfourvounie 94
Meall a Bhuiridh 94
Meall Beag 94
Meall Garbh 94
Meall Glas 94
Meall More 94
Meall na Caora 139
Meall nam Fuaran 122
Meall Odhar 94
Meall Uaine 94
Mearns 103
Mearns Cross 46
Megget Water 95
Megginch 78
Meg, Craigie 95
Meggernie 75
Meigle 95
Mekie, Craig 95
Meldrum 92
Melfort 62
Melrose 92, 115
Melvaig, Melvich 62
Melville 27
Menstrie 136
Menteith, Lake of 97
Merchiston 133
Merkland 86
Merse, The 96
Methil 95
Methlick 95

Mhadaidh, Creag 41
Mharcaonaich, A' 18, 93
Mhuillin, Loch a 96
Middleshade 120
Midlem 94
Midmar 7
Migdale 95
Migvie 94
Milford Haven 62
Millport 96
Milngavie 1, 6, 67
Milton 96
Minard 96
Mingary 67, 97
Minginish 101
Minigaig 56
Minishant 97
Minnigaff 97
Minto 50
Moidart 62
Moine 99
Monadhliath 97
Monadhruadh 69, 97
Moncrieff 97
Mondyne 97
Monega 97
Moness 30
Moniaive 66
Monifieth 99
Monimail 99
Monorgan 86
Montrose 114
Monymusk 99
Monzie 94
Monzievaird 94
Moonzie 94
Morangie, Glen 78
Morar 51
Moray 100
Morebattle 74
More Ben, Glen 98
Morlich, Loch 136
Morroch 100
Morsham 98

Mortlach, Mortlich 136
Morton 98
Morvern 100
Morvich 100
Mossburnford 99
Mossend 99
Mossgiel 99
Mosshope Fell 99
Mossmorran 99
Motherwell 132
Moulin 92
Mound, The 137
Mount Battock 97
Mount Blair 97
Mounth, Capel 93, 97
Mounth, The 73, 97
Mounth, White 65
Mount Florida 97
Mount Keen 97
Mount Stuart 97
Mount Vernon 97
Mount, The 97
Moy 94
Moyness 94
Muchalls 99
Muck 99
Muckhart 99
Muckraw 99
Mugdock 50
Mugdrum 99
Muick, Glen, Loch 99
Muillin, Glen, 96
Muirhead 98
Muir of Ord 104
Muirkirk 87
Muirton 98
Mull 58
Mull, Sound of 84
Mullach an Rathain 100
Mullach coire Mhic Fhearchar 100
Mullach Nan Coirean 100
Mull of Galloway 92
Mull of Kintyre 92
Mundurno 52

Munlochy 30
Murlagan 100
Murroch 100
Murthly 136
Musselburgh 32
Muthill 95
Myreside 96

N

Nab 137
Nairn 6
Naked Tam 112
Navar 101
Navitie, Navity 101
Neidpath 128
Nell, Loch 57
Ness, Loch, River 79
Nethergate 69
Nethermyres 95
Netherton 133
Nethy 65
Nevay 101
Nevis, Ben, Loch, River 27
Newark 103
Newbattle 74
Newbigging 103
Newburgh 103
Newcastleton 37
Newhaven 75, 103
Newmore 101
Newport-on-Tay 103
Newton 103, 133
Newtongrange 88
Newton Mearns 103
Newtonmore 98
Newton St Boswells 103
Newtyle 136
Niddrie 136
Nigg 139
Nithsdale 47
Norncalder 66
North Haven 75
Notmans Law 87

Nottingham 135
Nova Scotia 103

O

Oare, River 23
Oban 77
Ochil Hills 104
Ochiltree 104
Ochtertyre 22
Oder, River 28
Ogil, Glen 104
Ogilvie 104
Oich, Loch 23
Old Ladders 17
Old Maud 17, 41
Opinan 77
Onich 18
Orchy, Bridge of 32
Ord, Ord Bain, Ordhead 104
Ordie, Loch 104
Orkney 7, 58, 100
Ormiston, Ormistoun 133
Osmondwall 139
Osnaburgh 33
Ostaig 139
Overton 133
Oxgang 51
Oxnam 74
Oykell, River, Strath 104

P

Pabbay 57, 111
Padanaram 113
Paisley 55
Panbride 106
Panlathie 106
Panmure 106
Pannanich Wells 106
Papa Stour 57
Papay 111
Paphrie Burn 106

Pap of Glencoe, Jura etc. 52, 53
Pappert Hill, Law 107
Partick 107
Pathstruie 122
Patna 113
Pearsie 54
Peel Burn, Fell 106
Peffer, Peffery 106
Peffermill 106
Pencaitland 39, 107
Penicuik 107
Pennel 107
Pennyland 86
Penpont 107
Pentland 67, 86
Persey 54
Perter Burn 107
Perth 107
Peterhead 102
Petty 108
Pettycur 108
Pettymuck 108
Philiphaugh 77
Phones 60
Picktillum, Pickletillem 113
Pilmore, Pilmuir 106
Pilrig 106
Pilton 106
Pitblado 108
Pitcairn 108
Pitcaple 93, 108
Pitcarmick 108
Pitchirn 110
Pitcoig 108
Pitcorthy 124
Pitcrievie 43
Pitcullen 110
Pitfirran 122
Pitforthie 124
Pitfour 108
Pitgaveny 127
Pitgersie 72
Pitgobar 108, 139
Pitkeathly 108

Pitkennedy 108
Pitkerro 108
Pitlessie 68
Pitlochry 108, 124
Pitmillie 96
Pitsligo 121
Pittencrieff 43, 108
Pittentarrow 127
Pittenweem 108, 137
Philiphaugh 77
Plockton 134
Pluscarden 36
Plynlimmon 89
Pollock 109
Pollokshaws 109, 120
Pollokshields 109, 130
Polmadie 108
Polmaise 108
Polmont 109
Poltalloch 104
Polwarth 109, 141
Port a' Churaich 109
Port Askaig 109
Port Ellen 109
Port Gordon 71
Portland 109
Portknockie 109
Portmoak 109
Portmore 109
Portobello 109
Port of Menteith 109
Portpatrick 109
Portree 82, 109
Portsmouth 109
Portsoy109
Possil 132
Powfoot 109
Powgavie 109
Powmill 96, 109
Pressley 110
Preston 111
Prestonfield 111
Prestongrange 111
Prestonpans111

Prestwich 111
Prestwick 111, 140
Priorletham 87
Provan 55
Pultneytown 134

Q

Quaich, Glen, Water 105
Quair, River 135
Queensferry 81
Quinaig 105
Quiraing 8
Quoich, Glen 105

R

Raasay 57
Radernie 111
Raeburnfoot 49
Raecleuch 49
Raigmore 112
Raith, Raitt 112
Ramornie 111
Ranachan 110
Ranfurlie 86
Rannoch 29, 110
Rathelpie 111
Rathillet 111
Ratho 112
Rattray 112, 136
Ravenscraig 57
Reay 112
Redford 62
Redgorton 112
Redheugh 50
Renatton 22
Renfrew 62, 102
Rescobie 115
Restalrig 115
Rest and Be Thankful 112
Restenneth 115, 129
Rhiconich 82
Rhidorroch 44

Rhu, Rhue 116
Rhubodach 116, 141
Rigg, Riggend, Rigside 114
Riggin, The 114
Rhinns of Galloway 102
Rhynd 102
Rodel 48
Rohallion 112
Romanno 112
Ronaldsay 58
Rosehaugh 115
Rosehearty 114
Roseisle 114
Rosemarkie 93, 114
Roslin 115
Rosneath 101, 114
Rosque, Loch 46
Ross 114
Rossdhu 114
Rossie 115
Rosyth 114
Rotherham 115
Rotherhithe 75, 115
Rothes 59
Rothesay 58
Rothiemay 93, 112
Rothiemurchus 112
Rousay 58
Rowardennan 40, 116
Roxburgh 32
Roy, Glen 70, 115
Rubislaw 87
Ruchill 115, 138
Rum 57
Rumgally 111
Rutherford 115
Rutherglen 115
Ruthrieston 115
Ruthven 115
Ruthwell 115
Rynettin 22
Ryvoan 21

S

St Abbs Head 117
St Andrews 116
St Boswells 117
St Cyrus 55
St Enoch's 99
St Fergus 117
St Fillans 117
St Fort 117
St Gregory's 117
St Kilda 117
St Michaels 117
St Monans 117
St Ninians 117
St Vigeans 117
Salach, Glen 76
Salachan 44
Salen 118
Saline 118
Saltcoats 118
Sand 118
Sanda, Sandaig, Sanday 118
Sandbank 118
Sandbister 118
Sandend 118
Sand Fiold 118
Sandfordhill 118
Sandness 118
Sandsound 118
Sandwich 118
Sandwick 118
Sannox 118
Sauchen, Sauchie 44
Sauchieburn 44
Sauchiehall Street 77
Saughton 44
Scalloway 130, 138
Scalpa, Scalpay 57
Scapa 57
Scarba, Scarpa 57
Scarborough 119
Scarskerry 57
Scavaig 139

Schawpark 120
Schiehallion 120
Sciennes 27
Scone 123
Scoonie 123
Scores, The 119
Scorrie, The 119
Scotlandwell 66
Scotscalder 66
Scotston, Scotstoun 66
Scourie 21
Scrabster 123
Seabhag, Craig an t- 57
Seanspittal 121
Selkirk 82
Sellafield 58
Sgorr an Fhuarain 119
Sgurr Alasdair 119
Sgurr a' Mhadaidh 119
Sgurr a' Mhaim 119
Sgurr Dearg 119
Sgurr Eideadh nan Clach Geala 119
Sgurr Fiona 119
Sgurr na Ciche 119
Sgurr na Feine 119
Sgurr nan Fhuarain 122
Sgurr nan Gillean 119
Sgurr of Eigg 119
Sgurr Ouran 119, 122
Sgurr Voulin 96
Shambelly 112
Shank, Shankhead 103
Shaw 120
Shawbost 120, 123
Shawhead 120
Shawlands 120
Shawwood 120
Shee, Glen 120
Shelibost 21
Shellay 58
Shetland 58
Shiant Islands 74
Shieldaig 103
Shieldhill 130

Shillinglaw 130
Shotts 61
Sidlaws 87
Sithean, Ben an t- 120
Skara Brae 119
Skarskerry 57
Skeabost 123
Skegness 101
Skelbo 121
Skelister 121
Skelwick 121
Skene 123
Skibo 123
Skinnergate 69
Skipness 101
Skye 57
Slamannan 124
Slattadale 69
Sleach 61
Sleat 69
Slieve Donard 61
Sligachan 120
Sligcarnach 121
Sligo 121
Slioch 61
Slochd 52
Slug of Auchrannie 52, 110
Slugain, Sluggan 52
Sma' Glen, The 70
Smailholm, Smallholm 74, 77
Smiddy Green 72
Smithfield 72
Smithton 72
Smoo 137
Snizort 62
Soay 57, 139
Socach 102
Solway 98
Solway Moss 98
Sorbie 33
Sound 84
Soutars of Cromarty 72
Souterford, Souterhill, Souterton 72
Soutra 136

Sowerby 33
Spey 6
Spinningdale 48
Spittal, Spittalfield, Spittalhaugh 121
Springburn 122
Springfield 122
Stac Polly 109, 126
Stack Ben, Loch126
Stack of Handa 126
Staffa 122
Staffin 122
Stane 123
Stanley 113
Steall 54
Stenhousemuir 123, 130
Stenness 102
Stenton 123
Stevenston 133
Stirling 6
Stix 126
Stobcross 126
Stob Coir an Albannaich 126
Stob Coire nan Lochan 126
Stob Gabhar 126
Stobhall 126
Stobhill 126
Stobo 126
Stobs 126
Stobsmuir 126
Stockbridge 32
Stoer 57
Stonefield 123
Stonehaugh 123
Stonehaven 75, 124
Stonehouse 123
Stoneybridge 123
Stoneyburn 123
Stoneywood 123
Stonybeck 123
Stornoway 132
Straans, The 125
Stracathro 34, 125
Strachan 125
Strachur 45

Straloch, Stralochy 90
Stranraer 102
Strathaven 22
Strathblane 125
Strathbogie 24
Strathclyde 125
Strath Dee 125
Strathearn 56
Strathfarrar, Glen 125
Strathfillan 117, 125
Strathgartney 85, 125
Strath Glass 70
Strathhalladale 48
Strathkinlas 70
Strathkinness 112
Strathmartine 125
Strathmiglo 95
Strathmore 125
Strathpeffer 106
Strathtyrum 112
Strathyre 45
Stravithie 112
Strome Ferry 102
Stromness 102
Stronaclachar 72
Strone 102
Strontian 102, 120
Stroud 122
Struan 122
Struie, Struy 122
Strutherhill 122
Stuc, Stuic, An 126
Stuc a Chroin 125
Study, The 113
Succoth 102
Suilven 60
Sullum Voe 138
Sunart 62
Swanbister 123
Swanney 57
Swanston 57
Swinton 99
Swordale 48
Symington 133

T

Tain 128
Tamnavrie 76
Tanar 128
Tannach, Tannochside 16
Tannadice 16
Tannahill 16
Tantallon 45
Tarbat Ness 101, 127
Tarbert 126
Tarbet 126
Tarbolton 75, 134
Tarbrax 134
Tarff, River 127
Tarf, Water 127
Tarland 86, 127
Tarradale 127
Tarves, Tarvie 127
Tarvit 127
Tay 6
Taychreggan 130
Taynuilt 17
Tayvallich 130
Teallach, An 104
Teampull Chaon 129
Tee, Ben 120
Templand 129
Temple, Templeton 129
Tennet, Glen 129
Tentsmuir 98
Terpersie 131
Terregles 55
Tervin 131
Teviot 60, 70, 128
Threepland, Threipland 45
Threepneuk, Threepwood, Threipmuir 45
Threave 135
Thun 53
Thurso 128, 135
Tibbermore 131
Tiendrish 110, 131
Tighnabruaich 30, 130
Tillicoultry 136

Tilliecairn 136
Tilliedrone 136
Tinto,Tintock 129
Tipperary 132
Tipperlinn 131
Tipperty 132
Tiree 131
Tirinie 131
Tirnadrish 131
Titaboutie 131
Tobermory 131
Todhead, Todhills 77
Todrig 77
Tol an Lochain 132
Tollcross 132
Tollomuick 132
Tolmount 97, 132
Tomatin 136
Tomintoul 136
Tomnahurich 136
Tongland 103
Tongue 103
Torboll 123, 135
Torc, An 99
Torduff 134
Torlundie 134
Tormore 134
Torness 134
Torphichen 134
Torosay 135
Torphin 134
Torrance 135
Torridon 127, 135
Torrisdale 135
Torry, Torryburn 134
Tough 136
Toward 132
Towie, Towie Barclay 132
Towie Hill 132
Towiemore 132
Trabrown 135
Traigh Ban 135
Traigh Bhagh 135
Tranent 135

Traprain 135
Traquair 135
Treig, Loch 76
Trinafour 50
Trochry 112
Tromie, Glen, River 110
Trongate 69
Trool, Loch 122
Troon 102
Trossachs 47
Trotternish 101
Truim, Glen, River 110
Tullibardine 136
Tullibole 136
Tullibody 136
Tulloch 136
Tullochcurran 110
Tullochgorum 136
Tullybanchor 28
Tullybelton 136
Tummel 76
Turc, An 99
Turriff 134
Twa Havens 75
Twechar 45
Tweed 6
Tweeddale 70
Twynholm 76
Tyndrum 130
Tyne, River 128
Tyninghame 74
Tynwald 16
Tyrie 131

U

Uamh, Loch nan 137
Uddingston 133
Udny 17
Uig 139
Uigshader 119
Ulbster 41
Ullapool 108, 123
Ulva 41, 57

Unapool 123
Unst 57
Unthank 113
Uplawmoor 87
Urquhart 36
Usk, River 138

V

Vealoch, Loch a 26
Vennacher, Loch 28
Vorlich, Ben 24
Voulin, Sgurr 96
Vrackie, Ben 31

W

Wandsworth 141
Ward 120
Wardhill 87
Wardlaw 87
Waterloo 113
Waternish 101
Waukmill 96
Wedderburn 139
Wedderlairs 139
Wedderlaw 139
Wedderlie 139
Weem 137
Wells of Dee 122
Wemyss 137
Westruther 122
Wetherby 139
Wether Hill 139
Whalsay 58
Whitadder 29
Whitburn 28
Whitby 33
Whithorn 117
Whittingehame 74
Wick 139
Wigton 140
Wimbledon 53
Winchburgh 32

Windygates 69
Winthank 113
Wirren 122
Wishaw 120
Witch Hill, Lake 140
Wolstanton 41
Wolfhill 41
Wolflee 41
Wolverhampton 41
Woodhaven 75
Wormiston 133
Wormit 133
Wrath, Cape 102
Wyvis, Ben 76

Y

Yar, Yare 68
Yarrow 68
Yell 58
Yetholm 74, 77
Yoker 22
Ythan 65

Z

Zoar 113